Masters in Pieces

The English Canon *for* the Twenty-first Century

Michael Parker
and Fiona Morrison

CAMBRIDGE
UNIVERSITY PRESS

DEDICATED TO JAN MORRISON

. . .

CAMBRIDGE UNIVERSITY PRESS
Cambridge, New York, Melbourne, Madrid, Cape Town, Singapore, São Paulo

Cambridge University Press
477 Williamstown Road, Port Melbourne, VIC 3207, Australia

www.cambridge.edu.au
Information on this title: www.cambridge.org/0521671310

© Michael Parker, Fiona Morrison 2006

First published 2006

Designed and typeset by Mason Design
Illustrations by Bettina Guthridge
Edited by Susan Lee
Printed in Australia by BPA Print Group

National Library of Australia Cataloguing in Publication data
    Parker, Michael
    Masters in pieces: the English Canon for the twenty-first century.
    For NSW English year 10 and 11 students.
    ISBN-13 978-0-521-67131-6 paperback
    ISBN-10 0-521-67131-0 paperback
    1. English language – Textbooks. 2. English literature – Textbooks.
    3. Australian literature – Textbooks. I. Morrison, Fiona. II. Title.
428

ISBN-13 978-0-521-67131-6
ISBN-10 0-521-67131-0

Reproduction and Communication for educational purposes
The Australian *Copyright Act 1968* (the Act) allows a maximum of
one chapter or 10% of the pages of this publication, whichever is the greater,
to be reproduced and/or communicated by any educational institution
for its educational purposes provided that the educational institution
(or the body that administers it) has given a remuneration notice to
Copyright Agency Limited (CAL) under the Act.

For details of the CAL licence for educational institutions contact:

Copyright Agency Limited
Level 15, 233 Castlereagh Street
Sydney NSW 2000
Telephone: (02) 9394 7600
Facsimile: (02) 9394 7601
E-mail: info@copyright.com.au

Reproduction and Communication for other purposes
Except as permitted under the Act (for example a fair dealing for the
purposes of study, research, criticism or review) no part of this publication
may be reproduced, stored in a retrieval system, communicated or
transmitted in any form or by any means without prior written permission.
All inquiries should be made to the publisher at the address above.

Cambridge University Press has no responsibility for
the persistence or accuracy of URLs for external or
third-party internet websites referred to in this publication
and does not guarantee that any content on such
websites is, or will remain, accurate or appropriate.

Contents

Preface

Note to teachers

If we thought that this book was going to become a student's entire English experience for a year we would be appalled and try to have the book recalled. We want the units in this book to take their place alongside other film-based, multimedia-based and concept-based units in your programme, all of them rich with contemporary material. However, we do believe that a study of 'canonical' works should be woven into any programme delivered to students who may eventually attempt a higher-level English course for their external exam. Otherwise, the 'traditional' texts that almost all of these students will ultimately have to write about will appear to them as un-familiar, without context and therefore daunting. It is in this spirit that these units are presented to you here.

That each unit conforms to the syllabus outcomes and that it prepares your students for the final examination are, of course, centrally important. However, what we are equally concerned about is that your students go away from your class engaged by the ideas, enthusiastic about the texts and energised for more. We even have hopes that the students will read some of the full texts under their own steam.

We feel there are several ways that you can use this book:

- The first is to treat each literary period as a separate unit that takes between three and five weeks. If two literary periods are taught in Year 10, and another two in Year 11, this means that students will really have a sense of the rich contexts of the English canon. They will have been exposed to many of its most enduring works by the time they are to sit their external exams. In addition, they will have a strong critical perspective on the entire concept of a canon, as well as familiarity with the different ways of reading a text.
- The second is to base the extract studies on some of the seven critical perspectives offered in Unit 1: postcolonial, feminist, Marxist, psychoanalytic, new historicist and cultural materialist, deconstructionist and queer. Each critical perspective is linked to approximately five texts. Each of these texts has explicit questions or activities pertaining to that critical perspective. Thus, it is possible to have a very productive three weeks, for example, looking at feminist readings of English texts throughout history. We have included an 'alternative structure for units' (page vii) to use as a guide if you would like to take this approach.
- The third is to select a text from each period as a core (for example, a Shakespeare from the Renaissance period, *The Importance of Being Earnest* from the Victorian period or *Heart of Darkness* from the modern period) and then use this book to provide an extensive sense of the period's cultural and literary context.
- The fourth is simply to provide a smorgasbord of works from each of the periods as your own preference dictates. Themes (such as 'chivalry', 'love' or 'the horror') could be used to unify these.

Any of these approaches would provide students with a valuable literary grounding.

Additional information for teachers

Space dictated many of our choices. If you are concerned that Robert Browning, Lord Byron, Mary Shelley and the entire neoclassical period are not included in the book, we understand and sympathise and can only reply that we had 240 pages as our quite reasonable brief, not 2400. Similarly, our choice to concentrate on British writers means that we were unable to include other writers in English (from the USA, Canada, India and so on) or writers of other languages. We admit that we have made the inconsistent choice of including a chapter on Australian literature in a book otherwise about British writers. This is not an oversight: we simply could not bear to see this book go into Australian schools without our 'own' national literature as part of it.

There are three broad types of questions and activities in each unit:

¤ The first asks students to do a reasonably detailed language study of a piece.
¤ The second asks students to look at the broader implications of the piece. This may involve different theoretical approaches and ways of looking at the text.
¤ The third asks students to do activities based on the piece. These can take all sorts of forms, from re-enactments through to creative writing.

The balance of these questions and activities varies from extract to extract. They are certainly not all designed to be used in any one programme. Of the six or so pieces in a period, perhaps two or three will receive a detailed language/techniques treatment. You may want to use two or three as a springboard to do something creative, active or resistant. We have not specified whether each of the questions is for discussion, writing or group work. The balance of these approaches is up to you.

Similarly, some of the questions and activities are considerably harder than others. Many of the questions and activities may suit a Year 10 class of reasonable ability. However, a few questions and activities may really only be embraced by a strong Year 11 class. Again, you should be able to judge what is and is not appropriate for your class as you go through each unit. The medieval unit is possibly the least difficult (perhaps suitable for a Year 8 or 9 class), whereas the modern unit is possibly the most challenging (perhaps not suitable before Year 11).

Some of the texts in this book will be prescribed texts for your state's external exam. You will not be able to teach these parts of the unit in the preliminary years. We have included them regardless because each state's prescribed list is different and also because the prescribed texts change every few years.

Much of the backbone of the book comes from our approach to the whole idea of a canon. We have tried to interrogate it, appreciate it, question it, deconstruct it and, above all, thoroughly enjoy it. We do feel that several lessons on the idea of a canon are fundamental to prevent students falling into the old-fashioned trap of assuming these texts are simply some sort of humanistic guide to moral and literary perfection from the great minds of the past and the present.

We have applied a variety of approaches throughout the text, including new historicism, cultural materialism, deconstruction, Marxism and humanism. Hopefully, the units wear their critical clothing relatively lightly. Certainly, the book provides the tools to allow you to take as central or as attenuated a 'cultural studies/critical literacy' focus as you wish in your classes. Regardless, your students should feel that their analytical and critical facilities are being sharpened by exposure to each of the texts. In addition, we have provided grids that show how the syllabus outcomes are satisfied by the questions and activities. There is also a glossary and a bibliography.

Enough of apparatus. Enough of the syllabus. We would like to end on the point that is the most significant to us: our hope that you and your students have an invigorating, challenging and great time using this book.

Michael Parker and Fiona Morrison

Alternative structure for units

The following structure can be used by teachers who would like to use a theoretical perspective (such as feminism) as the organising principle for a unit of study.

Postcolonial criticism

The canon and literary criticism (Unit 1, pages 14–15)

Shakespeare and *The Tempest* (Unit 3, pages 79–81)

Alternative readings: the pastoral, English landscape and imperialism (Unit 4, pages 116–17)

Brontë and *Jane Eyre* (Unit 5, pages 145–8)

Conrad and *Heart of Darkness* (Unit 6, pages 165–9)

Visions of the outback: Harpur and Mackellar (Unit 7, pages 198–9 and 202–4)

Feminist criticism

The canon and literary criticism (Unit 1, pages 15–16)

Mystery plays and *Noah's Flood* (Unit 2, pages 40–4)

Sonnets: Sidney and Wroth (Unit 3, pages 63–5 and 68–9)

Milton and *Paradise Lost* (Unit 3, pages 81–4)

Austen and *Pride and Prejudice* (Unit 4, pages 117–22)

Tennyson and 'The Lady of Shalott' (Unit 5, pages 130–8)

Brontë and *Jane Eyre* (Unit 5, pages 145–8)

Woolf and *To the Lighthouse* (Unit 6, pages 183–7)

Stead and *For Love Alone* (Unit 7, pages 209–10)

Marxist criticism

The canon and literary criticism (Unit 1, page 16)

Chaucer and *The Canterbury Tales* (Unit 2, pages 31–7)

More and *Utopia* (Unit 3, pages 57–61)

Shakespeare and *King Lear* (Unit 3, pages 76–9)

Blake and *Songs of Innocence and of Experience* (Unit 4, pages 89–94)

Austen (Unit 4, pages 117–22)

Browning and 'Cry of the Children' (Unit 5, pages 125–6)

Dickens and *Hard Times* (Unit 5, pages 140–3)

Psychoanalytic criticism

The canon and literary criticism (Unit 1, pages 16–17)

Vision literature and St Julian of Norwich (Unit 2, pages 37–40)

Coleridge and 'Kubla Khan' (Unit 4, pages 104–8)

Rossetti and 'Goblin Market' (Unit 5, pages 149–53)

Eliot and 'The Love Song of J Alfred Prufrock' (Unit 6, pages 187–93)

Winton and *Cloudstreet* (Unit 7, pages 218–19)

New historicism and cultural materialism

The canon and literary criticism (Unit 1, pages 17–18)

Malory and the *Morte D'Arthur* (Unit 2, pages 44–9)

Sonnets: Wyatt and Sidney (Unit 3, pages 61–5)

Shakespeare and Renaissance scripts (Unit 3, pages 75–6)

Blake and *Songs of Innocence and of Experience* (Unit 4, pages 89–94)

Yeats and 'Easter 1916' (Unit 6, pages 172–5)

The Ern Malley affair (Unit 7, pages 210–13)

Deconstruction

The canon and literary criticism (Unit 1, page 18)

Shakespeare and 'Sonnet 18' (Unit 3, pages 65–6)

Marlowe and *Dr Faustus* (Unit 3, pages 71–5)

Tennyson and 'The Lady of Shalott' (Unit 5, pages 130–8)

Paterson and 'The Man from Snowy River' (Unit 7, pages 199–201)

Queer theory

The canon and literary criticism (Unit 1, page 19)

Shakespeare and 'Sonnet 18' (Unit 3, pages 65–6)

Wilde and *The Importance of Being Earnest* (Unit 5, pages 153–8)

New South Wales Stage 6 Outcomes

This table demonstrates which sections (and questions and activities) in each unit satisfy which outcomes from the New South Wales Year 11 and Year 12 syllabuses.

Outcomes	Introduction	Medieval
To describe and explain the relationship between composer, responder, text and context in particular texts	Challenges to humanism (pp. 10–11)	St Julian of Norwich (pp. 37–40)
To describe and explain relationships among texts		Malory's *Morte D'Arthur* (pp. 44–9); Cameron's *Terminator 2* (pp. 49–50)
To develop language appropriate to the study of English	Context: ways of seeing the canon (pp. 6–9)	*Beowulf* (pp. 25–31)
To describe and explain the ways in which language forms and features, and structures of particular texts shape meaning and influence responses	Introductory activity: rock and roll hall of fame (pp. 1–4)	Chaucer's *Canterbury Tales* (pp. 31–7)
To demonstrate an understanding of the ways various textual forms, technologies and their media of production affect meaning	Deconstruction (p. 18)	Mystery plays (pp. 40–4)
To engage with a wide range of texts to develop a considered and informed personal response		Review questions and activities (p. 51)
To select appropriate language forms and features, and structures to explore and express ideas and values	The American 'culture wars' (p. 12)	Chaucer's *Canterbury Tales* (pp. 31–7)
To articulate and represent own ideas in critical, interpretative and imaginative texts	Humanism and the canon (pp. 9–13)	St Julian of Norwich (pp. 37–40)
To assess the appropriateness of a range of processes and technologies in the investigation and organisation of information and ideas	The American 'culture wars' (p. 12)	St Julian of Norwich (pp. 37–40)
To analyse and synthesise information and ideas from a range of texts for a variety of purposes, audiences and contexts		*Beowulf* and Tolkien's *Lord of the Rings* (pp. 25–31)
To draw upon the imagination to transform experience into text	Introductory activity: rock and roll hall of fame (pp. 1–4)	Context of the period (pp. 21–5)
To reflect on own processes of responding, composing and learning	Challenges to humanism (pp. 10–11)	Mystery plays (pp. 40–4)
To demonstrate a capacity to understand and use different ways of responding to and composing particular texts	Challenges to humanism (pp. 10–11)	Malory's *Morte D'Arthur* (new historicist) (pp. 44–9)

Renaissance	Romantic	Victorian	Modern	Australian
Milton's *Paradise Lost* (pp. 81–4)	Blake's *Songs of Innocence and of Experience* (pp. 89–94)	Dickens's *Hard Times* (pp. 140–3)	Yeats's 'Easter 1916' (pp. 172–5)	Slessor's 'Five Bells' (pp. 207–8)
Donne (pp. 67–8); Wroth (pp. 68–9)	Keats's 'To Autumn' (pp. 113–17); Mackellar's 'My Country' (pp. 202–4)	Wilde's *The Importance of Being Earnest* (pp. 153–6); Monty Python satire of Oscar Wilde (pp. 157–8)	Review questions and activities (p. 194)	Paterson's 'The Man From Snowy River' (pp. 199–201); Richardson's *The Fortunes of Richard Mahony* (pp. 204–6); Mackellar's 'My Country' (pp. 202–4)
Marlowe's *Dr Faustus* (pp. 71–5)	Austen's *Pride and Prejudice* (pp. 117–22)	Rossetti's 'Goblin Market' (pp. 149–53)	Joyce's *Ulysses* (pp. 178–83)	Wright's 'At Cooloolah' (pp. 213–14)
Shakespeare's *King Lear* (pp. 76–9)	Coleridge's 'Kubla Khan' (pp. 104–8)	Dickens's *Great Expectations* (pp. 143–4)	Eliot's 'The Love Song of J Alfred Prufrock' (pp. 187–93)	Winton's *Cloudstreet* (pp. 218–19)
Sidney (pp. 63–5)	Shelley's 'Ozymandias' and photo of statue of Saddam Hussein (pp. 111–13)	Tennyson's 'The Lady of Shalott' and Waterhouse's paintings (pp. 130–8)		The Ern Malley affair: Malley v. Eliot (activities, pp. 211–12)
The Renaissance sonnet (pp. 61–9)	Review questions and activities (p. 123)	The rise of the novel (pp. 139–40)	Review questions and activities (p. 194)	'The great Australian novel' activity (p. 220)
More's *Utopia* (pp. 57–61)	Keats's 'To Autumn' (pp. 113–17)	Brontë's *Jane Eyre* (pp. 145–8)	Conrad's *Heart of Darkness* (pp. 165–9)	Harpur's 'A Midsummer Noon in the Australian Forest' (pp. 198–9)
Context of the period (pp. 53–7)	Wordsworth's 'Tintern Abbey' (pp. 94–104)	Wilde's *The Importance of Being Earnest* (pp. 153–6)	Context of the period (pp. 162–5)	Mackellar's 'My Country' (pp. 202–4)
Marlowe activity 4 (pp. 74–5)	Wordsworth's 'Tintern Abbey' (pp. 94–104)	Tennyson's 'The Lady of Shalott' (pp. 130–8)		'The great Australian novel' activity (p. 220)
Review questions and activities (pp. 84–5)	Review questions and activities (p. 123)	Review questions and activities (pp. 159–60)	Review questions and activities (p. 194)	Visions of the outback (pp. 197–206)
Milton's *Paradise Lost* (pp. 81–4)	Blake's *Songs of Innocence and of Experience* (pp. 89–94)	'Forge a poet' activity (activity 2, pp. 159–60)	Joyce's *Ulysses* (pp. 178–83)	Winton's *Cloudstreet* (pp. 218–19)
More's *Utopia* (pp. 57–61)	Keats's 'To Autumn' (pp. 113–17)	Tennyson's 'The Lady of Shalott' (pp. 130–8)	Joyce's *Ulysses* (pp. 178–83)	Mackellar's 'My Country' (pp. 202–4)
Shakespeare's *The Tempest* (postcolonial) (pp. 79–81)	Coleridge's 'Kubla Khan' (psychoanalytic) (pp. 104–8)	Dickens's *Hard Times* (Marxist) (pp. 140–3)	Woolf's *To the Lighthouse* (feminist) (pp. 183–7)	Paterson's 'The Man from Snowy River' (deconstruction) (pp. 199–201)

Victorian Units 1 and 2 Outcomes

This table demonstrates which sections (and questions and activities) in each unit satisfy which outcomes from the Victorian Year 11 syllabus.

Outcomes	Introduction	Medieval
1/1 On completion of this unit the student should be able to identify and discuss key aspects of a set text, and to construct a response in oral or written form	Introductory activity: rock and roll hall of fame (pp. 1–4)	St Julian of Norwich (pp. 37–40)
1/2 On completion of this unit the student should be able to create and present texts, taking account of audience, purpose and context	Context: ways of seeing the canon (pp. 6–9)	Malory's *Morte D'Arthur* (pp. 44–9*)*
1/3 On completion of this unit, the student should be able to identify and discuss, either in writing and/or orally, how language can be used to persuade readers and/or viewers	Queer theory (p. 19)	'The Pardoner's Tale' (pp. 33–36)
2/1 On completion of this unit the student should be able to discuss and analyse how texts convey ways of thinking about the characters, ideas and themes, and construct a response in oral or written form	Introductory activity: rock and roll hall of fame (pp. 1–4)	Chaucer's *Canterbury Tales* (including real estate advertisement) (pp. 31–7)
2/2 On completion of this unit the student should be able to create and present texts, taking account of audience, purpose and context	Challenges to humanism (pp. 10–11)	Mystery plays (pp. 40–4)
2/3 On completion of this unit the student should be able to identify and analyse how language is used in a persuasive text and to present a reasoned point of view in oral or written form	The American 'culture wars' (p. 12)	*Beowulf* (pp. 25–31)

Renaissance	Romantic	Victorian	Modern	Australian
Milton's *Paradise Lost* (pp. 81–4)	Blake's *Songs of Innocence and of Experience* (pp. 89–94)	Wilde's *The Importance of Being Earnest* (pp. 153–6)	Joyce's *Ulysses* (pp. 178–83)	Paterson's 'The Man From Snowy River' (pp. 199–201)
Shakespeare's *King Lear* (pp. 76–9)	Austen's *Pride and Prejudice* (pp. 117–22)	Bronte's *Jane Eyre* (pp. 145–8)	Eliot's 'The Love Song of J Alfred Prufrock' (pp. 187–93)	Winton's *Cloudstreet* (pp. 218–19)
Sonnets (p. 65)	Blake's 'London' (p. 92)	Dickens's *Hard Times* (p. 141)	Conrad's *Heart of Darkness* (pp. 168–9)	Lawson's 'The Drover's Wife' (p. 202)
More's *Utopia* (not media texts) (pp. 57–61)	Coleridge's 'Kubla Khan' (not media texts) (pp. 104–8)	Dickens's *Great Expectations* (not media texts) (pp. 143–4)	Review questions and activities (not media texts) (p. 194)	Mackellar's 'My Country' (not media texts) (pp. 202–4)
Sidney's *Astrophel and Stella* (pp. 63–5)	Shelley's 'Ozymandias' (pp. 111–13)	Tennyson's 'The Lady of Shalott' and Waterhouse's paintings (pp. 130–8)	Woolf's *To the Lighthouse* (pp. 183–7)	Stead's *For Love Alone* (pp. 209–10)
Marlowe's *Dr Faustus* (pp. 71–5)	Wordsworth's 'Tintern Abbey' (pp. 94–104)	'Forge a poet' activity (activity 2, pp. 159–60)	Conrad's *Heart of Darkness* (pp. 165–9)	The Ern Malley affair: Malley v. Elliot (activities, pp. 211–12)

Acknowledgments

The authors extend special thanks to Mary and Stephen Parker, without whom this book could not have been written.

IMAGES

Cover: © Photolibrary.com.
Pages 25, 35, 45, 118, 163, 183: © Photolibrary.com; **29:** Gerard Butler as Beowulf in *Beowulf and Grendel*. Courtesy of Sturla Gunnarsson/Equinoxe Films; **40:** Robert Chambers *Book of Plays* (1871); **58:** Portrait of Sir Thomas More by Hans Holbein the Younger. Copyright The Frick Collection, New York; **68, 112:** Shutterstock. com; **79:** Barry Otto as Prospero. The Company B production of *The Tempest*, directed by Neil Armfield, at the Belvoir Street Theatre, 1995. Photo by Heidrum Lohr; **82:** Illustration by Gustave Doré in John Milton's *Paradise Lost*. National Library of Australia Rbf 821.4 M662 (2242965); **90:** William Blake *Songs of Innocence and of Experience, shewing the two contrary states of the human soul*. National Library of Australia 821.7 B636s <006138207>; **95:** © Martin Craster; **103:** Courtesy NASA/HST Key Project Team; **110:** © Newspix/Diena and Brengola; **113:** © AFP Photo/Ramzi Haidar; **125:** 'Outdoor Relief' in James Grant *Sketches in London*. State Library of Victoria; **131:** Gustave Doré *The Doré Gift Book: Illustrations to Tennyson's* Idylls of the King (188-); **145:** Courtesy Phil Tully, www.shopsinripon.co.uk; **149:** Engraving by DG Rossetti in Christina Rossetti *Goblin Market and Other Poems*. National Library of Australia RB 821.8 R8292; **154:** © Ruperto Wite; **165:** Library of Congress [LC-USW33-031074-D]; **172:** © Australian Picture Library; **179:** © AP Photo/Maxwells; **197:** © Ged Unsworth; **199:** National Archives of Australia [A1200:L9007]; **201:** [Portrait of Henry Lawson] National Library of Australia an23352041; **207:** Frank Hurley [Ferry leaving Milson's Point] National Library of Australia an23477934; **213:** Photo by Graeme Rainsbury.

TEXT

Extracts from *The Lord of the Rings: The Fellowship of the Ring* Reprinted by permission of HarperCollins Publishers Ltd. © JRR Tolkien, 1954.

Dorothea Mackellar 'My Country' By Arrangement with the Licensor, c/- Curtis Brown (Aust) Pty Ltd.

Kenneth Slessor *Five Bells* from his *Selected Poems* reproduced with permission of HarperCollins Publishers.

Extracts from Christina Stead *For Love Alone* reproduced with kind permission of Margaret Harris.

Extracts from Ern Malley *The Darkening Ecliptic* reproduced with permission of Mr Lee Riley, executor of the estate of Harold Stewart, and Curtis Brown (Aust) Pty Ltd, on behalf of Mr Michael McAuley.

Judith Wright 'At Cooloolah' from *A Human Pattern: Selected Poems* (ETT Imprint, Sydney, 1995).

Extract from *Cloudstreet* by Tim Winton, published by McPhee Gribble, an imprint of Penguin Books Australia, 1991.

Extracts from *Beowulf* by Seamus Heaney reproduced with the permission of Faber and Faber Ltd.

Extracts from 'The Love Song of J Alfred Prufrock' and 'The Waste Land' by T S Eliot reproduced with permission of Faber and Faber Ltd.

Every effort has been made to trace and acknowledge copyright. The publishers apologise for any accidental infringement and welcome information that would rectify any error or omission in subsequent editions.

The Canon & Literary Criticism

Outcomes

By the end of this unit you should have:

¤ developed an understanding of the way historical, cultural and political forces shape the values and ideas in 'canonical' texts

¤ recognised the interrelationship between texts and their contexts

¤ analysed and questioned the idea of a 'canon' of great texts written in English by writers from England, Scotland, Wales and Ireland

¤ considered canonical texts on the basis of how writers produce them and also how they are received by readers and/or audiences

¤ developed an understanding of a variety of perspectives through which texts can be seen, such as Marxist and feminist

¤ gained enjoyment through engaging with ideas about texts.

Introduction to *the* canon

Introductory activity: rock and roll hall of fame

In 2004, the music magazine *Rolling Stone* produced a 'canon' of the top 500 rock and roll songs of all time. The list came from all pop music genres of the past fifty years, 'from Hank Williams to OutKast'. The first fifty songs on the list are shown in the table on pages 2–3.

Question

Before you look at the following list of the top fifty songs, jot down what you think some of the tracks on this list should be.

ROLLING STONE'S TOP FIFTY ROCK AND ROLL SONGS

Rank	Song title	Artist	Year
1	'Like a Rolling Stone'	Bob Dylan	1965
2	'(I Can't Get No) Satisfaction'	The Rolling Stones	1965
3	'Imagine'	John Lennon	1971
4	'What's Going on?'	Marvin Gaye	1971
5	'Respect'	Aretha Franklin	1967
6	'Good Vibrations'	The Beach Boys	1966
7	'Johnny B Goode'	Chuck Berry	1958
8	'Hey Jude'	The Beatles	1968
9	'Smells Like Teen Spirit'	Nirvana	1991
10	'What'd I Say' (Parts 1 and 2) (Stereo)	Ray Charles	1959
11	'My Generation'	The Who	1965
12	'A Change Is Gonna Come'	Sam Cooke	1964
13	'Yesterday'	The Beatles	1965
14	'Blowin' in the Wind'	Bob Dylan	1963
15	'London Calling'	The Clash	1980
16	'I Want to Hold Your Hand'	The Beatles	1963
17	'Purple Haze'	Jimi Hendrix	1967
18	'Maybellene'	Chuck Berry	1955
19	'Hound Dog'	Elvis Presley	1956
20	'Let It Be'	The Beatles	1970
21	'Born to Run'	Bruce Springsteen	1975
22	'Be My Baby'	The Ronettes	1963
23	'In My Life'	The Beatles	1965
24	'People Get Ready'	The Impressions	1965
25	'God Only Knows'	The Beach Boys	1966
26	'A Day in the Life'	The Beatles	1967
27	'Layla'	Derek and the Dominos	1970
28	'(Sittin' on) The Dock of the Bay'	Otis Redding	1968
29	'Help!'	The Beatles	1965
30	'I Walk the Line'	Johnny Cash	1956
31	'Stairway to Heaven'	Led Zeppelin	1971
32	'Sympathy for the Devil'	The Rolling Stones	1968
33	'River Deep, Mountain High'	Tina Turner	1966
34	'You've Lost that Lovin' Feeling'	The Righteous Brothers	1964
35	'Light My Fire'	The Doors	1967
36	'One'	U2	1991
37	'No Woman No Cry' (Live)	Bob Marley	1975
38	'Gimme Shelter'	The Rolling Stones	1969
39	'That'll Be the Day'	Buddy Holly	1957
40	'Dancing in the Streets'	Martha and the Vandellas	1964
41	'The Weight'	The Band	1968
42	'Waterloo Sunset'	The Kinks	1968
43	'Tutti Frutti'	Little Richard	1956

44	'Georgia on My Mind'	Ray Charles	1960
45	'Heartbreak Hotel'	Elvis Presley	1956
46	'Heroes'	David Bowie	1977
47	'Bridge over Troubled Water'	Simon and Garfunkel	1970
48	'All along the Watchtower'	Jimi Hendrix	1968
49	'Hotel California'	The Eagles	1976
50	'The Tracks of My Tears'	Smokey Robinson	1965

Rock and roll has existed for a little over fifty years. There are 500 songs on the complete *Rolling Stone* list. Distributed evenly, that would be about ten songs per year. Yet only three songs released during the seven years prior to the list being created (that is, during 1998–2004) made it into the top 500. These are:

¤ 'Stan' by Eminem 2000 (position: 290)

¤ 'Lose Yourself' (explicit) by Eminem 2002 (position: 166)

¤ 'Hey Ya!' by OutKast 2003 (position: 180).

Questions

1 a Make a tally of how many of the songs you knew.

b Now make a tally of the years in which these songs were produced. What do you notice about this?

2 Why do you think *Rolling Stone* would bother making a list such as this?

3 a How do you think *Rolling Stone* has defined 'rock and roll'?

b What types of popular music are included on this list?

c What types of popular music seem to have been excluded?

4 Recent songs appear to be underrepresented on the list. Rate the following possible reasons for this. Use a rating from 1–5 for persuasiveness, and justify your ratings:

a Rock is simply not as good now as it used to be. Its heyday was in the 1960s.

b The people who made the list are old and out of touch.

c We need to wait for some time after a song is released to determine whether the song is a classic.

d The people who made this list are hung up on guitars and don't like rap/urban.

e The people who made this list are racist against black people.

f *Rolling Stone* can see that the rock industry has sold out.

It is clear that this authoritative list of the 'best' popular songs did not come out of thin air. Instead, people made the list. So, who made it seems to be a vital question. This is how *Rolling Stone* describes its judging panel and explains some of the ways the song choices were made:

> Welcome to the ultimate jukebox: ... a celebration of the greatest rock and
> roll songs of all time, chosen by a five-star jury of singers, musicians, producers,

industry figures, critics and, of course, songwriters ... The editors of *Rolling Stone* called on rock stars and leading authorities to list their fifty favorite songs, in order of preference. The 172 voters, who included Brian Wilson, Joni Mitchell and Wilco's Jeff Tweedy, were asked to select songs from the rock and roll era. They nominated 2103 songs in virtually every pop-music genre of the past half-century and beyond, from Hank Williams to OutKast. The results were tabulated according to a weighted point system.

Questions

1 Which groups of people were included in the 'jury' that made the list? What do you think about including these groups?

2 List the groups of people who seem to be excluded from, or underrepresented in, the jury. Should these groups have been included or excluded? How do you think the list of songs would look if these groups had been included or more adequately represented?

3 Why do you think *Rolling Stone* used a 'weighted' point system?

Activity

Make up a class list of the best ten songs of the past five years. This will be your own 'musical canon'. You choose the rules as to how you are going to create this canon. Possible areas to consider:

a How are you going to weight the voting? For example, should some people (such as music students and people who play in a band) have more voting power than others?

b Should your teacher vote?

c Should there be a ban on songs you have only heard in the last few weeks?

d Are you going to vote for your favourite songs, or are you going to agree on a short list of, say, fifty songs?

A 'canon' of works of literature is a little like a rock and roll 'best of'. However, a canon of literary works has been a lot longer in the making and is not created by a single vote.

Questions

1 Reflect on how you made your list of favourite songs. How is the process the same as that used to make a canonical list of literary works? How is it different? In summary, what do you think are the key points to emerge from your reflection?

2 What did you learn from the *Rolling Stone* activity above?

3 Can there be any such thing as a 'best of' anything? What gets in the way of choosing a 'best of'?

»

4 What benefits and disadvantages can you see in studying a 'best of' anything?

5 When creating a 'best of' should we ignore what was made in a society that is different from ours (for example, one that existed fifty years ago) and say that it is not relevant to us? Why or why not?

What is the 'English canon'?

When this book refers to the 'canon' of English literary works it is discussing a body of selected works written in English over the last thousand years by writers from England, Wales, Scotland and Ireland; so it is really a 'British' canon. It is felt by many that these works have stood the 'test of time'. This means that the works are not only seen as having value and significance when they were written, but also that succeeding generations have regarded them as being worthy of reading. Some more recent works are also considered to be part of the canon because people believe strongly that those works will stand the 'test of time' and be valued by generations to come. However, the entire idea of a canon has come under sustained scrutiny over the last fifty years. We will explore some of these arguments below.

Many generations of readers have valued the works included on the canon.

It is important to note that other countries (such as the USA, France, Vietnam, Canada and China) also have their own equally vibrant national canons. Space prevents us from including these. There is one exception to this: an Australian 'canon' is included in Unit 7, and demonstrates the way in which lists of the 'great works' of national literature are formed. The British canon was itself formed as a list of 'masterpieces' in the vernacular (native language) that was meant to assert the importance of native British culture and compete with great works in Latin, Greek and French. By way of contrast, you may want to spend some time thinking about the US literary canon as a contemporary national canon that is experiencing upheaval and turmoil in terms of national authority and globalisation. The USA's position in contemporary world politics influences the way in which they see their own literary canon, and the way in which non-Americans react to the US canon, either positively or negatively.

'Canon' comes from a Greek word, meaning reed. (It is the same as our word 'cane'.) A reed or cane was used as a measuring stick (or yardstick), and certain works were said to 'measure up' to the idea of what literature should be. For example, some plays by Shakespeare quickly fitted the measure (according to his contemporaries). They became accepted into the literary canon quite early and stayed there. Other books, such as *Wuthering Heights*, were measured against the yardstick and discarded by reviewers and critics until about 100 years after their publication. So, in actuality, the canon has always been highly varied because the measuring yardstick changes over time according to the change in the criteria for what is valuable. The canon has undergone constant change because the conditions of production (publication) and reception (criticism and readership) are always changing.

If you want to know what a reasonably standard canonical list of English literature looks like, refer to the contents page of this book.

Origins of the canon

Opinions among scholars differ about exactly when the concept of the English canon began to form. Some critics suggest that as early as the sixteenth century certain writers were being recommended as especially valuable. Shakespeare was eulogised by his contemporary Ben Jonson as 'not of an age but for all time'. Although Jonson's comment indicates the relatively early significance in British literature of the idea of what might last or have universal appeal, it was not until the eighteenth century that the formation of what we think of today as the English canon really began. Until this time, the most valuable works of literature had generally been seen as those in classical languages. However, eighteenth-century critics, such as Samuel Johnson (one of the first of a class of 'professional' writers and critics), began to propose a canon of great English writers. Until that time, the classical texts had been used in schools and universities as guides to learning rhetoric (the art of using language effectively to please or persuade) and effective written style. In the eighteenth century, critics began to promote certain written works for their intrinsic aesthetic value and, above all, as examples of good taste and refined sensibility. These texts were recommended for use within the educational system and for the general reading public.

The growth of the canon was also related to economic and legal factors, as well as social and aesthetic ones. Publishing began to be privately financed, and made profitable by the income of the growing literate classes. In addition, copyright on books became limited to twenty-one years. Older books were out of copyright and cheaper, and thus more attractive. A reputable list of what one ought to read became newly important for the middle class as a form of 'cultural capital'.

There has always been disagreement and controversy about the canon, and there continues to be vigorous, even heated, debate about the existence and nature of the literary canon. The following material will give you an understanding of these arguments and provide a sharp 'lens' through which you can view the following units of this book.

Context: ways of seeing the canon

This book does not treat canonical works as museum pieces in glass cases to which we should all dutifully pay our respects. We do think there is much to appreciate in these works. However, it is vital to treat these works as texts that were produced by authors who were influenced by their times, and texts that are received by us as readers who are influenced by our times. This approach means we can see this literature as part of living culture in the twenty-first century instead of works that have passed their use-by date.

As times change, values change, cultural assumptions change and therefore meanings of texts change. The values of chivalry portrayed in the King Arthur stories, for example, would have had a very different meaning for a medieval peasant than for a twenty-first century banker. However, both meanings are relevant and valid. Like a chameleon, canonical texts reinvent

The canon is just a list made by old men who want everyone else to study what they studied at school.

The canon is a list of the fine literature of a culture that we can be proud of as a product of that culture.

A canon contains some of the most beautiful, stirring and exciting works ever written. Everyone should be able to savour it.

A canon is a representative sample of the writings of a culture that can be studied to understand the workings of that culture.

A canon is a distracting waste of time that gets in the way of teaching people how to secure a career.

A canon is an oppressive instrument that shines big spotlights on white male authors, but keeps women, working class people and other races in the dark.

The canon is irrelevant. Any piece of writing is as valid as any other piece.

A canon is a moral instrument that teaches people how they should behave.

Differing views on the canon.

themselves to suit the new times. If meanings change, this indicates that there is the possibility of there being as many readings, or interpretations, as there are readers.

Literary critics have accepted, to a certain extent, that when anyone interprets a text they bring their own subjectivity and bias to the task; it is inevitable. There is no one ultimately 'correct' interpretation (though there can be some very unsustainable and poorly argued interpretations). This means that it is still useful to read rigorously the list of 'great' literary works, but in new and critical ways.

A traditional reading list is a window that shows us a lot about what is dominant and powerful in a culture. It also indicates what may be resistant or subversive. In addition, it allows us to study and speculate about the culture, as well as the contents, of the reading list. By looking closely at some of the units in this book you will see how the connection between the literary canon and culture works in practice. As Cathy N Davidson argues in *Revolution and the Word: The Rise of the Novel in America*, 'literature is one way in which values are taught in society and canonisation is the mechanism for that larger enterprise'. Edward Said makes a similar connection between canon and culture in the introduction to his book *Culture and Imperialism*:

> The novels and other books I consider here I analyse because first of all I find them estimable and admirable works of art and learning, in which I and many other readers take pleasure and from which we derive profit. Second, the challenge is to connect them not only with that pleasure and profit but also with the imperial process of which they were manifestly and unconcealedly a part; rather than condemning and ignoring their participation in what was an unquestioned reality in their societies, I suggest that what we learn about this hitherto ignored aspect actually and truly *enhances* our reading and understanding of them.

Said is making a powerful suggestion here: there are many reasons for us to be attracted to the canon (including pleasure, value and status) and this attraction is always going to involve us in political and even imperial processes.

When we study a literary canon, we study what sort of work 'made it in' (inclusions) and what sort of work was left out (exclusions). This study is political. We look at how inclusion on the list gives a text cultural privilege and power, and makes people feel that they 'should' read it. We can also think about how we, as readers, by our very acts of reading, are part of this process of inclusion and exclusion—whether we like it or not.

We can look at the canon in order to study three broad areas: literacy, cultural production and artistic production. Everyone needs to study something to learn about these areas. The works accepted as a part of the canon are as good (or sometimes perhaps even better) to study as anything else. The works in this book all have sufficient complexity to repay close study. Complexity offers an educational challenge, as well as teaching analytic technique and providing pleasure. The inclusion of these 'great' works 'on the list' will certainly affect how you read them.

So what can the canon do for you? The canon allows you to ask questions about why anyone produces art in the first place, and how it functions throughout different cultures and down the ages. Studying literature as part of an historical context gives you insights into language, times and other consciousnesses that you would not have otherwise. Finally, the canon allows you to explore works that many people have read and loved and been amazed by over the centuries. Perhaps you will love them and be amazed by them too.

Humanism and the canon

Humanism is a body of thought that emerged in the Renaissance when many people stopped looking only to God for teachings about matters such as ethics and morality and decided to focus their attention as well on the human spirit and the history of human progress. Many humanists regarded the human spirit as the most important source of enlightenment and knowledge. They believed that if one is going to look to humans for education about greatness, morality, ethics and so on then the best place to search is the writings of humans. This way one could see into the minds of the most profound and ethical humans who ever lived, and their learning and wisdom might be transferred to the reader.

For several centuries the mediums that provided insights into the human condition were 'great' works of poetry and drama. By the late nineteenth century, novels could also count as masterpieces. The quality of the writing and the stirring actions of the heroes and heroines (such as King Arthur, Elizabeth Bennett and Aragorn) might inspire us to become better people ourselves. On the other hand, texts showing the downfall of villains (including Faustus, Macbeth and Becky Sharpe) could act as cautionary tales. In this vein, the poet and critic Matthew Arnold (1822–1888) insisted that, apart from having aesthetic and pleasing qualities, literature had something important to teach us. Arnold thought that literature saved people from being philistines (narrow-minded and materialistic) and that it elevated their understanding and moral sense.

Famous twentieth-century humanists, such as FR Leavis and QD Leavis, suggested that this potential for improvement of the reader was a major determinant of whether a work is judged to be great. The great author is great because he or she has managed to convey 'an authentic vision of life' that would communicate a deep moral vision and train the feelings, sensibilities and reasoning power of those who studied that author's work.

Questions

1 RECAP: What did humanists think were the benefits of studying the canon?

2 Where did you learn your set of values? Were any key books, plays and/or poems involved in establishing your values? If so, how were they involved?

3 Make a list of some of the most famous fictional characters you know. (They can be from film or written texts.) What values could these characters 'teach' you?

4 Do you think literature should aim to teach morality and ethics? Why or why not?

Challenges to humanism

Westminster Abbey: a symbol of societal structures that people are influenced by but over which they have little control.

Humanists believe that individuals are the most powerful agents in their own fate. Thus, the individual is free to improve him or herself. For humanists, literature is an important tool in this process of improvement. Marx, Nietzsche and Freud (see Unit 6, pages 163–4) were nineteenth and early twentieth-century thinkers who challenged the concept that individuals were free and self-governing. Collectively, they suggested that people participated in, and their lives were shaped by, large social, political and cultural structures over which they did not have control. These structures could be described as systems of class and economic inequality (as Marx suggested) or of religion (as Nietzsche suggested) or could even be the manifestations of unconscious psychology (as Freud suggested). If this is true, then people can read all the literature they like as part of self-directed freedom and improvement, but the results will be ultimately futile because it is the system, rather than the individual, that needs to be changed.

Anti-humanist critics argue that literature can cleverly present and promote an ideology that falsely makes people believe that justice will be done and that individuals can improve themselves in the current system. (For example, Dickens's Oliver Twist improved himself by being delightful and honest. Austen's Elizabeth Bennett held out for love and got her man.) This may mean that people will be fooled into not agitating for wholesale changes in the unfair way that society has been set up. In other words, far from delivering moral lessons and self-improvement, literature often supports the dominant ideology (system of belief) by silencing opposition to it, or at least making the ideology seem 'natural'. Also, every act of inclusion in the canon is also an act of exclusion. Every voice we hear is another voice silenced. It is no surprise that the silenced voices are often those from the margins of society: women, servants, labourers, immigrants and slaves.

In addition, complex theories (such as postmodernism and post-structuralism) emerged during the 1950s and 1960s and challenged the whole basis of a literary canon. These theories were based on philosophical insights about how the very structure of language itself is unstable. If language is unstable, these theorists wondered, how could meaning ultimately be decided, and how could anyone confidently value any one piece of writing over any other? These theories further established that bias, stereotypes and excluded voices were inevitable aspects of constructing any canon. Today, most critics start by assuming that literary texts cannot avoid being part of what Michel Foucault called a 'discourse', or a system of ideas with a particular vocabulary that carries social power. This means that we understand from the outset that the canon is a problematic way to select and represent certain kinds of writing. We also understand that for as many dominant and privileged readings of texts, there are an equal number of possible resistant and alternative readings.

The English canon seems to have many attractions, but also many problems (including the humanist versus anti-humanist debate). How do we deal with this? Perhaps we need to do a double manoeuvre: we should embrace a literary canon—appreciate it, benefit from it and love it—while always remaining suspicious of it. We should perhaps rejoice that the canon is a source of lively debate and cultural turmoil, and acknowledge that our aim is to read critically and widely rather than to seek to resolve the debate.

Questions

1 RECAP: Explain, in your own words, the main challenges to a humanistic view of the canon.

2 Do you think there is anything wrong with literature supporting an ideology, such as free market capitalism? Explain your answer.

3 Imagine that you are living in a fascist dictatorship in which all the literature you had read since you were a child supported the dictatorship's belief system (ideology). Do you think you would support this ideology? Justify your response.

4 Can the act of studying an *English* canon be oppressive to people of other cultures? Do you think a canon can help create a situation in society where certain people are excluded from social and cultural power?

The American 'culture wars'

In the 1980s and 1990s, the USA experienced what has become known as the 'culture wars', when humanist academics launched a counterattack on the various vigorous challenges to humanism. The literary canon was the battlefield. The defence of humanism and the traditional canon was spearheaded by Harold Bloom. He asserted his view about the aesthetic and spiritual greatness that excellent literature can communicate. Such greatness, he argued, embodies values that should be treasured and protected by the West. Bloom and others felt that post-structuralism was eroding the great traditions of western learning with which they had grown up. They felt that the great aspects of western culture were being sucked into a quagmire of truthlessness, pop culture, relativism, advertising headlines and tokenistic multicultural criticism. Bloom objected to the position that the writing on a chip packet (which is how he saw the direction of post-structuralist analysis) should take place alongside the complete works of Shakespeare. He wrote *The Western Canon* (1996) in this context.

Many readers have seen Bloom as a necessarily feisty and heroic defender of western art against a truthless, valueless and superficial postmodern condition. Equally, many critics have felt that Bloom didn't provide informed counter-arguments to the insights of postmodernism; he just dismissed them. Some expressed disappointment that instead of agreeing that different histories can operate side by side, Bloom felt the need to argue for one 'totalising', timeless and authoritative literary history.

It seems that trying to raise one more orthodox list against another is not really fruitful. Rather, we might continue to debate the terms and teaching practices that make the canon such an interesting and touchy subject and not just a squabble about a list. Indeed, many contemporary readers and critics have tended to be interested in discussing literature in terms of how cultural identity is constructed through writing and other forms of representation. Individual works of literature give us a chance to study and analyse language and creativity. The literary canon is an extension of this opportunity, providing the added possibility of speculating more widely about culture, tradition and ethics.

Questions

1 With whom do you agree more: Bloom or his critics? Explain the reasons for your response.

2 Who should have the most influence on the western canon: Harold Bloom, your teacher or Oprah Winfrey? Why?

3 How do you think the explosion in visual technologies (such as film and the web) will affect the canon? Will the canon survive it?

4 Choose one category of representation that is not literature (such as films, cartoons or journalism). List at least five great works from your selected category and explain your choices.

5 Should there be a 'canon' of photographs and websites, for example? Explain your answer.

»

Literary critical perspectives

One important area of thought that has continued to fuel the challenges to humanism since the 1950s relates to how ideologies (systems of belief) operate in texts. The idea that the literary canon is a list of masterpieces that will stand the test of the ages because they are timelessly appealing and excellent has been robustly challenged by the view that we all read from particular positions. These positions are inevitably biased and dependent on contextual factors, such as class, race and gender. Since the current view seems to be that there is no single way of reading works of literature, it is useful to know something about the various critical perspectives for reading literature that have emerged in the twentieth century. The following summaries of literary critical perspectives are intended to help students understand that there is a range of possible readings of texts. The summaries also provide students with an introduction to the overall concepts and technical language of these reading positions. These summaries are often referred to in later activities in this book.

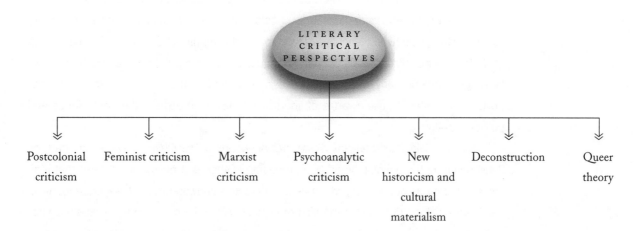

Literary critical perspectives.

Note: The following sections intentionally use some of the metalanguage that is necessary for the communication of the ideas contained in many of the literary critical perspectives. (Metalanguage refers to the language or vocabulary used to describe or analyse language.)

Postcolonial criticism

Postcolonial criticism attempts to understand the problems posed by European colonialism and its aftermath and its inescapable effects on literary production. Postcolonial literature consists of a body of writing from continents and countries whose political existence has been shaped by the experience of colonialism. These include Africa, India, Canada, the Americas, Australia and New Zealand. One can also study literature from Britain using a postcolonial focus.

Postcolonial criticism looks at questions of:

¤ History: Postcolonial criticism is interested in foregrounding the often-invisible accounts of the process and experience of colonisation and the postcolonial world.

¤ Identity and its formation: Postcolonial criticism highlights the way in which the process and experience of colonisation affects the way in which people identify themselves and others.

¤ Ethnicity and race: This is one of the most significant aspects of identity in postcolonial criticism because it relates to the way in which certain people are empowered or oppressed.

¤ Gender: This is another significant aspect of identity in postcolonial criticism because it can never be separated from any other facet of identity, and because it relates to the way in which women, in particular, are empowered or oppressed.

¤ Hegemony: This refers to the way in which certain social and political groups (colonial power) come to dominate with the seeming consent of the oppressed (colonised people).

¤ Discourse: This is an area of social knowledge made up of specific statements and vocabulary. Colonialism and imperialism are examples of such areas of knowledge.

¤ Hybridity: The idea of a crossing or grafting between two things takes a variety of forms in postcolonial criticism, including linguistic, cultural, political and racial forms.

¤ Ambivalence: Colonised peoples often have a fluctuating and contradictory relationship with the colonising power that never simply amounts to either opposition or complicity.

Language is one of the most crucial aspects of postcolonial criticism because language is a zone where the effects and accounts of colonisation can be identified and analysed. For example, Creole is a hybrid language created out of the conditions of colonialism in the south of North America. Dispossession of native language and the requirement to use the imperial language is one of many kinds of dispossession created by the colonialist project. It leads postcolonial writers to use a range of linguistic strategies to express their experience and political position.

Edward Said's *Orientalism: Western Conceptions of the Orient* (1978) examined the construction of the oriental 'other' by Europeans. ('Other' is a philosophical term that indicates the opposite of the 'self', which helps to create self-awareness and separate identity.) Said's work helped to establish the field of postcolonial criticism. Since the 1980s, debates in postcolonial criticism have centred on the way in which colonial and postcolonial subjects are represented and discussed.

Postcolonial criticism has a number of common ideas:

¤ Postcolonial literature may provide versions of colonial experience that contest European versions; that is, colonised people may write their own history.

¤ The language of the colonial power (such as English) is used but is varied to better reflect the colonised country. As a result, distinctive variant forms of that language arise. Postcolonial writers writing in English may reject the correct or standard rules of grammar, and choose to work with native dialect. This is known as abrogation. These writers may also use the forms and genres of English and modify them for their own, often subversive, purposes. This process is referred to as appropriation.

¤ Postcolonial literature may seek to awaken political and cultural nationalism.

¤ Writers explore the tensions between the centre of the colonising power (such as London) and those that have been colonised (such as India). This is sometimes described as the power struggle between the 'metropolitan centre' and the 'margins'.

¤ Postcolonial writers may present their own examples of women's experience, which is often hidden in colonial literature.

Postcolonial criticism continues to address ideas about culture, representation and the post-colonial world.

Feminist criticism

There are numerous positions and controversies within feminist criticism. Many of these are part of the wider range of feminist thinking in relation to society as a whole and are not specific to literature. On the other hand, literature is seen as a particular focus for the preconceptions and prejudices that can be discovered by feminist analysis, and an array of special terms and concepts have been defined to aid these investigations.

A tenet of feminist thought is that masculine (patriarchal) ways of perceiving and ordering are 'inscribed' into the prevailing ideology of society. Analysing texts from a feminist perspective can demonstrate how patriarchal assumptions are communicated.

In patriarchal societies, language contains binary oppositions of qualities, such as active/passive, adventurous/timid or reasonable/irrational. It is argued that the feminine is always associated with the less desirable words in the listed pairs. Other pairs include head/heart, reason/feeling and strength/weakness. Women are subordinated because the language used to describe them is inherently negative.

In patriarchies, areas of human achievement are defined in terms of masculine ideas and aspirations, and the presumption that advances in civilisation have always been brought about by men. Women are thus conditioned to enter society accepting their own inferiority. Literary texts may depict women in terms of stereotypes of womanhood (such as polarising them into virgins and whores) or marginalise female characters (and readers) by supporting the higher value of masculine endeavours and interests. One related political idea is that femininity is a construction of society rather than an inherent or essential set of qualities. One task of feminist criticism is to examine and re-evaluate literature in light of this perception.

Another important debate within feminism is between the ideas of essentialism and performativity. Those who believe there are certain timeless characteristics of femininity (essentialism) disagree with those who believe that gender is something that is repeatedly acted out or 'performed' on a daily basis, and really has no essential basis at all.

A feminist approach to literary criticism

Early feminist literary criticism investigated the position of women as readers of patriarchal texts by analysing how these works addressed and positioned women readers.

Feminist literary criticism went on to investigate the position of women as writers within patriarchy. This involved demonstrating that there was a rich history of women's writing, and asking whether there is a specific way in which women write about female experience.

Feminist literary criticism then began to ask questions about the cultural constructions of gender, based on binary oppositions. This has involved thinking about:

¤ identifying patriarchal bias—questioning whether women are considered automatically inferior
¤ re-evaluating the representations of women in texts
¤ uncovering discrimination in language.

Contemporary feminist literary criticism is engaged in debates in an area loosely described as feminisms of difference, in which the idea of difference rather than sameness has become central to discussions about sexuality, gender, ethnicity, race, class and culture.

Marxist criticism

Marxist literary criticism, which began to emerge in the 1920s, is based on the economic and political theories of Karl Marx. Marx proposed a model of history in which economic and political conditions determined social conditions. Marxist literary criticism considers literature in terms of how it reflects class struggles and economic conditions. It also looks at how texts might distort a picture of society by showing it from the point of view of only the upper and/or middle class. For the Marxist critic, literature must be understood in relation to the determining forces of society: history, economics, politics, class and ideology. If economics forms the basis of our existence and shapes our lives, then how and why do people write literary texts?

More recent Marxist criticism has been concerned with how human beings are created through ideological structures, such as schools and governments. It has also focused on the significant role of hegemony (domination by consent) in shaping cultural and economic life.

In this capitalist age, the means of production are owned by the bourgeoisie (middle class). Bourgeois ideology (capitalism, hard work, reward for 'talent' and so on) has been devised to keep power from the working class. This ideology permeates every aspect of society, thought and culture, including criticism, education and, significantly, literature.

Psychoanalytic criticism

Psychoanalytic literary criticism emerged in the middle of the twentieth century, based on the theories of Sigmund Freud and his followers (such as Jacques Lacan). Freud developed the discipline of psychoanalysis as a means of curing neuroses in his patients, but its concepts were expanded so that they could be used to understand human behaviour and culture generally. Freud's ideas include the concept of the unconscious mind, the importance of dreams, and the idea of sublimation to artistic processes. Freudian theory regards the fundamental motivation of all human behaviour as the avoidance of pain and the gaining of pleasure. These theories influenced many writers, artists and critics in the early decades of the twentieth century.

Literature, for Freud, is produced by the same mechanism as dreams. Desires that are in conflict with social norms are censored and relegated to the subconscious; they are repressed. However, they do not stay there. Instead they re-emerge in forms that are modified, disguised and all but unrecognisable to the conscious mind. There are various common forms for this distortion in dreams and literature. Sexual symbolism is the most widely recognised of these. This gives rise to the concept of the Freudian symbol; that is, something that resembles a sexual object is seen to represent sexual desire. For example, a cylindrical object can be interpreted as a representation of the penis. Psychoanalysis has had a significant impact on literary studies, both as a means of interpretation and as a theory about human beings and language.

The critical application of Freudian concepts generally falls into three categories:

¤ emphasising the author's psychological conflicts as evidenced in his or her work
¤ focusing on the way in which the texts allow readers to access hidden desires and fears
¤ analysing the characters in a text as if they were real people.

Such an analysis of the characters may involve the reader finding the subtext (the unconscious, or covert, motives and feelings) communicated in the characters' speech or action. It may also cause the reader to look for the characters' psychoanalytic symptoms. These may include:

¤ repression—pushing a deep desire into one's unconscious
¤ sublimation—having a deep desire reappear in a different way
¤ the Oedipus complex—a male experiencing sexual love for his mother and, subsequently, feeling competitive jealousy with his father
¤ transference and projection—seeing in other's behaviour something that actually tells one more about one's own behaviour.

Psychoanalytic literary criticism may also discover conflict and competing desires in a text. This could involve looking for images, symbols, metaphors, conceits, superstitions, myths and objects that have sexual connotations.

While important, these Freudian approaches can produce dated applications of psychoanalytic theory. Later psychoanalytic theories have proved useful for literary critics who want to speculate about human beings, writing and desire. In terms of literary criticism, it is the work of Lacan that is most important because of his view that the human subject is the *effect* rather than the *cause* of language.

New historicism and cultural materialism

In the 1980s, the American new historicists and the British cultural materialists began to read literary texts with a strong focus on the society in which it was produced; that is, the context of production. Today, these critics look at how texts reflect their society and, more importantly, how the texts can reinforce the dominant social structures of that society. They perceive texts as 'artefacts' that are part of the circulation of power in a society.

American new historicists come from a liberal democratic tradition and are content with pointing out the power relations that were in play when a text was produced. British cultural materialists come from a stronger socialist tradition than the American new historicists. They pursue an additional interest in the possibility of genuine dissidence and in the usually conservative roles that cultural icons, such as Shakespeare, have been made to play in later times.

These theories came about after the digestion of post-structuralist theory, because it was then that people saw literature as integral to a much wider cultural and ideological context. This shift involved a return to acknowledging the important role of history in literary criticism, but not in the same old way; that is, the approach was broadened beyond trying to understand and explain texts by knowing the story of the writers' lives.

New historicists and cultural materialists work with a series of questions and problems rather than a systematic map for the interpretation of literary works. They believe that:

¤ history is textual and texts are always situated within a historical context
¤ literature makes visible ongoing contests for social and cultural power, as well as contests between values, discourses and ideas
¤ the study of literary texts should not be separated from a study of non-literary texts.

Cultural materialists are interested in how we interpret past texts in terms of contemporary power relations and contemporary ideologies.

Deconstruction

Deconstruction is a mode of analysis that identifies and criticises the hierarchical binary oppositions that have structured western thought. (Examples of binary oppositions include nature/culture, man/woman, mind/body, speech/writing and absence/presence.) Often misunderstood as meaning to simply 'analyse' (understand the constituent parts), deconstruction is a specific analytic method pioneered in the work of Jacques Derrida. Coming to prominence in the late 1960s, Derrida was one of the most significant post-structuralists.

Post-structuralism is a term used to describe theoretical discussions that question the possibility of objective knowledge and subjective self-mastery. Structuralists view language as a set of solid tools with which to convey ideas. However, post-structuralists see that language is an unstable medium, with no final guarantee of meaning to stabilise it.

To 'deconstruct' a binary opposition is to demonstrate that each word in the pair (such as man/woman) is defined by the other, and that one term is dominant over the other. Deconstructionists point out that while this hierarchy is often invisible and looks natural, it is not, in fact, natural, and is indeed very significant. The purpose of this close analysis of binaries is to see why one term (man, in the previous example) is dominant. Working deconstructively involves investigating the inconsistencies, contradictions and complexities that are at the heart of dominant terms and, therefore, of dominant ideologies. For this reason, deconstructive reading is useful when attempting to uncover and understand what holds some discourses together; in other words, what creates and binds certain values, beliefs and ideologies.

Queer theory

Just as the experience of colonisation is a key point of reference for postcolonial literary critics, queer theory is a critical perspective that can be used to address and understand texts. The emphasis for queer theorists is on the forms and ideologies of sexuality.

The word 'queer' is used to transform a word meant as a homophobic insult into a term of pride, and to mark the difference from the study of gender.

Following the work of Michel Foucault in *A History of Sexuality* (1976), queer theorists suggest that sexuality is not a 'natural' occurrence; that is, inevitable because it is a part of nature. Instead, they view sexuality as a historical construction, meaning something that cultures have created particular languages and terms in order to describe and control.

Foucault argued that sexuality represents a powerful force that always threatens authority. Therefore, the history of sexuality is the history of the various forms of repression of sexuality. One example of this repression was the gradual marginalisation and criminalisation of homosexuality. British queer theorists identify these sites of repression of sexuality as important and powerful moments in history, with the potential for powerful subversive force.

Foucault's argument has become the springboard for the work of queer theorists, who use the marginalised position of the homosexual as a vantage point from which to criticise the norm of heterosexuality in western culture. Theorists such as Eve Sedgewick and Judith Butler have continued to question the cultural construction of sexuality. They work deconstructively on the binary category of heterosexual/homosexual. Butler, in particular, sees that sexual orientations are not fixed essential identities but are repeated performances of sexuality.

Queer critics work with literary texts in a number of ways. Queer literary criticism:

¤   is interested in highlighting and analysing the history of lesbian and gay writing

¤   locates textual examples of queer desire and analyses how this desire operates as a rejection or subversion of mainstream heterosexuality

¤   analyses homophobia within a text by reading texts resistantly, or against the grain

¤   points out that heterosexuality is the sexuality we commonly accept as the norm, and that this bias creates political and literary oppressions and marginalisations that must be scrutinised

¤   analyses texts in light of the notion that sexuality is a matter of performance rather than essential identity—based on the idea that there is no 'natural' sexuality.

Knights, Floods & Dragons

MEDIEVAL LITERATURE

Highlights

¶ *Hero rips arm off man-eating monster*

¶ *Beast and wizard do battle*

¶ *Thieves fight over loot—kill each other*

¶ *Woman sees God—sixteen times*

¶ *King impales son, hurls sword into lake*

¶ *Weather: rain—for forty days and nights*

Outcomes

By the end of this unit you should have:

¤ developed an understanding of the relationship between the texts and the context of the medieval era (including the literary, cultural and historical contexts)

¤ gained an appreciation of the way in which the texts can be seen as cultural products of both their authors and their times

¤ engaged in detailed textual interpretation of a number of medieval pieces and developed an understanding of how language forms and/ or techniques shape the meaning of these pieces

¤ challenged and evaluated some of the cultural assumptions that exist in medieval texts and considered alternative readings of some texts

¤ come to a personal view about valuing the texts and the medieval period based on your own context and preferences

¤ engaged with the texts in a number of ways, including writing essays and dialogues, participating in discussions and giving drama presentations

¤ gained enjoyment through exposure to the texts and their ideas and contexts.

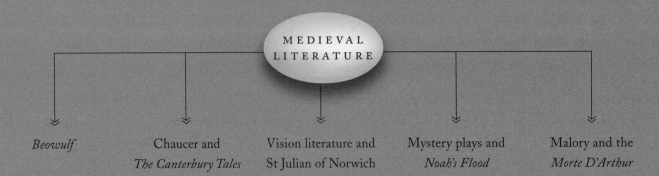

MEDIEVAL
LITERATURE

Beowulf Chaucer and *The Canterbury Tales* Vision literature and St Julian of Norwich Mystery plays and *Noah's Flood* Malory and the *Morte D'Arthur*

Context *of* the period

In this section we will focus on the historical development of medieval language, writing and culture. We will also examine how works have risen up from the medieval past to become part of 'the canon' today.

Historical context

The period covered by the 'medieval' extends from approximately 700 AD to 1485 AD. Scholars divide this period into Old English (until 1066) and Middle English (after 1066). The medieval period begins with the Viking invasions of England. It ends with the introduction of the printing press and the ascension to the throne of the Tudor king Henry VII. The medieval period is characterised by the combination of dynamic changes in beliefs, language, law and leadership and an increasingly established and powerful Christian Church.

The Vikings first attacked England at the monastery in Lindisfarne in 793. In 865, a 'great army' of mainly Danish Vikings conquered much of England and the entire central section of England became known as 'the Danelaw'. In 1066, a successful French invasion was led by William the Conqueror and resulted in the establishment of Norman feudalism across England. Under the feudal system, ordinary farmers (serfs) and local lords owed each other obligations. The lord owed his local population protection. Serfs owed their lord allegiance and a proportion of their harvest. The lord had an enormous capacity to exploit his serfs. The lord essentially owned his serfs, and this entrenched the importance of the 'local principle'—very few people moved out of their immediate village or town during their lifetime. This meant that ideas and literature spread very slowly.

In addition, during this time a large number of civil wars and other battles were fought in pursuit of the throne. Many monarchs were killed in these clashes, among them Richard III, Henry IV, Henry VI and Edward IV. The Hundred Years War—the series of wars fought between France and England from 1338 to 1453—was a particular influence on the literature of this period as it prevented the sort of political stability that is conducive to literary production. The bubonic plague also cut a swath through villages across England, wiping out a third of the population by 1348.

Literary context

Until the printing press was introduced to England in 1474, if a written text existed it had been written by hand. Before the twelfth century, works were written on vellum, which was the dried skin of domestic animals. It was primarily the monasteries, full of willing and able monks, where collections of written works were created and transcribed. Often these transcribers were artists themselves, creating elaborate and beautiful illuminated manuscripts in their scriptoriums (writing rooms).

This method of production produced an artificial skewing of the way in which written works were valued. Monks were more likely to value a work about the transcendent value of prayer than they were to value a work about the earthly joys of family life and children.

(Interestingly, some monks were actually barely literate, and could not always understand what they were transcribing.) These values determined what was produced, transcribed and maintained. Thus, it not surprising that much of the work that exists from the Middle Ages is religious or devotional in nature; although there are secular (non-religious) exceptions, such as *The Battle of Maldon*.

Nonetheless, all books were valued as precious objects. A library was a rare and wonderful thing indeed. All that needed to happen was a fire, a flood, a pillage, or even a spillage, and a 'major' work of English literature could be lost for all time. For example, almost all we have of the original versions of medieval Anglo-Saxon verse exist in just four manuscript copies. We can only guess how many other books of poetry were lost. The sole copy of *Beowulf* almost burnt to ash in a house fire in 1731. How many equivalent poems were lost in this and other fires?

Many works from this time would never have been written down in the first place. Paper and vellum were expensive and beyond the reach of most. Half the medieval English lyrics we have come from a single manuscript called Harley 2253, which was produced in the early 1300s. Much verse, particularly English secular verse that was culturally marginalised, would have been retained orally amongst an illiterate population from generation to generation. Some of this survives as folk music and ballads, but most of this literature is unavailable to us. It is sometimes difficult, but incredibly useful, to think about what it would have been like to participate in a culture where people remembered rather than read things.

Medieval language and literature

During the medieval period there were two different 'broad' languages. The first is Old English, a Saxon language that is almost entirely Germanic and was brought to England with the Viking invaders. The second is Middle English, which is a combination of Old English and French. Modern English was established soon after the introduction of the printing press in the late fifteenth century.

FEATURES OF OLD ENGLISH LITERATURE

Most stories in Old English were written in alliterative verse and in medieval times were spoken to the accompaniment of a harp. These performances were conducted by a scop: a learned man who had a high social standing. Furthermore, only a small amount of the verse was ever written down. Popular language devices used in Old English epics include metonymy, where the name of a feature of a thing is used instead of the name of the thing itself (such as 'keel' for ship), and kenning, where two words are substituted for one (such as 'whale road' for sea).

Many of the stories are conservative, harsh and heroic. They describe legendary figures who are fiercely loyal to their kings as well as kings who, in return, are extremely generous to their knights and others who serve them loyally. In these epics, glory, honour and kinship are all. (See the following extract from *Beowulf*.) Women are almost completely absent from this particular world view.

Note: Old English also produced some sombre Christian meditations, such as *The Seafarer* and *The Dream of the Rood*.

FEATURES OF MIDDLE ENGLISH LITERATURE

Middle English literature is more diverse than Old English literature. This is partially as a result of the language fragmenting; that is, different types of English being used in different regions. Instead of (or as well as) alliteration, new types of metre and rhyme were used in Middle English literature.

In this period the 'romance' was established. These are heroic tales that tell not only of war and battle but also of romantic love and noble, chivalric behaviour. In these stories, the knights tend to gain worth through noble deeds rather than high birth. The tales were usually adapted from French sources and, in comparison with Old English literature, allowed for more magical and imaginative deeds.

There was also an emphasis on God and religious themes. Those works intended for the priesthood were generally written in Latin, while those for transmission to the laity (general population) were in English ('the vernacular'). In the fifteenth century, mystical writing also arose, in which people wrote of their visionary experiences of God. God was also the major theme for medieval drama; the only Middle English plays we have records of either told biblical stories (mystery plays) or reflected on Christian virtues (morality plays).

Questions

1 RECAP: The survival of a medieval work was dependent on a number of factors. What were they?

2 RECAP: Make up a mind map of the major types of literature in Old English and Middle English. What were the major characteristics of each?

3 Choose a film that you think is a modern-day example of a romance story. Justify your choice. Listen to the choices from several other people from your class and choose the film that you think corresponds most closely to a medieval romance as described above.

4 Who held power in these times? How do you think this may have shaped the sort of work being produced in the medieval period?

Activities

1 Draw a circular target. In the centre of it, write the subjects that would have been written about and preserved during medieval times. Further out from the centre, write the subjects that would have been marginalised. Make a list of the societal forces and other factors that you considered when making these choices.

2 Make up some of your own kennings (see the explanation on page 22) for the following words:
a mall
b ballet
c rugby
d celebrity
e eunuch.
Choose four difficult words and give them to the person next to you to turn into kennings. »

3 Look at this evening's television programmes. Compare and contrast the subjects of medieval writing with this evening's offerings on television.

How do your findings reveal what is valued in each age?

DIALECTS AND OTHER LANGUAGES

During the Middle Ages, Britain would have felt like a much larger place than the whole world is now. Today, no place on the globe is currently more than a day or two of travel away from any other—and, with the Internet, information can travel instantly. By contrast, to get news, goods or people from the north of Britain to the south in medieval times would have taken over a week. The local principle was all-important and most people rarely travelled out of their village. This was particularly so for feudal serfs bonded to a particular nobleman and area. It was common for people to have never in their lives been to a town that may be only ten or twenty kilometres away.

In this context, many local dialects of English were maintained and strengthened. If people only spoke to a small pool of others who all lived in the same area, it was very simple for local variations in the language to become commonly used and entrenched. The situation became more pronounced after the Norman invasions in 1066. Before 1066 there was a semi-standard language called Late West Saxon, but after the overthrow of the Saxons by the French, a number of different dialects arose, and each was quite distinct. There was the Midland dialect, the West England dialect, the Staffordshire dialect and the North dialects, amongst others. These were almost separate languages, all within one country. This was an issue for any scholar writing for an English audience: in whose English should the work be written?

Most people simply did not write in English at all. Latin was the preferred language of the Church and many scholars. The Venerable Bede, John of Salisbury and Geoffery of Monmouth, for example, all wrote in Latin. French was the national language of the aristocratic court for hundreds of years after 1066; most of the aristocratic court from William the Conqueror onwards were French. Indeed, for almost 200 years the kings of England could not even speak English. For much of this time, English prose and poetry mainly existed in the margins of society. Each new 'major' text that was written in English rather than in French or Latin was a conscious cultural act in the medieval period. By writing in English, the author was emphasising the local over the aristocratic or the ecclesiastical (the Church). (Examples of these English-language texts are Geoffrey Chaucer's *The Canterbury Tales* and Thomas Malory's *Morte D'Arthur*, both of which are discussed later in this unit.) National identity, and its relationship to a national language, has always been integral to the making of a literary canon.

Questions

1 RECAP: What does the above section tell you about the development of English as a language?

2 Geoffrey Chaucer makes it into the literary canon (and this book). He wrote »

The Canterbury Tales in Midlands English, which is the basis for the English language we use today. During the Middle Ages, Midlands English was used in London, as well as the two university towns: Oxford and Cambridge. *Sawles Warde* was written in the thirteenth century by monks who lived in Worcester and Hereford. It was written in Wigmore English, a local version of English. (For example, the Wigmore English sentence 'Fondunges to wrestli steale-wurplich toyein de deofles swenges' translates to 'Wrestle valiantly in times of temptation against the devil's assaults'.) Except for a few scholars, people cannot read Wigmore English in the original any longer. For this reason, *Sawles Warde* is not in the canon, and not in this book.

What does this tell us about how cultural and historical factors influence what we read and value? Should inclusion in the canon be influenced by the dialect in which the text is written?

Beowulf

Introduction to *Beowulf*

Beowulf is an epic poem of approximately 3000 lines that was written somewhere in the midlands of England and some time between the eighth and tenth centuries AD. In the poem, the young hero, Beowulf, goes to help the Danish king, Hrothgar. Hrothgar's problem is that each night a foul monster, Grendel, steals into Hrothgar's Great Hall, rips off the heads of several of the king's loyal kinsmen, and then eats them. Beowulf vows to rid Hrothgar of Grendel and so lies in wait for the monster. One night, Grendel appears. Beowulf wrestles with him, and defeats the monster by tearing Grendel's arm out of its shoulder socket. The next night, Grendel's mother arrives at the hall to revenge herself on Beowulf. Beowulf tracks her back to where she lives and kills her too.

Fifty years pass. Beowulf has become king of the Geats (a Scandinavian tribe). In the twilight of his life, Beowulf is called upon to defend his country against a dragon that has been attacking his people. He fights with the dragon by a stone arch in the dragon's fiery lair. Both of them are killed in the fight.

A page from the only extant copy of *Beowulf*.

The poem *Beowulf* almost did not survive into the twenty-first century. The journey from its original 'creation' to the present day is almost as tortuous as the trials that Beowulf himself encounters. It tells us much about how texts were produced and received through the ages.

First, *Beowulf* was originally composed as an oral tale: something told from the storyteller's memory. This was because it was not possible to write down stories in preliterate societies. *Beowulf* would eventually have been written down when the technology of writing was adopted by certain parts of Anglo-Saxon culture (such as the monasteries), but we do not have that first written version. Over the centuries it would have been translated from person to person, each of whom transcribed and copied the poem. As with a game of Chinese whispers, the meaning and words inevitably changed in the process. Also, vellum was so valuable that many older texts were erased and written over.

Second, the form in which the poem exists is written in a type of Old English that is difficult to understand and translate into Modern English. An example is given below.

> Oft Scyld Scefing sceapena preatum,
> monegum maegpum meodosetla ofteah,
> egsode eorl[as], syddan aerest weard
> feasceaft funden; he peas frofre gebad

According to Seamus Heaney, the above lines from *Beowulf* translate as follows.

> There was Shield Sheafson, scourge of many tribes
> A wrecker of mead-benches, rampaging among foes.
> This terror of the hall-troops had come far.
> A foundling to start with, he would flourish later on.

Third, the only surviving manuscript copy of *Beowulf* almost burnt in 1731, before anyone had translated it into Modern English. In fact, the fire destroyed the entire building in which the manuscript was housed, and the manuscript itself was seriously damaged.

If *Beowulf* is such a significant piece of literature, it begs the question as to why there was only one copy of it in existence in 1731. This is because *Beowulf* has only been valued much more recently. As we have seen, the canon is not something set in stone forever. *Beowulf* was so seriously marginalised in the seventeenth century that almost no-one had heard of it. Over the eighteenth and nineteenth centuries *Beowulf* became better known as people's interest in antiquarian texts grew. However, at this time it was mainly known as a translation exercise from the Old English, and also for its many historical and Christian references, allusions and moral lessons.

One man is primarily responsible for bringing *Beowulf* into prominence as a work of literature: JRR Tolkien. An Oxford University professor (who wrote some fantasy fiction in his spare time), Tolkien composed an article called 'Beowulf: the Monsters and the Critics' in 1936. Tolkien's argument was that the poem's historical references that everyone had been looking at for a century were merely additional colouring that elevated Beowulf's heroic stature. Instead, what made *Beowulf* such a significant piece were the daring battles with the monsters. Tolkien's view of *Beowulf* is the way in which the poem has been 'read' since the 1940s. In the twenty-first century we may find yet another way of reading *Beowulf*.

In the section leading up to the extract on page 27, Grendel has broken into the Great Hall that Beowulf is guarding.

1 RECAP: Outline the reasons given for why we may not be reading *Beowulf* in exactly the same way that the original author intended. Can you think of any other reasons?

2 In the introductory section (page 22), *Beowulf* is described as an 'epic' poem. Using the story of *Beowulf* (see page 25) and Tolkien's view (see the second last paragraph on page 26), what features do you think an epic poem has?

BEOWULF

The captain of evil discovered himself   750
in a handgrip harder than anything
he had ever encountered in any man
on the face of the earth. Every bone in his body
quailed and recoiled, but he could not escape.
He was desperate to flee to his den and hide   755
with the devil's litter, for in all his days
he had never been clamped or cornered like this …

ooooo

the two contenders crashed through the building.   770
The hall clattered and hammered, but somehow
survived the onslaught and kept standing: …

ooooo

The story goes
that as the pair struggled, mead-benches were smashed   775
and sprung off the floor, gold fittings and all.
Before then, no Shielding elder would believe
there was any power or person upon earth
capable of wrecking their horn-rigged hall
unless the burning embrace of a fire   780
engulf it in flame. Then an extraordinary
wail arose, and bewildering fear
came over the Danes. Everyone felt it
who heard that cry as it echoed off the wall
a God-cursed scream and strain of catastrophe,   785
the howl of the loser, the lament of the hell-serf
keening his wound. He was overwhelmed,
manacled tight by the man who of all men
was foremost and strongest in the days of this life …

»

Then he who had harrowed the hearts of men
with pain and affliction in former times
and had given offence also to God   810
found that his bodily powers failed him.
Hygelac's kinsman kept him helplessly
locked in a handgrip. As long as either lived,
he was hateful to the other. The monster's whole
body was in pain, a tremendous wound   815
appeared on his shoulder. Sinews split
and the bone-lappings burst. Beowulf was granted
the glory of winning; Grendel was driven
under the fen-banks, fatally hurt,
to his desolate lair.   820

Questions

1 How does the writer use language to build up
our revulsion for Grendel? (Look particularly at
the variety of names he gives, such as 'captain of
evil' in line 750.)

2 How are God, religion and religious imagery
used in this passage to guide our responses?

3 In this extract, what is heroic about Beowulf's
victory? How is this heroism made clear to the
reader?

Activities

1 Imagine you are the author of *Beowulf*. You have
told the story of Grendel to your bloodthirsty
yet temporarily hushed listeners around a
campfire somewhere in the moors of Mercia in
750 AD. However, once you are finished, your
audience is not happy. They complain that the
climax—the scene where Grendel has his arm
torn off—goes by in a flash (see lines 816–17).
They want to hear more. They want more action,
more reaction, and more horror. Unless you give
it to them, they threaten to re-enact the scene
themselves around the campfire, with you as
Grendel … The pressure is mounting. Write
another ten lines of *Beowulf*, in the style of the
extract above, that gives your listeners what they
ask for. It should be possible to insert easily your
lines into lines 816–17 above.

2 Experiment with rewriting this excerpt using
a different point of view, by writing an official
letter from Beowulf to Grendel's mother,
informing her of the incident leading to the fatal
wounding of her son. Include in your letter a
justification for your actions.

»

3 In this task the religious context of *Beowulf* is considered. It is believed that this poem originally came from the Vikings who settled in Midland England and who were converted to Christianity. There are many references to the Old Testament in *Beowulf*. For example, Grendel is described as a descendent of Cain (Book of Genesis) and Grendel finds a story about how a race of giants was destroyed by the Flood (also from the Book of Genesis). By contrast, there are no references to the New Testament. Speculate on what the religious references say about the attitudes and beliefs of the Vikings.

4 What cultural assumptions about 'manliness' are made in *Beowulf* by its Viking originators? Make a reading of this extract (and some other sections of the epic) that challenges these assumptions.

Tolkien and *Beowulf*

JRR Tolkien wrote his article about *Beowulf* in 1936. In August 1940, he wrote the first draft of the chapter 'The Bridge of Khazad-dûm' in his trilogy *The Lord of the Rings*. This is the chapter in which the wizard Gandalf fights a monster called the Balrog and appears to fall to his death. Tolkien's initial plot sketch of this chapter had Gandalf fighting a Black Rider on the bridge. It was only later (in 1940) that he changed the opponent to a dragon type of creature: the Balrog.

Look at the following passages from *The Lord of the Rings* and from *Beowulf*. Then answer the questions on page 31.

Gerard Butler as Beowulf in the film *Beowulf and Grendel*.

THE LORD OF THE RINGS

From The Fellowship of the Ring, *part 1 of* The Lord of the Rings *trilogy*

[The Balrog] came to the edge of the fire and the light faded as if a cloud had bent over it. Then with a rush it leaped across the fissure. The flames roared up to greet it, and wreathed about it; and a black smoke swirled in the air. Its streaming mane kindled, and blazed behind it. In its right hand was a blade like a stabbing tongue of fire; in its left it held a whip of many thongs …

The Balrog reached the bridge. Gandalf stood in the middle of the span, leaning on the staff in his left hand, but in his other hand Glamdring gleamed, cold and white. His enemy halted again, facing him, and the shadow about it reached out like two vast wings. It raised the whip, and the thongs whined and cracked. Fire came from its nostrils. But Gandalf stood firm.

'You cannot pass', he said …   »

The Balrog made no answer. The fire in it seemed to die, but the darkness grew. It stepped forward slowly on to the bridge, and suddenly it drew itself up to a great height, and its wings were spread from wall to wall …

'You cannot pass!' [Gandalf] said.

With a bound the Balrog leaped full upon the bridge. Its whip whirled and hissed …

At that moment, Gandalf lifted his staff, and crying aloud, he smote the bridge before him. The staff broke asunder and fell from his hand. A blinding sheet of white flame sprang up. The bridge cracked. Right at the Balrog's feet it broke, and the stone upon which it stood crashed into the gulf, while the rest remained, poised, quivering like a tongue of rock thrust out into emptiness.

With a terrible cry the Balrog fell forward, and its shadow plunged down and vanished. But even as it fell it swung its whip, and the thongs lashed and curled around the wizard's knees, dragging him to the brink. He staggered and fell, grasped vainly at the stone, and slid into the abyss. 'Fly, you fools!' he cried, and was gone.

BEOWULF

Hard by the rock-face that hale veteran, …
saw a stone arch and a gushing stream   2445
that burst from the barrow, blazing and wafting
a deadly heat. It would be hard to survive
unscathed near the hoard, to hold firm
against the dragon in those flaming depths …

ooooo

Pouring forth
in a hot battle-fume, the breath of the monster
burst from the rock …
the outlandish thing   2560
writhed and convulsed and viciously
turned on the king, whose keen-edged sword,
was already in his hand …

ooooo

The serpent looped and unleashed itself.
Swaddled in flames, it came gliding and flexing
and racing towards its fate …   2570

》

> [Beowulf] threw
> his whole strength behind a sword-stroke
> and connected with his skull. And Naegling snapped.
> Beowulf's ancient iron-grey sword   2680
> let him down in the fight …
>
> ∞∞∞
>
> Then the bane of that people, the fire-breathing dragon,
> was mad to attack for a third time.
> When a chance came, he caught the hero   2690
> in a rush of flame and clamped sharp fangs
> into his neck. Beowulf's body
> ran wet with his life-blood: it came welling out.

Questions

1 Identify the language in the Tolkien passage that sounds a little old-fashioned to you (for example, 'smote'). What is the overall effect of this language? Why do you think Tolkien wrote in this way?

2 What similarities in plot, style and/or tone do you notice between these sections of *The Lord of the Rings* and *Beowulf*?

3 How do you think Tolkien's study of *Beowulf* may have influenced his writing of *The Lord of the Rings*? You should refer closely to the settings and language of both passages in your answer.

4 How does the *Beowulf* text change (and stay the same) when set by Tolkien in a different context?

Chaucer and *The Canterbury Tales*

Geoffrey Chaucer (c. 1343–1400)

Chaucer was born in about 1343 to a prosperous wine merchant. He secured a position in his teenage years as a page in the aristocratic house of the Countess of Ulster. This placement allowed Chaucer to learn the customs of the aristocracy. In turn, this set him up for a career in the medieval civil service. Chaucer held various positions during his lifetime: controller of customs, diplomat, parliamentarian, deputy forester of the King's Forest at Petherton and clerk of the King's Works. He also organised the building of the nave of Westminster Cathedral. In addition, Chaucer spent some time in the army, during which he was taken prisoner by the French and ransomed.

Writing fiction did not become a professional occupation until the eighteenth century. This explains why Chaucer, the most prominent writer of the medieval period, did not (or could not) devote himself to his craft. However, civil service work had its advantages. It was on a diplomatic mission to Genoa and Florence in 1372–73 that Chaucer came into contact with the writings of the Italian Renaissance, such as those of Boccaccio (whom he probably used extensively in *The Canterbury Tales*). Before Chaucer wrote *The Canterbury Tales*, his major works included a long love poem called *Troilus and Creseyde* (c. 1385), and a recount of a dream vision called *The Parliament of Fowls*. However, *The Canterbury Tales* is his best-known work.

The Canterbury Tales

Begun in about 1387 and probably worked on by Chaucer until his death in 1400, *The Canterbury Tales* is about twenty-nine pilgrims who are travelling from Southwark to Canterbury to visit the grave of the martyr Thomas à Beckett. Their host suggests that they make the journey more pleasant by telling two tales each on the way there and another two on the way back. They agree. *The Canterbury Tales* is incomplete as only twenty-four of the proposed 116 stories were ever written. However, even these stories make for a detailed tapestry of medieval concerns, opinions and life. They range from the heroic deeds of classical characters, to the tragedy of fallen biblical figures, to ribald stories of bed-hopping rogues. Many of the stories are borrowed from French, Italian or classical sources, such as Boccaccio's *The Decameron* and Plutarch. This wholesale 'borrowing' was common in medieval times.

Chaucer usually wrote in what are called 'heroic couplets', which are pairs of rhyming lines in iambic pentameter. Iambic pentameter refers to lines of ten syllables each where the stress falls on the second, fourth, sixth, eighth and tenth syllables. An example is given below. Iambic pentameter was used regularly by poets after Chaucer and employed famously by Shakespeare.

From 'The Miller's Tale', lines 639–40

Who <u>rubbeth now</u>, who <u>froteth now</u> his <u>lippes</u>
With <u>dust</u>, with <u>sond</u>, with <u>straw</u>, with <u>cloth</u>, with <u>chippes</u>

The narrative structure of a storytelling pilgrimage allowed Chaucer to mix the 'estates' of the people he wrote about. (Estates were similar to classes. There were three estates: the aristocracy, the Church and all others.) A pilgrimage was one of the few places where it was possible to find a knight rubbing shoulders with a cook and a carpenter. This device allowed Chaucer to give a more complete picture of the whole of medieval society. The pilgrimage story also allowed for a single overarching story: that of twenty-nine pilgrims interrupting each other, fighting with each other, telling stories just to spite each other and so on.

1 How does the language form of iambic pentameter help shape the meaning in the two-line extract from 'The Miller's Tale' provided opposite?

2 As we saw from the discussion of Chaucer's sources, in medieval times stories were recycled over and over again.

   a Do you think this is plagiarism? Explain your response.

   b Use what you know about medieval society to explain why scholars do not appear to be particularly worried by this phenomenon.

   c How (if at all) have values shifted regarding the issues of originality and plagiarism over the last 700 years?

   d How would you compare this 'borrowing' with rap artists sampling the hook lines of other songs?

3 In Chaucer's tales the knights experience noble, courtly and honourable love (as in 'The Franklin's Tale', for example). By contrast, the lower-class tradespeople tend to have riotous and sex-filled romps (as in 'The Miller's Tale'). What could this indicate about Chaucer's cultural assumptions when writing? How would your knowledge of this affect your reading of these tales?

Activity

Iambic pentameter was used to convey information as well as express poetic sentiment. Write a heroic couplet in which you:

   a Ask the teacher if you may go to the bathroom.

   b Stage a protest march.

   c Tell your boyfriend/girlfriend that it's over.

'The Pardoner's Tale'

The tale that the Pardoner tells is of three lowlife louts who are attempting to hunt down and kill Death. They find a pot of gold under a tree (strategically left there by Death) and decide to guard it for a while and then split it three ways. The youngest lout agrees to go to town to buy some wine to drink while they are guarding the gold. The two older louts then plan to murder the youngest one when he returns.

> **THE PARDONER'S TALE**
> *Translated into Modern English*
>
> This youngest rogue who'd gone into the town,
> Often in fancy rolled he up and down
> The beauty of those florins new and bright.

'O Lord,' thought he, 'if so be that I might   840
Have all this treasure to myself alone,
There is no man who lives beneath the throne
Of God that should be then so merry as I'.
And at the last the Fiend, our enemy,
Put in his thought that he should poison buy   845
With which he might kill both his fellows; aye,
The Devil found him in such wicked state,
He had full leave his grief to consummate;
For it was utterly the man's intent
To kill them both and never to repent.   850
And on he strode, no longer would he tarry,
Into the town, to an apothecary,
And prayed of him that he'd prepare and sell
Some poison for his rats, and some as well
For a polecat that in his yard had lain,   855
The which, he said, his capons there had slain,
And fain he was to rid him, if he might,
Of vermin that thus damaged him by night.
The apothecary said: 'And you shall have
A thing of which, so God my spirit save,   860
In all this world there is no live creature
That's eaten or has drunk of this mixture
As much as equals but a grain of wheat,
That shall not sudden death thereafter meet;
Yea, die he shall, and in a shorter while   865
Than you require to walk but one short mile;
This poison is so violent and strong'.
This wicked man the poison took along
With him boxed up, and then he straightway ran
Into the street adjoining, to a man,   870
And of him borrowed generous bottles three;
And into two his poison then poured he;
The third one he kept clean for his own drink.
For all that night he was resolved to swink
In carrying the florins from that place.   875
And when this roisterer, with evil grace,
Had filled with wine his mighty bottles three,
Then to his comrades forth again went he.
What is the need to tell about it more?
For just as they had planned his death before,   880
Just so they murdered him, and that anon.

                                                                 »

And when the thing was done, then spoke the one:
'Now let us sit and drink and so be merry,
And afterward we will his body bury'.
And as he spoke, one bottle of the three   885
He took wherein the poison chanced to be
And drank and gave his comrade drink also,
For which, and that anon, lay dead these two.

Questions

1 What is your initial overall impression of this piece?

2 Explore the images and other language features that are used to make the louts seem ribald and earthy.

3 Chaucer makes the actual scene where the three die very brief. Why does he do this? What effect is gained by the brevity?

4 a How are medieval Christian theology and values present in the description of the younger lout's 'evil' plan (lines 840–50)?

b What are some ways in which his actions could be explained based on the values of contemporary society?

c How does this highlight the difference between the values of medieval and contemporary society?

d How are these medieval values shaping this text?

THE PARDONER: LITERATURE'S FIRST PUSHY SALESMAN

Medieval society spawned a number of occupations, such as the pardoner, that hovered at the fringe of the Church. A pardoner was a roving agent authorised by the Pope to forgive sins ('grant indulgences'). Dying with sins on one's soul could consign one to an eternity of hell. The pardoner could forgive people these sins wherever they were … for a price. In addition, many pardoners carried fake holy relics (physical objects connected with religious events, such as the Crucifixion) like religious souvenirs. The pardoner would let people look at, pray before and purchase his relics.

The Pardoner

The Pardoner in Chaucer's story carries around crystal jars full of rags and bones, which, he asserts, are relics. He even has a magical mitten, which multiplies the grain of any farmer who puts it on. After the Pardoner tells his tale, he attempts to encourage his fellow pilgrims to purchase his pardons, suggesting that they could die at any moment through sudden mishaps, such as falling off a horse.

The Pardoner from Chaucer's 'The Pardoner's Tale'.

THE PARDONER'S TALE: THE EPILOGUE

'But, sires, oo word forgat I in my tale:
I have relikes and pardoun in my male
As faire as any man in Engelond,
Whiche were me yiven by the Popes hond.
If any of you wol of devocioun
Offren and han myn absolucioun,   635
Come forth anoon, and kneeleth here adown,
And mekely receiveth my pardoun, ...

ooooo

Looke which a suretee is it to youw alle
That I am in youre felaweshipe yfalle   650
That may assoille you, bothe moore and lasse,
Whan that the soule shal fro the body passe.
I rede that oure Hoste shal biginne,
For he is most envoluped in sinne.
Com forth, sire Host, and offre first anoon,   655
And thou shalt kisse the relikes everichon,
Ye, for a grote: unbokele anoon thy purs.'

Questions

1 Study the real estate advertisement for a house
(which is a combination of several genuine ads).
Compare the Pardoner's selling techniques with
those in the advertisement alongside. What
persuasive techniques could the Pardoner and
the real estate agents who wrote this ad learn
from one another?

2 Re-read the section about Marxist criticism in
Unit 1 (page 16). What do you think a Marxist
critic would find interesting to study in *The
Canterbury Tales*? In your answer, look at the
background to the tales as well as both the
extracts provided.

Renovator's Delight!

Don't miss out on this one! Plenty of scope for you to
make this your dream home. Come in and add your
own vision to this freestanding 2/3 bedroom house set
within a pleasant garden. Conveniently situated within
30 seconds' walk of bus and train transport to work and
shops. This house has 'Value Add' written all over it.
Be quick or regret it later. Open your chequebooks!

1 Translate as much of the preceding passage as you can into Modern English.

2 The Pardoner is transported into contemporary society, and decides to mount a modern campaign to sell his relics and absolutions (forgiveness for sins). He employs you as his advertising agency. In groups, write and present to the class one of the following items for him:

a a promotional pamphlet

b a thirty-second television advertisement

c a web homepage

d a newspaper advertisement

e the opening paragraphs of a speech he will give to an audience at a nursing home

f the opening dialogue of his appearance on a 'home shopping' television programme.

Vision literature and St Julian of Norwich

Another important type of medieval writing is literature that described the visions of the authors or of characters. Chaucer related visions in works such as *The Parliament of Fowls*, which is about a group of birds that meet to choose their partners on St Valentine's Day. One of the best-known examples of medieval vision literature is *A Book of Showings* by St Julian of Norwich in which she describes her visions of God.

St Julian of Norwich was an anchoress (religious hermit). This meant that, in order to devote her life to contemplation and prayer, she agreed to be walled up in a single room for the rest of her life. There were quite a few anchoresses (and indeed anchorites—the male equivalent) in the Middle Ages, and their cells could often be found on the side of churches. One window in the cell would look out to the world the anchoress had left behind, the other would look into the church. Indeed, to add weight to the idea that anchoresses were 'buried alive', they even had mock funerals as part of the ceremony to become an anchoress. St Julian was not the actual name of the anchoress being written about; instead, it was simply the name of the church in Norwich in which she was interred.

Sitting in a cell for the rest of her life meant that St Julian had some time on her hands. She spent it contemplating, studying and writing about a set of sixteen holy visions she had experienced. These visions had come to her at the age of thirty when she was on the very point of death with illness. Her decision to become an anchoress may well have been as a result of the visions she had at these times. In her writings she calls herself a 'simple' and 'unlettered' person, but this piece of modesty belies the attributes of her work. Her writings show that she had an extensive knowledge of both the Bible and medieval religious writings (in English and Latin). Her references to these works were also very prudent; to be claiming direct access to Christ bordered on heresy in a time when all matters religious had to go through the established Church hierarchy.

Question

The male authors we focus upon in this unit (Chaucer and Malory) seemed to lead full lives as international diplomats, commanding officials, wily politicians and buccaneering soldiers. The female author lived in a cell. What conclusions about the nature of the society can (and can't) we draw from this? What extra information would you want before you came to stronger conclusions? In what way has this question been phrased to influence your response?

A BOOK OF SHOWINGS TO THE ANCHORESS JULIAN OF NORWICH

And when I was thirty years old and a half, God sent me a bodily sickness in which I lay three days and three nights; and on the fourth night I took all my rites of Holy Church and thought not to have lived until day …

Thus I endured until day, and by then my body was dead from the middle downwards, as it felt to me …

After this my sight began to fail and it was all dark about me in the chamber as if it were night, save in the image of the cross wherein I beheld a common light, and I knew not how …

After this the other parts of my body began to die so quickly that I soon had only feeling, with shortness of breath. And then I thought surely to have passed. And, in this, suddenly all my pain was taken from me and I was whole, and namely in the other parts of my body, as ever I was before …

In this I suddenly saw the red blood trickling down from under the garland, hot and freshly and plenteously, as it were in the time of his passion that the garland of thorns was pressed down on his blessed head, as both God and man, the same that suffered thus for me. I conceived truly and mightily that it was himself [who] showed it to me without any means …

And I said 'Benedicte domine!' This I said, for reverence in my meaning with a mighty voice; and full greatly was astonished for wonder and marvel that I had, that he that is so reverend and dreadful will be so homely with a sinful creature living in wretched flesh …

In this he brought our blessed lady[1] to my understanding. I saw her ghostly likeness, a simple maid and meek, young of age and little grown above a child, in the stature that she was when she conceived…

In this sight I understood surely that she is more than all that God made beneath her in worthiness and grace; for above her is nothing that is made but the blessed manhood of Christ, as to my sight.

In this same time our lord showed to me a ghostly sight of his homely loving. I saw that he is to us everything that is good and comfortable for us. He is our clothing that for love wraps us, embraces us and all encloses us for

»

tender love, that he may never leave us, being to us everything that is good, as to my understanding. Also in this he showed a little thing, the quantity of a hazel nut in the palm of my hand; and it was as round as a ball. I looked thereupon with the eye of my understanding and thought: 'What may this be?' And it was generally answered thus: 'It is all that is made.' I marvelled how it might last, for I thought it might suddenly have fallen to nothing for its littleness, and I was answered in my understanding: 'It lasts and ever shall, for God loves it; and so all things exist by the love of God.'

1 Lady Saint Mary

Questions

Answer either 1–4 and 6 OR 5 and 6.

1 St Julian used the term 'homely' twice to describe God. What is unusual about this and what effect do you think she was intending to convey with this choice of diction? What effect does it actually have on you?

2 What impression do we get of Mary in this extract? How does St Julian use language to convey this impression?

3 Explain how St Julian uses simile and paradox in the description of the 'little thing' in her hand. What point is she trying to make about God here?

4 Explain, in your own words, what St Julian means in the last three sentences of the piece.

5 Write an extended piece showing how St Julian uses language to make her visions both vivid and profound.

6 Julia Kristeva argues that female mystics expressed forbidden sexual desire in the form of ecstatic visions. Re-read the section on psychoanalytic criticism in Unit 1 (pages 16–17). (In particular, Freud's ideas of sublimation may be useful to consider here.) What evidence in the passage can you find to support Kristeva's view? What is your opinion about her view?

Activities

1 Write another vision of St Julian in which she is propelled forward to the centre of the central business district of a major city in the twenty-first century. Try to use as much of her language style as possible to evoke how she would have perceived the CBD. Also use her medieval mind-set to comment on what she sees.

2 Similar visions to St Julian have been recounted by contemporary people in contemporary contexts. They are called 'near-death

experiences'. Read some of these recounts on the Near-Death Experiences and the Afterlife website. Dianne Morrissey's is one of those at the site (www.near-death.com/morrissey.html). Access others from the home page (www.near-death.com). Compare these visions with those of St Julian. What similarities and differences do you notice? What conclusions can you draw about the different cultural and religious contexts of the two societies?

≫

Mystery plays and *Noah's Flood*

Medieval England was devoutly religious. It was also largely illiterate, which meant that most families could not read the Bible. This meant that other ways were needed to communicate the stories from the Bible. One such way was to dramatise the stories and perform them. These dramatisations were known as mystery plays. They dealt with many of the major stories of the Bible from the Creation, to the expulsion of Adam and Eve, to the Last Judgment. The major New Testament stories were the Birth, the Crucifixion, the Harrowing of Hell (books from the Bible in medieval times in which Jesus descends into Hell for three days after the Crucifixion) and the Ascension into Heaven.

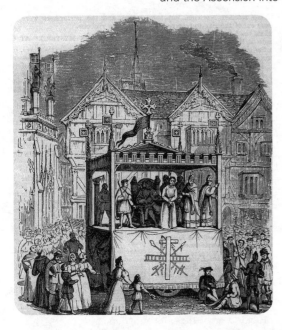

Chester mystery play.

Each play was performed in many of the major towns of England during the Summer Festivals—either Whitsuntide or Corpus Christi, both of which occurred about two months after Easter. Each set, or 'cycle', of plays contained at least a dozen plays; sometimes they contained up to forty-eight plays. The atmosphere would have been more like a modern fete than a modern trip to the theatre. The plays were performed on the street. Many of the plays were performed simultaneously, so whichever street corner the people went to they would quite probably be able to watch a play. Furthermore, each of the plays was usually performed on a portable wagon or cart. In many towns the cast on the cart would stop, perform the play, roll on to the next venue and start performing all over again. This meant that someone could stand on a particular street corner and over the course of a day watch an entire 'cycle' of plays without having to move. The most elaborate carts contained sets and costumes as well as the stage and cast. The plays started as early as 4.30 in the morning.

These plays were not performed by professional actors, but by tradespeople. Thus, they were often called 'trade plays'. Indeed, the term 'mystery play' does not refer to a 'mystery' in the story but the 'mestier' or 'trade' of the performers. The plays were often performed by professions, or 'guilds', that could be associated with the story. For example, *Noah's Flood* (see pages 41–3) was performed in York by the 'fishers and mariners' and in Chester by the 'water leaders and drawers in Dee' (those who took water from the River Dee and sold it to people in the city). In York, *The Last Supper* was played by the bakers while *The Crucifixion* was played by the sellers of nails.

Each town had its own scripts. Many of them were developed over hundreds of years by clergymen, directors and actors, which is why we cannot attribute any of the scripts to one person. Most of the plays are now lost. We do still have five of the plays from the town of Chester. The last time they were performed (before recent times) was 1575, and the script version that we have was written down after this. Mystery plays went into hibernation after the Protestant Revival and Reformation in the sixteenth century. The Reformers did not like seeing idols or religious pageants. The secular content of some of the plays also aroused suspicion.

Questions

1 Imagine you are the organiser of the 1575 Chester mystery cycle. A papal envoy (representative of the Pope) has come to find out more about the plays. Explain to him why you have the mystery cycle and how it works.

2 What is significant about biblical material being in the textual form of a play?

Activity

In groups, imagine that you are organising a play cycle day for your school. Work out:
a the aim of the day
b what venues around the school will be used
c how you will divide up the plays (by year groups, houses or sports teams, for example)
d a list of what cycle of stories you want to tell (such as historical or current events, school-based stories or sport-based stories) and why you would want to tell them
e how you would enthuse people to act, and encourage other people to come to watch.

How does doing this activity make you reflect on the festivals of the Middle Ages?

Noah's Flood

Noah's Flood is from the Chester cycle of plays. Noah has built a boat to save two of each animal from the flood that God is to send. Jaspeth, Shem and Ham are his sons.

NOAH'S FLOOD
Note: Some words have been modernised

JASPETH'S WIFE	And here are doves, ducks, drakes,	
	Redshanks running through the lakes;	190
	And each fowl that singing makes	
	In this ship man may find.	

»

NOAH	Wife, come in. Why stands thou there?
	Thou art ever forward; that dare I swear.
	Come, in God's name! Time it were, 195
	For fear lest that we drown!
NOAH'S WIFE	Yea, sir, set up your sail
	And row forth with evil luck;
	For without any doubt
	I will not out of this town. 200
	Until I have my gossips[1] every one,
	One foot further I will not gone.
	They shall not drown, by Saint John,
	And I may save their life.
	They loved me full well, by Christ. 205
	But thou will let them into thy ship,
	Else row forth, Noah, when thee list
	And get thee a new wife.
NOAH	Shem, son, lo thy mother is wrow[2];
	By God, such another I do not know. 210
SHEM	Father I shall fetch her in, I trow[3]
	Without any fail.
	Mother, my father after thee send
	And bids thee into yonder ship wend[4].
	Look up and see the wind, 215
	For we be ready to sail.
NOAH'S WIFE	Son, go again to him and say
	I will not come therein today.
NOAH	Come in, Wife, in twenty devils way,
	Or else stand there without. 220
HAM	Shall we all fetch her in?
NOAH	Yea, son, in Christ's blessing and mine,
	I would ye hied you betime,
	For of this flood I stand in doubt.
	SONG
THE GOOD GOSSIPS	The flood comes fleeting in full fast 225
	On every side that spreadeth full far.
	For fear of drowning I am aghast;
	Good gossip, let us draw near.
	And let us drink ere we depart.
	For oftentimes we have done so. 230
	For at one draught thou drink a quart,
	And so will I do ere I go.
NOAH'S WIFE	Here is a pot of sweet wine good and strong;
	It will rejoice both heart and tongue.

》

	Though Noah think us never so long,	235
	Yet we will drink at once.	
JASPETH	Mother, we pray you all together—	
	For here we are, your own childer—	
	Come into the ship for fear of the weather,	
	For his love that you bought!	240
NOAH'S WIFE	That I will not for all your call	
	But I have my gossips all.	
SHEM	In faith, mother, yet thou shall,	
	Whether thou will or nought. *[Drags her aboard.]*	
NOAH	Welcome, wife, into this boat.	
NOAH'S WIFE	*[Slaps him]* Have thou that for thy note[5].	

1 Friends   3 Trust   5 Trouble
2 Angry   4 Go

Questions

1 What is your overall impression of this work as a piece of drama?

2 Before the beginning of the extracted section, there are thirty lines listing the animals in the ark. Why do you think the list was included?

3 What language features have been used to add interest to Jaspeth's wife's lines at the beginning?

4 Why doesn't Noah's wife board the ship? How persuasive do you find her reasons?

5 Mystery plays were supposed to achieve the twin functions of entertainment and piety (humble devotion to God's teachings). To what extent do you think these were achieved in this extract? Justify your answer.

Activities

1 How would you stage the last section of this extract to ensure a maximum response from the crowd watching you on the street corner in Chester? Act it out.

2 You and three friends have gone back in time to Chester in the fifteenth century, a day before the Feast of Corpus Christi. The four people who were originally going to act out the Old Testament story of the creation of heaven and earth have sadly died of plague. You are asked to step in and take their place. The story, which is told in Chapter 1 of Genesis, can be found at the University of Virginia Library's Electronic Text Center (etext.lib.virginia.edu/ebooks/subjects/subjects-bible.html). Devise and act out a short version of this mystery play. You will need a narrator and three people to enact the story of the Seven Days.

Alternative reading: Noah's wife and the role of women

Much of the male hierarchy of the medieval church was what we would now see as misogynist (anti-female). They believed that women were predominantly sensual creatures whose aim was to divert man from his proper contemplation of the divine and instead make him concentrate on the earthly and the physical. The famous St Augustine (whose book of Christian doctrine, *The City of God*, was written in the fifth century) deplored any sexual relations with women. He also wrote, 'Women should not be enlightened or educated in any way. They should, in fact, be segregated'. This view is consistent with the biblical figures of Eve and Mary Magdalene being regarded as temptresses and with the saintly Mother Mary being a virgin.

Another central misogynist stereotype of women in medieval times was as shrewish gossips who verbally batter their poor, henpecked menfolk. Often, 'shrew' was another name for a woman who exerted informal kinds of power, such as folk wisdom and local remedies. The fear of female power led to the Church's brutal suppression of those women it had accused of practising witchcraft.

Questions

1 Noah's wife is not featured in the biblical story of Noah's Ark. Re-read the preceding 'light-hearted' portrayal of Noah's wife with your knowledge of the medieval conceptions of women and the Church.

  a Does the passage 'read' any differently to you now? Justify your answer.

  b What 'hidden' values about women and male–female relationships are being conveyed by this text?

  c What would be the effect on you if you were to read this play without an alert feminist eye? What could have been the effect on a medieval audience?

2 Read the section about feminist criticism in Unit 1 (pages 15–16), in particular the ideas about bias, women's inequality and stereotyping. What conclusions do these ideas allow you to draw about the preceding passage?

King Arthur, Malory and the *Morte D'Arthur*

Social context and the chivalric tradition

When many people think of the Middle Ages in Britain, the image that comes to mind is one from the Arthurian tradition: that of knights in armour galloping nobly through verdant green countryside on their way to a quest or to save a damsel in distress. This is representative of the chivalric tradition in which the ruling group (the knights) were governed by the virtues of honour, duty and obedience to the king. Of course, this bears little resemblance to the various accounts of the Middle Ages available from contemporary historians and archaeologists. For many, as the philosopher Hobbes later suggested, life was 'nasty, brutish and short'. Even many of the 'noble' knights in question would have had painful sicknesses, such as tooth decay, and suffered from the difficulties of life as a semi-nomad. Yet this chivalric tradition of 'knights and castles' has a powerful hold on much of the world's perception of Britain's medieval past. The chivalric tradition was a powerful social ideology. The feudal system was changing from the warrior code of the heroic age to something more modern. The stories of the chivalric tradition made these changes appear to be more virtuous and noble.

King Arthur's knights prepare to depart on their quest for the Holy Grail.

The stories of King Arthur, a semi-mythical king of England, played a significant role in creating this chivalric tradition. These stories have their origin in the Dark Ages—up to 1000 years ago—when Arthur was not really directly represented, but rather alluded to. The Welsh and the French are responsible for taking sketchy accounts of him from the ninth and tenth centuries and building the Arthurian romances out of the mists. Arthur's legitimacy (that is, his right to the throne) was divinely ordained because he had pulled the sword Excalibur out of a stone. He set up an ideal medieval court in Camelot, and his round table emphasised the equality of the knights, the king's humility and an interest in non-barbarian justice. Arthur's wife, Queen Guinevere, epitomised feminine fairness and beauty, and Arthur's greatest knight, Lancelot, suitably and tragically adored her. The quest on which Arthur sends his knights is to find the Holy Grail (the cup from which Jesus drank at the Last Supper). This mission emphasises Arthur's Christian piety and his knights' determination and obedience (a medieval European, rather than Celtic, emphasis).

The Arthurian cycle has provided material for literature since the twelfth century. Each literary period has touched on the topic of Arthur in some way, and this continues with unabated enthusiasm in the present. Nostalgia for the structures and 'gallantry' of the chivalric tradition continues to grow. It is easy to forget that these were important aspects of a culture and systems of government in a time of considerable change.

Questions

1 RECAP: Describe, in your own words, the chivalric tradition. Why is it significant that it is always placed in the past?

2 Why do you think people create a chivalric tradition? What needs does it fulfil?

3 Is there a 'chivalric past' for our contemporary society? If so, what is it? What does this say about the way in which values have changed and stayed the same since the medieval period?

Activity

Describe creatively a chivalric past for your school: an age gone by lost in the mists of time, where the teachers were noble, the students were virtuous and there was no litter in the playground. Write a page describing the school, using elements of the chivalric tradition. As part of this past, you can include elements that are mythical and slightly magical, such as an equivalent of the story of the sword in the stone.

Thomas Malory and the *Morte D' Arthur*

Malory, in the *Morte D'Arthur* (the Death of Arthur), wrote about noble, chivalric knights doing fair deeds and honourably rescuing fair maidens. This is quite ironic, as he was probably a barbaric pillager. In fact, he wrote all of the *Morte D'Arthur* from prison. The first record of Malory finding himself in trouble is his attempt to ransack a monastery in Lincolnshire in 1451. In the years after this he was jailed for, amongst other things, extorting money, breaking out of gaol, and plundering the Abbey at Coombe (twice). When in prison he missed out on two general amnesties (pardons) from King Edward IV—more evidence that he was a hardened case.

Malory appears to have adapted the *Morte D'Arthur* from French romances while in prison between 1469 and 1470. The *Morte D'Arthur* consists of eight books. Book One is about the establishment of the Arthurian Kingdom and Book Two is about Arthur's campaign for Rome. Books Three to Seven are about the adventures of individual knights. Book Eight is about the break-up of Arthur's fellowship and the death of Arthur at the hands of his illegitimate son, Mordred. Malory died (probably in prison) the year after finishing the book. The manuscript was then picked up, edited and printed by the first English printer, the merchant William Caxton, in 1485. A copy of Malory's untampered manuscript was only uncovered in Winchester College almost 500 years later, in 1934 (in a safe in the warden's bedroom).

Malory is considered to be the first English writer to make prose as rich a form as poetry. The prose form and style also gives the work a sense of historical realism. The characters speak realistically and use understatement throughout. The story itself is a combination of historical and magical material. The historical story tells of a Roman–British king defending the British people in the period after Rome had abandoned Britain. Fused into this are many pre-Christian magical elements: sorcerers, poisoned garments and a sword in a stone that can only be drawn by the one 'true king'. The combined effect is to create a world that is both magical and yet 'real'.

Questions

1 RECAP: Explain, in your own words, the contrast between Malory's writings and his life.

2 Malory wrote in 1469 during a bitter civil war. Book Two of the *Morte D'Arthur* is thought to parallel famous victories won fifty years earlier when England was united under the popular King Henry V. Link these facts with what was written above about chivalry being situated in the past. In what ways could this make the *Morte D'Arthur* a cultural product of its time?

3 The Thomas Malory described above is Sir Thomas Malory, knight of Newbold Revel in Warwickshire and Winwick in Northamptonshire. There is some speculation that there were actually two Malories. What if an old chest of documents turned up to show that this is, in fact, a case of mistaken identity, and the author of the *Morte D'Arthur* was actually a different Malory: a timid and law-abiding citizen who was never involved in politics? Does it matter anymore? If it does not, should scholars research this 'new' Malory, or should they quietly put the documents back in the chest?

Morte D'Arthur

In this extract, Arthur and his army are fighting a battle with his son, Mordred.

MORTE D'ARTHUR

Then the king took his spear in both hands and ran towards Sir Mordred, crying, 'Traitor, now is thy death day come'. And when Sir Mordred heard Sir Arthur he ran at him with his sword drawn in his hands. And there King Arthur smote Sir Mordred under the shield with a thrust of the spear, through the body more than a fathom[1]. And when Sir Mordred felt that he had his death wound, he thrust himself with the might that he had up to the burr of King Arthur's spear. And right so he smote his father Arthur, with his sword held in both hands, on the side of the head, [so] that his sword pierced the helmet and the side of the brain, and with that Sir Mordred fell stark dead to the earth. And the noble Arthur fell in a swoon to the earth, and there he fainted many times. And Sir Lucan the butler and Sir Bedevere many times heaved him up. And so, weakly they led him between them both to a little chapel not far from the seaside.

'Therefore,' said Arthur unto Sir Bedevere, 'take Excalibur my good sword and go with it to yonder water side. And when you get there, I charge you throw my sword in that water and come back and tell me what you saw there' …

So Sir Bedevere departed, and along the way he beheld that noble sword, [how] the pommel and the haft was all of precious stones, and then he said to himself, 'If I throw this rich sword in the water, thereof shall never come good, but harm and loss'. And then Sir Bedevere hid Excalibur under a tree, and so as soon as he might he returned to the king and said he had been at the water and had thrown the sword into the water.

'What did you see there?' said the king.

'Sir,' he said, 'I saw nothing but waves and wind'.

'That is untruly spoken,' said the king. 'Therefore go lightly again and do my commandment, as you are to me beloved, and there spare not but throw it in.'

Then Sir Bedevere returned again and took the sword in his hand, and then thought, sin and shame to throw away that noble sword, and so again he hid the sword and returned again and told the king that he had been at the water and done his commandment.

'What saw you there?' said the king.

'Sir,' he said, 'I saw nothing but the waters wap and waves wan'.

'A traitor untrue,' said King Arthur. 'Now have you betrayed me twice. Who would have thought that you who have been to me so beloved

»

and dear, and you are named a noble knight, and would betray me for the richness of a sword. But go again lightly for your long tarrying puts me in great jeopardy for my life. For I have taken cold, and if you do [not] now as I bid thee, if ever I may see thee I shall slay thee [with] my own hands, for you would for my rich sword see me dead'.

Then Sir Bedevere departed and went to the sword and lightly took it up and went to the waterside, and there he bound the girdle around the hilt and then he threw the sword as far into the water as he might. And there came an arm and a hand above the water and met it, and caught it and so shook it thrice and brandished [it] and then vanished away the hand with the sword in the water.

[Arthur is then taken by Bedivere to a barge by the waterside, where they are met by women, including three queens, wailing and shrieking, who will transport Arthur to the mystical Isle of Avalon.]

Thus of Arthur I find no more set down in books, nor any more of the very certainty of his death I never read, but that he was led away in a ship wherein were three queens [who tended to him] …

Yet some men say in many parts of England that King Arthur is not dead, but has been taken by the will of our Lord Jesu into another place. And these men say that he shall return and shall win the Holy Cross. And these men say that there is written upon his tomb this verse: [translated] Here lies Arthur, who was King once and king will be again.

1 Six feet

Questions

1 What is your overall impression of this piece of writing? Explain your answer.

2 Explain, in your own words, how Arthur and Mordred wounded each other.

3 Excalibur is the main symbol of the legitimacy of Arthur's rule. Why do you think he wishes to 'return' it to the lake? What is noble and 'chivalric' about this deed?

4 Comment on Malory's prose style in the paragraph where the arm in the lake takes the sword. Comment carefully on the cumulation of verbs.

5 Explore the parallels that you can you find to Christ's death in this narrative. (You could choose to discuss the promise of return, the mystical, the role of women and/or Bedevere's denial.)

»

6 Re-read the section about new historicism in Unit 1 (pages 17–18). Then look at the final inscription on the tomb of Arthur in the text. The week after Caxton printed this book in London, Henry Tudor landed in Wales and unfurled the red dragon banner of King Arthur. A week later, after defeating King Richard III on Bosworth field, Henry Tudor became King Henry VII of England. How could the Arthurian tradition in general and the *Morte D'Arthur* in particular have helped Henry Tudor? What does this tell you about contextual factors in the construction of texts? Link your answer to the culturally materialist concepts raised in the introductory section (such as the circulation of power).

Activities

1 Write five diary entries from the point of view of Sir Bedevere in which you recount and reflect on the events in the extract. In your diary entries, try to use the language and ethos of chivalry as much as you can.

2 What cultural assumptions does the code of chivalry make about men and women? Use your twenty-first century views of men and women to comment on (and perhaps resist or challenge) the presumed roles of masculinity and femininity in the scene in the extract.

Terminator 2: Judgment Day

The following script extract is from James Cameron's movie *Terminator 2*, which was released in 1991. The extract is from the closing moments of the film. The Terminator robot has to destroy itself in order to save the future of humanity. The woman, Sarah, and her child, John, are people with whom Terminator has formed a relationship. In the scene below, Terminator has just been stabbed through the chest with a pole, and has pulled himself through it in order to kill his attacker. He is now above a pit of molten lava and about to lower himself in.

TERMINATOR 2: JUDGMENT DAY
Terminator looks at Sarah. They both know what must be done. John shakes his head.

JOHN

No!

TERMINATOR

I'm sorry, John.

JOHN

No, no no!! It'll be okay. Stay with us!

»

TERMINATOR

I have to go away, John.

JOHN

Don't do it. Please ... don't go—

Tears are streaming down his face.

ooooo

TERMINATOR

It must end here ... or I am the future.

JOHN

I order you not to!

Terminator puts his hand on John's shoulder. He moves slightly and the human side of his face comes into the light. He reaches toward John's face. His metal finger touches the tear trickling down his cheek.

TERMINATOR

I know now why you cry. But it is something I can never do.
(to both of them) Goodbye.

Sarah looks at TERMINATOR ... They lock eyes. Warriors. Comrades.

SARAH

Are you afraid?

TERMINATOR

Yes.

He turns and steps off the edge. They watch him sink into the lava. He dissapears ... the metal hand sinking last ... at the last second it forms into a fist with the thumb extended ... a final thumbs up. Then it is gone.

Questions

1 The script hints at the story of King Arthur. What is the effect of these Arthurian hints on the end of the *Terminator* film?

2 How do the different forms—prose and film script —shape your response to the death of the characters in the *Morte D'Arthur* and *Terminator 2*?

3 Do you think film-makers should echo 'traditional' texts in this way? How do these appropriations affect your response to both the original and the newer text?

4 For those of you who know *Terminator 2*, what other elements of the chivalric tradition can you find in the film's story and characters?

1 In what ways do the texts you have studied in this unit reflect and challenge the attitudes that prevailed during the medieval period? In your response, refer in detail to the language forms and features of at least two medieval texts.

2 'A medieval text can be valued by us in the twenty-first century for the questions it poses far more than its certainties.' Use this view as a starting point of an exploration of the medieval texts you have studied.

3 Watch the film *Monty Python and the Holy Grail*. What aspects of medieval society that we have studied does it satirise? How does it use the resources of film to do this? In particular, compare:

a the 'black knight' scene with Malory and chivalry

b the 'burn the witch' scene with the section about portrayal of women

c the 'peasant proletariat' scene with the social context

d the 'appearance of God' scene with the visions of St Julian.

4 You have been asked on to a community radio station to discuss the topic 'medieval literature: why bother?' Your interviewer wants to know your opinions but is also sceptical about the value of studying medieval literature. Script the dialogue that takes place over the airwaves.

5 Draw a Trojan Horse. Inside it write all the cultural assumptions that you have looked at in the medieval texts you have studied in this unit. Outside it, draw and/or write the challenges to these assumptions that have been presented in this unit. Why is a Trojan Horse an appropriate image for cultural assumptions?

6 'In the midst of the horrendous social conditions and endless barbarity of the medieval age, it is a true testament to the human spirit that such a wealth of profound, delicate and wonderful works of literature was created.' What is your opinion of this view? In your answer, refer to at least two works in detail.

Lovers, Monsters & Devils

RENAISSANCE LITERATURE

Highlights

¶ *Shakespeare writes love poetry to men*

¶ *Death dies in freak metaphysical accident*

¶ *Man sells soul to devil—is taken to hell*

¶ *King abused by his own daughters*

¶ *Woman gives birth to dog*

Outcomes

By the end of this unit you should have:

¤ developed an understanding of the relationship between the texts and the context of the Renaissance era (including the cultural and historical contexts)

¤ gained an appreciation of the way in which the texts can be seen as cultural products of both their authors and their times

¤ engaged in detailed textual interpretation of a number of Renaissance pieces and developed an understanding of how language forms and/or techniques shape the meaning of these pieces

¤ challenged and evaluated some of the cultural assumptions that exist in Renaissance texts and considered alternative readings of some texts

¤ come to a personal view about valuing the texts and the Renaissance period based on your own context and preferences

¤ engaged with the texts in a number of ways, including writing essays and newspaper reports, participating in drama readings and preparing storyboards

¤ gained enjoyment through exposure to the texts and their ideas and contexts.

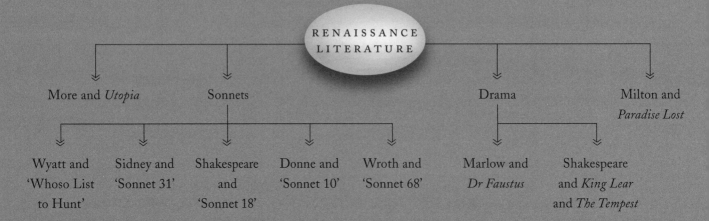

RENAISSANCE LITERATURE

More and *Utopia*   Sonnets   Drama   Milton and *Paradise Lost*

Wyatt and 'Whoso List to Hunt'   Sidney and 'Sonnet 31'   Shakespeare and 'Sonnet 18'   Donne and 'Sonnet 10'   Wroth and 'Sonnet 68'   Marlow and *Dr Faustus*   Shakespeare and *King Lear* and *The Tempest*

Context of the period

The Renaissance period in Britain occurred in the late fifteenth to mid-seventeenth centuries and is often viewed as a major cultural turning point for British culture. Religious and political conditions emerged that produced literature which was vibrant and rich with free thinking. The invention of the printing press meant there was so much more available to read. The emergence of the philosophy of humanism (see Unit 1, page 9) meant there was so much more to read about. And the expansion of English drama from one-off plays during religious festivals to fully-fledged Elizabethan theatres meant there was so much more theatre to see. The loose form of the medieval chivalric romance made way for the craft and art of lyric poetry, and the new kind of poet who wrote it.

Historical context

Wealthy patrons and leaders, such as the Medici Family in Florence, encouraged a rebirth in interest in the writing, arts and culture. They took as their models the subject matter and forms that had been prominent in classical society; that is, ancient Greece and ancient Rome. However, England was a cultural backwater compared with continental Europe. This was because much of England was preoccupied with the endless, petty wars of succession between the Houses of York and Lancaster. This reached its low point with King Richard III, who murdered his allies and enemies to attain the throne in 1483 and then (probably) murdered his child nephews in order to keep it. It was not until the Earl of Richmond killed Richard III in 1485 to become Henry VII, the first Tudor king, that there was enough political stability to allow the ideas of the Renaissance to begin to filter through.

As a result of commercial treaties that Henry VII made with Europe, there was more trade and communication with the continent after 1485. Medieval feudalism was declining in England due to the invention of firearms, which somewhat superseded the swords wielded by noble knights. Urbanisation was on the increase due to new farming methods. London's population increased from 50 000 people in Chaucer's time (the late 1300s) to 225 000 in 1605. The establishment of the printing press, initially by William Caxton in 1474, meant that ideas could be circulated much more widely (and by this time half the population could read). All these factors meant that the ideas of the Renaissance were able to flourish in the sixteenth century.

Philosophical context

One of the key philosophical elements of the Renaissance was the rise of humanism. This rise had enormous implications that we are still feeling in society today. For 1000 years, humans had been convinced (often by the Church) that we were worthless, sinful creatures, tarred by the original sin of Adam, and would be fortunate not to be consigned to hell. An eternity of heaven or hell awaited each person, and the short span of life on earth was little more than a prelude to this ascension or descent. Humanists, on the other hand, said that life on earth could be worth living for its own sake. They also said that humans had dignity and were full of great capacities—such as curiosity, wit and intelligence—which should be celebrated, not hidden away. Humans were at the centre of the earthly endeavour. We could even be comfortable with our faults. As the humanist philosopher Desidirus Erasmus stated: 'Now I believe I can hear the philosophers protesting that it can only be misery to live in folly, illusion, deception and ignorance, but it isn't—it's human'. This view involved a radical rethinking of both humanity and its role in the world.

As a result, there was a huge expansion in the range of subjects that authors wrote about. Even when medieval writings did not explicitly mention God, the emphasis on chivalry and nobility was often moralistic; these medieval writings taught people how to be more pleasing to God. Much Renaissance writing, by contrast, showed humans as they were and society as it was. Shakespeare's Hamlet, Juliet and Macbeth and the speakers in Donne's poems are all complex, multilayered and fully involved in what it is to be human. They may not teach us a great deal about going to heaven, but they are interesting in and of themselves.

Religious context

Coupled with the rise of humanism was a Reformation within the Church itself. Much of this began in 1517 with Martin Luther and his campaign against a corrupt church in Germany. There was also the issue of intercession. The Catholic Church believed strongly that priests acted as interlocutors (or middlemen) between ordinary people and God. The emerging Protestants believed that the middleman could be eliminated. They thought each person could have his or her own relationship with God, as long as that person faithfully read the Scriptures. The Protestants thought that the Church itself had become corrupt and idolatrous. The Catholics thought that a priest who had studied the Scriptures all his life had a much better idea about the Scriptures than would an illiterate farmer, and thus priests should act as interlocutors between the farmer and God. In addition, Catholics generally believed that people needed to cleanse themselves of Adam's original sin through work and atonement. Protestants believed that a person could be cleansed by faith alone.

Religion remained at the forefront of political and cultural life in the early sixteenth century. Henry VIII (who reigned during 1509–47) split from the Catholic Church in 1536 after it refused to allow him to divorce his wife, Catherine of Aragon. He created a 'Church of England' with himself as its head. The new church was influenced by Protestantism, and Catholics were executed. For good measure, Henry ransacked most of the monasteries and kept their money. Six years after Henry died, his daughter Mary Tudor came to the throne. She was devoutly Catholic and burnt Protestants at the stake for the next five years. After Mary's death in 1558 her half-sister, Elizabeth, ascended to the throne. She was Protestant, and so England reverted once again to persecuting Catholics. To complicate matters, there were the Puritans in England at the same time. They were a more extreme form of Protestant who combined rebellion from the Church with a severe, austere code of personal morality.

Questions

1 RECAP: Create a mind map diagram that outlines the major features of the Renaissance and how they were established in England.

2 What links can you make between Protestantism and humanism? (To assist you with this task, refer to the section on humanism in Unit 1, page 9.)

Political context

The relative political stability and protective cultural umbrella offered by the reigns of Henry VII and Henry VIII were strengthened under Elizabeth I. (Catholic agitation, Irish rebellion and threatened Spanish invasion notwithstanding.) This was partly because of the length of her reign (1558–1603), partly because of the canny firmness of her rule and partly due to her genuine interest in the arts.

Elizabeth knew that one of the ways to strengthen her rule was to make herself into a cultural icon so that people naturally associated Britain with her. In the latter half of her reign she set great store in being the 'Virgin Queen' who never married because England itself was her spouse. She also encouraged flattering portrayals of herself, both in art and poetry. Possibly the most extreme example of this was Edmund Spenser's poem about Elizabeth entitled *The Faerie Queene*, which is 33 000 lines of tightly packed and usually very flattering rhyme.

The entire Elizabethan court worked on patronage. Elizabeth had a few favourite ministers, such as Cecil, Leicester and Essex. These ministers then distributed favours to courtiers who wished to be bureaucrats, diplomats, judges and so on. By having the patronage system work so tightly, Elizabeth ensured greater loyalty among the members of her aristocracy. Unless one was already a well-connected noble, having a patron in court was vital to advancing in society.

Queen Elizabeth died in 1603. Her successor, James I (who reigned during 1603–25), continued her association with literature and was the patron of Shakespeare's theatre company. He also commissioned an authoritative English-language Bible, which is still known as the King James Bible. Fear of Catholics continued, made worse by the Gunpowder Plot, in which some Catholics in 1605 tried to blow up parliament and the king.

The major split of the first half of the seventeenth century was between the Protestant royalists (led by King Charles since 1625) and the Puritan rebels. Decades of covert, then overt, agitation and rebellion by the Puritans led to the overthrow and execution of King Charles in 1649. These Puritans believed that most art and literature was appallingly hedonistic (pleasure seeking). They had all the theatres in London closed down in 1642 and literature went into something of a deep freeze during the decade in which they were in power.

Activities

1 Research and compare the reign of Henry VIII with a contemporary tyrannical regime of your choice. What similarities and differences do you find? How do these comparisons affect your views of both current and sixteenth-century regimes?

2 Imagine that you are one of the top publicists of the twenty-first century, sought after by superstars and rock gods. Queen Elizabeth brings you back in time and asks you to make her 'the pre-eminent cultural icon of the millennium'. You refuse, citing previous engagements. She shows you her torture chamber. You accept her request.

Research the cultural context of the Renaissance further. Then use your knowledge of her times and ours to write Queen Elizabeth a campaign brief that will resound through the Elizabethan era and beyond. Make sure you link

»

each idea you come up with to why you think it will work in the late sixteenth century. Consider:

a the intellectual ideas prominent at the time that you can use

b the mediums available to you (no television or radio, obviously).

Write the campaign brief in the form of a proposal. Multimedia presentation software (such as PowerPoint) may be useful to make your presentation.

3 Watch the *Blackadder II* episode 'Potato'. Details are available at the BBC website (www.bbc.co.uk/comedy/blackadder/epguide/two_potato.shtml). How does this episode satirise Elizabeth and the patronage system that existed in Elizabeth's court?

Cultural context

So, influence and being noticed equated closely with power. How was one to be noticed at court? One way was to write what we now call 'literature', particularly poetry. The literature in question was usually in the form of praise of the patron. This dramatically increased the power that could be gained from writing, but turned writing explicitly into a means to an end, rather than an end in itself. Some Renaissance poetry seems like overblown flattery (to twenty-first century eyes at least). For example, John Donne favourably compares one of his patrons, the Duchess of Bedford, with God.

Connected to this is the idea that many writers wrote poetry as a supplementary activity to their work as statesmen or diplomats. There usually was not enough money in writing to support oneself. If someone did write professionally he or she was even more bound to write flattering pieces and dedicate the work to financial patrons. Indeed, some writers had books published with several front plates, each one dedicating the book to a different patron.

In Renaissance society, publication was generally unprofitable for writers. Royalties did not exist, and so writers such as Ben Jonson and Edmund Spenser had to sell their works for one-off (and low) sums.

Second, there was no copyright, so once a poet's work was out in society any other printer could also print the work without obligation to pay the poet. Indeed, the book that made English sonnets well known (see page 61), *Tottel's Miscellany* (1557), simply consisted of poems by various poets, including Thomas Wyatt and Henry Howard, that were never meant for publication at all. Shakespeare actually attempted to suppress publication of his plays for much of his life.

Third, to publish was often an act that diminished one's reputation. For many nobles it was beneath them. John Donne stated, on publishing *Anniversaries*, 'I confess I wonder how I declined [lowered myself] to it and do not pardon myself'.

Fourth, once a writer was published he or she had to risk censorship, questioning by humourless officials, and worse. John Stubbs wrote a pamphlet in 1579 advising Queen Elizabeth not to marry the Duke of Anjou. (Elizabeth did not go on to marry the Duke.) For writing the pamphlet, the unfortunately named Stubbs had his right hand cut off with a butcher's cleaver, after which, according to *The Norton Anthology of English Literature*, he raised his hat in his remaining hand and called out 'God save the Queen'.

1 On the basis of the brief overview here, what societal conditions do you feel are best for the production of literature? How do the cultural features of a society shape the texts that are written in it?

2 In the English Renaissance period, writing poems was one way to participate in a powerful

elite. Does this challenge your idea of what poetry is about and why it is written? Explain your answer.

3 What social conditions in your school promote or impede the confident, independent production of creative work among students?

Activity

Copy the following table and fill it out to compare how the Elizabethans thought about art and literature compared with how we think about them.

DOMINANT VIEWS ON ART AND LITERATURE

Elizabethan cultural context	Our cultural context
Artificiality is a desirable quality. It is good to improve on nature.	
Writing is a great craft, in common with cooking or planting a garden.	
Regularity and geometric forms are desirable qualities in writing, music, planting gardens and so on.	
Avoid being too original. Instead, look to classical writings and transform or improve on them.	

More and *Utopia*

Sir Thomas More (1477–1535)

Sir Thomas More was the son of a judge who studied at Canterbury College, Oxford, and became a very successful barrister. He became a trusted member of Henry VIII's court and was one of Henry's closest friends. Politically, he rose to the post of Lord Chancellor (the most senior legal post in England) in 1529. He held this post for three years before retiring to

Sir Thomas More.

the country and losing his income. He retired because of his deep misgivings about Henry breaking away from the Catholic Church.

However, Henry VIII soon came after him, insisting that More sanction his establishment of the Church of England. More refused in 1534 to take an oath that recognised the children of Henry and his new wife, Anne Boleyn, as heirs to the throne. For this he was thrown in the Tower of London for fifteen months, beheaded, and then had his head exhibited on London Bridge. Being Henry VIII's most trusted adviser and friend for many years clearly did not keep one safe when one disagreed with this monarch. More was made a saint in 1935.

Utopia

Utopia is about the traveller Hythloday who returns from South America with tales of a strange land called Utopia, the 'ideal' state. The place is a liberal fantasy land: no money, schools for all, six-hour working days, good hospitals, no fashion, and all religions living side by side in perfect harmony. There are few laws; the society does not need them because everyone is so naturally good. This is contrasted with England during the time *Utopia* was written, in which there was a great deal of deceitful moneymaking, poverty and crime.

So it seems unusual (to utopian liberals at least) that More wrote *Utopia* as a satire. The title comes from the Greek word 'ou-topos' ('no place') as a pun on 'eu-topos' ('a place where all is well'). Hythloday is very close to Greek for 'babbler'. This makes *Utopia* ambiguous. It appears to be the description of an ideal state and a satire of it at the same time. Perhaps part of the answer is seeing *Utopia* as a sort of 'festival' of ideas. More might not have liked the England of his day, but this does not mean that *Utopia* was meant to be a programme for reform of England. All it may be is a light-hearted look at an alternative.

Many scholars feel that More has created a worthy but dull society. Hythloday says about the towns, 'When you've seen one you've seen them all'. All the towns are made on a grid. People eat in long dining halls. It certainly provided a sterile contrast to the bawdy and riotous, but lively, world of London at the time.

Utopia is a key Renaissance text because it shows segments of English society wrenching their gaze away from heaven (although More was deeply religious) and instead contemplating life in the here and now. It is humanistic. Second, it is revolutionary because it is actually thinking about the health, welfare and happiness of the entire society, not just the ruling elites. By outlining difference in a hypothetical society, *Utopia* generates the sense that progressive change really is possible. *Utopia* may be light-hearted and ironic, but it also can be seen as profound, optimistic and setting the stage for centuries of social debate.

Three extracts from *Utopia* are presented here, each on a different subject.

Gold and silver

Anyone can see, for example, that iron is far superior to either [gold or silver]; men could not live without iron, by heaven, any more than without fire or water. But gold and silver have, by nature, no function with which we cannot easily dispense. Human folly has made them precious because they are rare …

While they eat from earthenware dishes and drink from glass cups, finely made but inexpensive, their chamber pots and all their humblest vessels for use in common halls and even in private homes, are made of gold and silver. The chains and heavy fetters of slaves are also made of these metals … Thus they hold up gold and silver to scorn in every conceivable way. As a result, if they had to part with their entire supply of these metals, which other people give up with as much agony as if they were being disemboweled, the Utopians feel it no more than the loss of a penny.

Marriage customs

Whether she be a widow or virgin, the bride-to-be is shown naked to the groom by a responsible and respectable matron; and similarly some respectable man presents the groom naked to his prospective bride. We all laughed at this custom, and called it absurd, but they were just as amazed at the folly of all other peoples. When men go to buy a colt … they won't close the deal until saddle and blanket have been taken off, lest there be a hidden sore underneath. Yet in the choice of a mate, which may cause either delight or disgust for the rest of their lives, men are so careless that they leave all the rest of the woman's body covered up with clothes and estimate her attractiveness from … the face, which is all they can see.

Religions

[King Utopus decreed] that every man might cultivate the religion of his choice, and proselytize[1] for it too, provided he did so quietly, modestly, rationally, and without bitterness towards others. If persuasions failed, no man might resort to abuse or violence, under penalty of exile or slavery … [Utopus] suspected that God perhaps likes various forms of worship and has therefore deliberately inspired different men with different views. On the other hand, he was quite sure that it was arrogant folly for anyone to enforce conformity with his own beliefs by threats of violence. He supposed that if one religion is really true and all the rest are false,

»

> the true one will sooner or later prevail by its own natural strength if men will only come to the matter reasonably and moderately. But if they try to decide things by fighting and rioting, since the worst men are always most headstrong, the best and holiest religion will be crowded out by foolish superstition, like grain choked out of a field by thorns and briers.

1 Preach

Questions

1 Do you think the way *Utopia* deals with the above three subjects are good approaches for a society? Discuss what would happen if they were implemented in our society.

2 In what ways is More's society similar to or at odds with our liberal democratic society? What would a Marxist or a religious fundamentalist make of some of these ideas? (See the section on Marxism in Unit 1, page 16.)

3 How has More used language features to engage the reader's interest in the paragraph beginning,

'Anyone can see, for example, that iron is far superior to either …'? In your answer, you may like to consider simile, variation of sentence length and cumulation.

4 How would you describe More's style overall? Do you find it engaging? Why?

5 How do you think that More's style and subject matter reflect the emerging spirit of the Renaissance? (For this question, revisit the introductory notes about the Renaissance on pages 53–7.)

Activities

1 You are a journalist in Utopia. Imagine (as More did) that another race of people who loved gold, silver and finery visited Utopia and tried to impress the inhabitants by parading around the town wearing their finest clothes and jewellery. Write a newspaper report of their visit for publication in Utopia's newspaper.

  a For this activity, try to use desktop publishing software, such as InDesign.

  b Think carefully about the presentation of your report, such as layout, choice of images and banner headline. Check a newspaper to establish the conventions.

  c Use a journalistic voice.

  d Use the material in this book about the Utopians to form your views. You may also want to research More's story about the Anemolians visiting Utopia.

2 In More's *Utopia*, when children choose a profession that differs from their parents' profession they are adopted out to a new family. In addition, families are encouraged not to eat together. Before *Utopia* was published, More wrote to his publisher, Peter Gilles, explaining why the writing of the book was delayed. He says:

»

You see, when I come home, I've got to talk to my wife, have a chat with my children, and discuss things with my servants. I count this as one of my commitments, because it's absolutely necessary, if I'm not to be a stranger in my own home. Besides, one should always try to be nice to the people one lives with, whether one has chosen their company deliberately, or merely been thrown into it by chance or family relationship—that is as nice as one can be without spoiling them.

a Link More's personal values and attitudes about family with his suggestions for Utopia.

b How persuasive do you find his views?

c How do his cultural assumptions about families contrast with your own, and how does this affect your reading?

3 What are your overall opinions about More's ideas? How have these opinions been shaped by your current political views about contemporary society?

The Renaissance sonnet

Sonnets have been a very common form in which to write poetry in English for centuries. They actually began life in Italy almost 200 years before the English took them up. The most famous Italian sonneteer was Petrarch, who established the form in the mid-1300s.

How to spot a Sonnet

· · ·

¤ It has fourteen lines.

¤ Each line is ten syllables long.

¤ The rhythmic stresses when you read them out are on the second, fourth, sixth, eighth and tenth syllables; that is, it is in iambic pentameter.

¤ A Shakespearean (English-style) sonnet is usually divided up into three linked four-line stanzas that state and develop an idea (the quatrains) and two lines at the end that tie it all together (a rhyming couplet).

¤ A Petrarchan (Italian-style) sonnet is usually divided into one eight-line section that states an idea (the octave) and one six-line section that responds to the idea (the sestet).

¤ A Shakespearean sonnet usually has the rhyme scheme *abab cdcd efef gg*.

¤ A Petrarchan sonnet usually has the rhyme scheme *abba abba cdcdcd* or *abba abba cdecde*.

Note: English poets also wrote Petrarchan sonnets.

Thomas Wyatt (1503–1542)

The sonnet form was picked up from Italy by the Englishman Sir Thomas Wyatt in the early 1500s. Wyatt was a diplomat who (when he was not in gaol for treason) served King Henry VIII and was appointed to a number of missions to Italy. He translated some Italian sonnets and adapted others. One of Wyatt's most famous pieces is the following sonnet, 'Whoso List to Hunt'. It is probably an adaptation of Petrarch's 190th sonnet. It is about Wyatt's infatuation with Anne Boleyn, a woman who eventually married King Henry VIII. Wyatt compares courting her to a hunt in which he has no chance of catching the deer. Wyatt, by all accounts, never actually had a relationship with Anne Boleyn. However, this did not prevent him from being thrown into the Tower of London, accused of having an affair with her. Wyatt was eventually released, but Anne Boleyn herself was executed by Henry VIII for alleged adultery. Wyatt watched her execution from his cell.

WHOSO LIST TO HUNT

Whoso list[1] to hunt, I know where is an hind[2],
But as for me, alas, I may no more.
The vain travail hath wearied me so sore
I am of them that farthest cometh behind.
Yet may I, by no means, my wearied mind   5
Draw from the deer, but as she fleeth afore,
Fainting I follow. I leave off therefore,
Since in a net I seek to hold the wind.
Who list her hunt, I put him out of doubt,
As well as I, may spend his time in vain.   10
And graven[3] with diamonds in letters plain
There is written, her fair neck round about,
'*Noli me tangere*[4], for Caesar's I am,
And wild for to hold, though I seem tame.'

1 Cares
2 Deer
3 Inscribed
4 *Noli me tangere quia Caesaris sum* (touch me not for I am Caesar's) was apparently written on the collar of Caesar's hinds. If caught, these animals would be set free by the hunter.

Questions

1 Check Wyatt's sonnet against the criteria in the 'How to spot a sonnet' box (page 61). What sort of sonnet is it?

2 Why can't Wyatt hunt the hind anymore? How far back in 'the pack' is he? What is his advice to other hunters/suitors?

3 What is the effect of comparing the hunt with holding the wind in a net?

4 Discuss the possible connotations of a diamond collar around the hind's neck.

》

5 This is a love poem that is also dangerously political. Re-read the section about new historicism and cultural materialism in Unit 1 (pages 17–18). Apply some of those ideas to the study of this poem.

6 What would you say is the overall tone and attitude of Wyatt in this sonnet?

Sir Philip Sidney (1554–1586)

As we have seen, writing poetry was one of the sixteenth-century ways of winning patronage and positions around the court. Although sonnets were about the expression of creativity, they were also very much about the circulation of power. A sonneteer had to follow the rules concerning rhyme, rhythm and development of argument, all within the space of fourteen lines, in order to demonstrate the writer's cleverness. Thus, writing a sonnet was like solving a puzzle. The three core areas studied at English grammar schools at this time were the trivium: logic, rhetoric and grammar. Sonnets were seen as a pure way of displaying all three of these areas of learning.

Sir Philip Sidney is a good example of a courtier with the right range of accomplishments, including the ability to write poetry. He was born to a very noble, wealthy family who regularly hosted literary functions and parties. He had travelled extensively through Europe on diplomatic missions for Queen Elizabeth, and was the ambassador to the German emperor. None of his poetry was published in his lifetime.

In 1585, he went to Europe to fight against Spain. He was wounded in the thigh in battle and lingered for twenty-six days before dying at the age of thirty-two. In that battle, apparently, he refused to wear thigh armour because he did not want to be better armed than the marshall of the camp. As he was being taken wounded from the field, he even handed his water bottle to a(nother) dying soldier, saying 'Thy necessity is yet greater than mine'.

His sonnet sequence, *Astrophel and Stella*, is allegedly about his devotion to the lady Penelope Devereux, who married the rather appropriately named Lord Rich. Like most sonnet sequences it has a plot of sorts, in which Astrophel is first attracted to the beauty and perfection of the lady Stella and then is forced to endure all the trials and joys of love: from crushing despair to soaring hope. Stella is often portrayed as something of a Renaissance ice queen who does not share Astrophel's enthusiasm for love in general, or love for him in particular. Over the span of 108 poems, which includes 'Sonnet 31', Astrophel receives only a single kiss. Even worse, Astrophel steals it from Stella in her sleep.

SONNET 31

With how sad steps, O Moon, thou climb'st the skies,
How silently, and with how wan a face!

»

What, may it be that even in heavenly place
That busy archer[1] his sharp arrows tries?
Sure, if that long-with-love-acquainted eyes   5
Can judge of Love, thou feel'st a Lover's case;
I read it in thy looks: thy languished grace,
To me that feels the like, thy state descries.
Then even of fellowship, O Moon, tell me
Is constant *love* deemed there but want of wit?   10
Are beauties there as proud as here they be?
Do they above love to be loved, and yet
Those lovers scorn whom that *love* doth possess?
Do they call *virtue* there ungratefulness?[2]

1 Cupid
2 What Astrophel sees as Stella's ungratefulness is seen by society as virtue

Questions

1 Is Sidney using a Petrarchan or English sonnet structure?

2 Astronomical imagery is used in this poem. Indeed, the name Astrophel means 'star lover', and Stella means 'star'.
   a How is apostrophe combined with astronomy in this sonnet? (Apostrophe is personification in which the inanimate object itself is addressed.)
   b Would this sonnet have been as effective if Sidney had chosen to apostrophise the sun instead of the moon? Why?

3 In the sestet, what complaints does Sidney mount about earthly love?

4 Re-read the text about the political and cultural contexts of the Renaissance period (pages 55–7). Then re-read the section about new historicist criticism in Unit 1 (pages 17–18). How can Sidney's sonnet be linked to his political situation in particular and the ideas of new historicism in general? Pay particular attention to the culturally materialist concepts of the 'historical situation' of texts and contemporary power relations.

Activities

1 You are Stella and you have just read 'Sonnet 31'. Write a sonnet (or a letter) back to Astrophel, explaining why you may appear to be cold and uninterested. (Keep in mind that relationships with men at that time could lead to pregnancy, disease and the destruction of a woman's reputation.) Use a female voice to disrupt some of the patriarchal assumptions about women in Sidney's poem. Refer to the section about feminist criticism in Unit 1 (pages 15–16) before you write this reply.

»

2 Construct a collage that is a homage to a man or woman of your dreams. Include images and words. Locate copyright-free images by using a search engine (such as the picture search function of Google <images.google.com>) and selected sites (such as the Corbis site <www.corbisimages.com>). Keep it PG rated. Use related symbolic images (such as stars) as well as images of people.

William Shakespeare (1564–1616)

Due to the plague, the Elizabethan theatre was regularly closed. It was during these times that Shakespeare turned to writing poetry, and this included a sequence of 154 sonnets. These sonnets, circulated among his friends, were published in 1609. The sonnet form had been familiar to readers for several generations before Shakespeare began writing them. So he toyed with a number of their conventions.

First, many of his expressions of love, devotion and praise are not directed towards an icy woman, but instead to a young man. Indeed, the speaker tells the man to make sure he marries so that he can have children and thus ensure his beauty is preserved. Shakespeare meditates on the corrosive effects of time on the young man's beauty, but comes to his rescue by writing poems about him and thus immortalising his beauty. However, it turns out that the boy exploits his looks immorally and Shakespeare ends up disgusted by him. The young man in the sonnet sequence is conjectured to be (amongst others) Henry Wriothesley, the Earl of Southampton.

The second convention Shakespeare played with was the type of woman he addressed, when he did so. The woman referred to in the latter part of the sonnet cycle is a dark, vivacious mistress: the 'dark lady'. This represents a substantial change from the virginal, unavailable women of previous sonnet cycles, who are praised for marble skin, fair hair and red lips. It is suggested in this sonnet sequence that the 'dark lady' ends up bedding none other than the young man, to the horror of the speaker in the poems. The following sonnet is one of Shakespeare's most lyrical.

The title page from an early edition of *Shakespeare's Sonnets*.

SONNET 18

Shall I compare thee to a summer's day?
Thou art more lovely and more temperate:
Rough winds do shake the darling buds of May,
And summer's lease hath all too short a date:

»

Sometime too hot the eye of heaven shines   5
And often is his gold complexion dimmed;
And every fair from fair sometimes declines,
By chance or nature's changing course untrimmed;
But thy eternal summer shall not fade,
Nor lose possession of that fair thou ow'st[1];   10
Nor shall death brag thou wander'st in his shade,
When in eternal lines to time thou grow'st:
So long as men can breathe, or eyes can see,
So long lives this, and this gives life to thee.

1 Shows

Questions

1 Use the 'how to spot a sonnet' guide (page 61) to determine whether this is an English or a Petrarchan sonnet.

2 What does Shakespeare say is wrong with comparing his love to a summer's day?

3 Explore the ways in which time and death are used by Shakespeare in this sonnet.

4 Explain, in your own words, the meaning of the rhyming couplet at the end of the poem. By discussing this poem in class have you helped to achieve Shakespeare's aim as stated in this couplet?

5 What is your overall impression of this poem?

6 How do the meanings of this sonnet change when you read it without the assumption that it is addressed by a man to a woman? This is an example of a form of resistant reading used by queer theorists. Re-read the section on queer criticism in Unit 1 (page 19) before you answer this question.

Activity

Deconstruction is a contemporary literary theory that asks us to view texts as constructed artefacts, rather than timeless pieces of beauty. (Read the section on deconstruction in Unit 1, page 18.) It asks us to look for what texts leave out and also what language may be concealing. This is often called the 'gap'. Tilottama Rajan, in her article 'Songs and Sonnets as Self-Consuming Artefact', claims that many sonnets actually call attention to themselves as constructed texts. Rajan states that they are 'not only the story of an emotional relationship, but also the narrative [story] of their own construction [creation]'.

You are not expected to become an authority on deconstruction after a one-paragraph introduction. However, imagine you are Tilottama Rajan and write a paragraph supporting your quote above. Use the Shakespearen sonnet you have studied to do this.

John Donne (1572–1631)

On the one hand, John Donne wrote clever, amorous poems that offered elaborate seductions of women. On the other hand, he wrote devotional poetry to God with great piety. John Donne himself was aware of the distinction between these two forms and once wrote in a letter that there were two Donnes: 'Jack Donne', who wrote bawdy love poetry, and 'Dr Donne', dean of St Paul's church, who wrote religious poetry.

Donne's own life was one of thwarted ambition. He was not of a 'noble' family. He began promisingly enough on the fringes of the Elizabethan court, but committed professional suicide when he married the seventeen-year-old niece of his patron, Sir Thomas Egerton. For this, Donne was sacked and thrown in prison. 'John Donne, Anne Donne, Undone' he wrote to his wife at the time. After his release he spent a dozen years in the courtly wilderness, during which time his writings included a pamphlet in defence of suicide, so we can conclude he may have been quite dispirited.

John Donne posing in his death shroud.

He eventually clawed his way back to the fringes of the court, but the new king, James, saw him 'only' as a churchman and preacher, and so a churchman he remained. In his lifetime he was most famous as a stirring preacher. (The famous lines 'No man is an island' and 'Never send to know for whom the bell tolls; it tolls for thee' are from his sermons.) His poetry only circulated in very select circles, for much of it had the potential to compromise his religious standing. He is an example of a poet for whom publication was something to be avoided rather than courted.

Donne is famous for his poetic conceits (extended similes often associating dissimilar images). He pushed poetic metaphor to be more elaborate, more intellectual and more original. His poetry became identified as 'metaphysical' because of its intellectual and argumentative qualities. The argumentative vigour in Donne's poetry can also be seen in his religious sonnets and writings. For example, he give orders to Death ('Death thou shalt die') and asks God to make violent love to him ('Nor ever chaste until you ravish me').

SONNET 10

Death be not proud, though some have called thee
Mighty and dreadful, for though art not so;
For those whom thou think'st thou dost overthrow
Die not, poor Death, nor yet canst thou kill me.
From rest and sleep, which but thy pictures be,   5
Much pleasure; then from thee much more must flow,
And soonest our best men with thee do go,

»

Rest of their bones, and soul's delivery.[1]
Thou art slave to fate, chance, kings, and desperate men,
And dost with poison, war, and sickness dwell,   10
And poppy[2] or charms can make us sleep as well
And better than thy stroke; why swell'st though then?
One short sleep past, we wake eternally
And death shall be no more; Death, thou shalt die.

1 Soul going to heaven
2 Opium

Questions

1 Donne apostrophises Death here. What is the effect of this?

2 How does Donne make Death appear powerless in the quatrains?

3 Explain the paradox in the final couplet.

4 1 Corinthians 15:54–5 says 'Oh death where is thy sting? O grave where is thy victory?' In 'Sonnet 10', is Donne simply extending this and being pious, or do you find his tone arrogant? Alternatively, do you have a different reaction? Explain your view about the tone of the poem.

5 What is your overall reaction to this poem?

Lady Mary Wroth's use of a woman as the subject (and thus the creator) rather than merely the admired object was revolutionary.

Lady Mary Wroth (1587–1651)

Very few women in Renaissance England had the opportunity, as Mary Wroth did, to be associated with literature. Her father, uncles (and even her aunt) were the foremost literary patrons of the day. One of her uncles was Sir Philip Sidney. Wroth wrote plays, sonnets and, in 1621, what was probably the first ever published novel by a woman. It caused a scandal because it made vague references to the court, and Wroth withdrew it. However, she continued to be a figure around court, until her illegitimate children, fathered by her cousin, caused another scandal.

Lady Mary Wroth did something revolutionary with her sonnet sequence, *Pamphilia to Amphilanthus*: she wrote it from a woman's point of view. For a woman to actually have the voice in the sonnet, rather than simply be the admired object, is a large shift indeed. She becomes the subject (and thus the creator of all the feeling, cleverness and artistry) rather than merely the object.

SONNET 68

My pain, still smothered in my grievèd breast,
Seeks for some ease, yet cannot passage find
To be discharged of this unwelcome guest:
When most I strive, most fast his burdens bind,
Like to a ship on Goodwin's[1] cast by wind,   5
The more she strives, more deep in sand is pressed,
Till she be lost; so am I, in this kind[2],
Sunk, and devoured, and swallowed by unrest,
Lost, shipwracked, spoiled, debarred of smallest hope,
Nothing of pleasure left; save thoughts have scope,   10
Which wander may. Go then, my thoughts, and cry
Hope's perished, Love tempest-beaten, Joy lost:
Killing Despair hath all these blessings crossed.
Yet Faith still cries, Love will not falsify.

1 Goodwin Sands is a dangerous sea entrance to the Strait of Dover in the south of England
2 Manner

Questions

1 What emotion does this poem address? Explain with close reference to the poem.

2 Explain and explore the conceit of the ship used in the sonnet.
   a How is it developed?
   b What, in your view, is the most effective aspect of the conceit?

3 In your view, does the sonnet's female voice deal with emotion differently from the sonnets you have read that use a male voice? Is it communicating anything that patriarchal voices do not? (Before you answer this question, re-read the section on feminist criticism in Unit 1, pages 15–16.)

Renaissance drama

Types of drama

Several types of plays were popular during the Renaissance, although of course fashions shifted during the period that we are discussing. The structure and form of the plays were affected by classical (that is, ancient Greek and Roman) models. First, there was comedy, which did not simply mean a funny play, but instead could involve any element of satire, common life, noble love, happy resolution and moral improvement. There were several types of comedy (such as domestic, satiric and city) and the most famous Renaissance comedies include

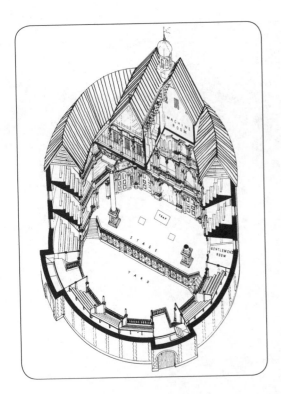

The Globe Theatre, erected in London in 1599. Many of Shakespeare's plays were performed here.

Thomas Middleton's *A Chaste Mayd in Cheap-side*, Ben Jonson's *The Alchemist* and William Shakespeare's *A Midsummer Night's Dream*.

Tragedies also took hold of the Renaissance imagination. There were revenge tragedies, based on the influence of the ancient Roman tragedian Seneca, in whose works there was much bloody violence and many heroic speeches. In these plays the revenger usually destroyed himself or herself as well as everything that he or she surveyed. Examples of this genre include Thomas Kyd's *Spanish Tragedy*, William Shakespeare's *Hamlet* and John Webster's *The White Devil*. Another major form of tragedy was Aristotelian, in which a 'great' man is brought undone by a fatal flaw in his own character. Aristotle, in his *Poetics*, described it as 'a man ... whose misfortune is brought upon him not by vice or depravity but by some error in judgment'. The audience can be appalled at the result, but at least know the main character brought much of it upon himself or herself. Examples of this kind of tragedy include Christopher Marlowe's *Dr Faustus* and Shakespeare's *King Lear*.

Historical context

Before the Renaissance, one of the only forms of drama in England was the occasional religious mystery play (see pages 40–1). In fact, it was the humble 'school play' in the mid-sixteenth century that sowed the seeds of Renaissance drama. The first known English comedy, *Ralph Roister Doister* (first performed in about 1552), was written by the headmaster of Westminster School, Nicholas Udall, and probably acted by and performed for the students of this school.

Professional theatre had a long journey to respectability. Permanent theatres began to be built in the late 1560s, many on the south bank of the Thames River. This was to avoid the puritan, prudish Corporation of London on the north bank. The Corporation of London, which was not unlike the local government, thought that all public performances, and particularly plays, were hotbeds of sin, crime, bawdiness and death. The entrepreneur Phillip Henslowe didn't help the reputation of theatre when he built his major theatre (The Rose) in the yard of his brothel.

Censorship didn't help matters. In 1598, a performance at The Swan of the play called *The Isle of Dogs* by Thomas Nashe was banned for being offensive and its lead actors (including Ben Jonson) were thrown into Marshalsea Prison and tortured. Further, the Privy Council ordered that all playhouses be pulled down. Other elements that made theatregoing rather adventurous for the public were the risks of fire, and of catching plague and dying an agonising death. In fact, the threat of plague was sufficiently severe for all theatres to be closed down between 1592 and 1594.

As no women were allowed on stage, acting was done by companies of men who had to find a nobleman as a sponsor and were then technically his servants. If nobody sponsored them, they were deemed by a 1572 Act of Parliament to be 'rogues, vagabonds and sturdy beggars', for which they could be punished. There were several companies, including 'The Admiral's Men', 'Lord Strange's Men' and 'The Chamberlain's Men'. Writers attached themselves to companies; Christopher Marlowe worked with 'The Admiral's Men' and Shakespeare worked (and managed, and produced and acted in) 'The Chamberlain's Men'.

Going to most theatre was not dissimilar to attending a football game today. Audience members could sit, or buy standing tickets towards the front. They could wander about and buy food during the performances. The people on stage had very few sets or props, but did have elaborate costumes. Often the performance took place in the open air in the afternoon as theatres could not be lit.

Questions

1 RECAP: Create a mind map of the main types of comedy and tragedy present in Renaissance theatre.

2 Speculate about why theatre and actors may have had such a bad reputation during the Renaissance.

3 Contrast the world of theatre as outlined in this chapter to what you know of the world of theatre today. What has changed? Which do you think makes for 'better' theatre and why?

Marlowe and *Dr Faustus*

Christopher Marlowe (1564–1593)

Christopher Marlowe's is an extreme example of the short, turbulent life of many in the theatre profession during the Renaissance. In the late 1580s, he was a spy for Her Majesty's secret service, but an unreliable one. In 1589, he was in a brawl where his opponent was killed by a fellow poet. Marlowe was jailed for this. In 1591, the playwright with whom Marlowe was living, Thomas Kyd, accused him of atheism and treason. Marlowe was brought before the Privy Council on these charges and, as a result, was not allowed to leave London, pending further investigation. He was rapidly becoming a liability to the secret service. In 1593, he was stabbed and killed in a pub, apparently in an argument over the normally sedate game of backgammon. However, the people who killed him were double agents. It has been speculated that he was coldly murdered, conspiracy style, to prevent him giving public evidence. Marlowe's plays include *Tamburlaine*, *The Jew of Malta* and *Dr Faustus*.

Frontispiece of *Dr Faustus*.

Dr Faustus

Dr Faustus is the story of a man who sells his soul to the devil for twenty-four years of power on earth. It embodies one part of the spirit of the Renaissance because Faustus yearns for more than science or philosophy can ever show him; he wants knowledge and happiness here on earth (not in the afterlife). Once he receives this power from the devil's servant, Mephistopheles, he squanders it and becomes a sort of medieval Monty Python member, turning horses into hay and throwing fireworks about the pope's chamber. The drop in quality in the middle section of the play is probably due to the work being 'padded' for the stage, and it is thought by many that these sections were not written by Marlowe at all. At the end of the play Faustus's twenty-four years are over, and, in a flood of terror and remorse, he realises to what he has signed himself. He pleads to be saved, but to no avail. The extracted section is Faustus's desperate monologue just before he is dragged to the fires of hell.

DR FAUSTUS
Scene 13

FAUSTUS: Ah Faustus.	55
Now hast thou but one bare hour to live,	
And then thou must be damned perpetually.	
Stand still, you ever-moving spheres of heaven,	
That time may cease, and midnight never come.	
Fair Nature's eye, rise, rise again, and make	60
Perpetual day, or let this hour be but	
A year, a month, a week, a natural day,	
That Faustus may repent and save his soul.	
Oh lente, lente currite, noctus equii[1]	
The stars move still, time runs, the clock will strike,	65
The devil will come, and Faustus must be damned.	
O, I'll leap up to my God! Who pulls me down?	
See, see where Christ's blood streams in the firmament!	
One drop would save my soul, half a drop: ah my Christ—	
Ah, rend not my heart for the naming of my Christ;	70
Yet I will class on him—O spare me, Lucifer!	
Where is it now? 'Tis gone: and see where God	
Stretcheth out his arm, and bends his ireful brows!	
Mountains and hills, come, come and fall on me,	
And hide me from the heavy wrath of God.	75
No, no?	
Then I will headlong run into the earth:	
Earth, gape! O no, it will not harbor me:	
You stars that reigned at my nativity,	
Whose influence hath allotted death and hell,	80

»

Now draw up Faustus like a foggy mist
Into the entails of yon laboring cloud,
That when you vomit forth into the air,
My limbs may issue from your smoky mouths,
So that my soul may but ascend to heaven.   85

[The watch strikes.]

Ah, half the hour is past: 'twill all be past anon.
O God, if thou wilt not have mercy on my soul,
Yet for Christ's sake, whose blood hath ransomed me,
Impose some end to my incessant pain:
Let Faustus live in hell a thousand years,   90
A hundred thousand, and at last be saved.
O, no end is limited to damned souls!
Why wert thou not a creature wanting soul?
Or why is this immortal that thou hast?
Ah, Pythagoras' *metempsychosis*[2]—were that true,   95
This soul should fly from me, and I be changed.
Unto some brutish beast:
All beasts are happy, for when they die,
Their souls are soon dissolved in elements;
But mine must live still to be plagued in hell.   100
Cursed be the parents that engendered me:
No, Faustus, curse thy self, curse Lucifer,
That hath deprived thee of the joys of heaven.

[The clock strikes twelve.]

O it strikes, it strikes! Now body, turn to air,
Or Lucifer will bear thee quick to hell.   105

[Thunder and lightning.]

O soul, be changed into little water drops,
And fall into the ocean, ne'er be found.
My God, my God, look not so fierce on me!

[Enter DEVILS.]

Adders and serpents, let me breathe awhile!
Ugly hell gape not! Come not, Lucifer!   110
I'll burn my books—ah, Mephastophilis!

[Exuent with him.]

1 Go slowly, slowly, you horses of the night
2 A theory that stated that when the human soul left the body at death it took on some other form of life

Questions

1 RECAP: Outline and explain the seven different pleas that Faustus makes in order to avoid his damnation.

2 How does Faustus's pleading become more desperate? How are language features used to increase this sense of desperation?

3 How is vocabulary used to emphasise the nature of eternity in the lines beginning 'Let Faustus live in hell a thousand years ...' (lines 90–4). In what ways does this section make you reflect on 'eternity'?

4 How much sympathy do you have for Faustus and his situation? Explain your answer with close reference to the passage.

5 How can this speech be seen as a heartfelt embodiment of and plea for the spirit of the Renaissance? In what ways could this speech be said to be reinforcing medieval values? (See the introductory section in Unit 2, pages 21–4.)

6 What is your personal response to this piece? How is it affected by your own beliefs and cultural context?

7 Re-read the section on deconstructive criticism in Unit 1 (page 18).

a Identify what you consider to be the important binary oppositions in the *Dr Faustus* extract. These oppositions should be made up of positive and negative pairs.

b Now read the extract about Satan from John Milton's *Paradise Lost* (pages 82–3). What binaries exist in this text?

c Could a resistant reading see the negative terms (that is, hell and damnation) in these texts as something other than fearful? If so, what does this do to the dominant ideology of Renaissance Christianity?

d Re-read the biography of Marlowe (page 71) and read the biography of Milton (pages 81–2). Can you see anything in the biographies that may explain a sympathy with rebellious characters and subversions of Renaissance Christianity?

Activities

1 Read sections of this speech aloud. Try to capture the sense of desperation and fear.

2 How would you stage (or film) this extract in the twenty-first century to give it maximum impact? Analyse the cultural factors of your audience in the twenty-first century (such as being less religious than a Renaissance audience) that will make the task more difficult.

3 The Faustian story was given a comic twist by Dudley Moore and Peter Cook in the film *Bedazzled* (1967), in which the devil gives Stanley Moon seven wishes in return for his soul, and then sets about cunningly ruining each wish. Watch this film (or the 2000 remake with Brendan Fraser and Liz Hurley). How does it subvert and play with the Faustian story? How does the seriousness of the core idea change as a result of its reuse in a different cultural and social context?

4 Some scholars believe that Shakespeare was an illiterate theatre manager and that Christopher Marlowe actually wrote all the plays that are attributed to William Shakespeare. »

Research this theory. The websites
www.zenigmas.fsnet.co.uk/marlowe.htm and
www.shakespeare-oxford.com/guide.htm are
places to begin. How credible do you find this
theory? How credible and appropriate do you
find these two websites? Explain your answer.

Shakespeare

Brief introduction to Shakespeare

Shakespeare is a major figure in the English literary canon, and many readers and students deal with book-length studies on 'the Bard' alone. Shakespeare's world flourished as part of the cresting wave of peace and prosperity that followed the English defeat of the Spanish Armada in 1588. One legacy of a sometimes brutal Tudor rule was a degree of stability, which, in turn, allowed a wonderful period of late Renaissance questioning, debate and cultural production to flourish in Britain.

A portrait of Shakespeare from the First Folio.

Shakespeare's early interest in history plays and kings as leaders, heroes and humans led to an increasingly sophisticated development of character and motive and moving portraits of vulnerable humanity (both male and female). He remained constant in his emphasis on the importance of power being held centrally by strong individuals, but the individual kings had to be worthy characters. Individuality was a new force in relationships with Church and State, and this shift in power relations was also reflected in the mix of poetry, action and debate that dramatised portraits of ambition, power and love. Shakespeare was indeed subject to the dynamics of cultural and social power that characterises any literary and theatrical milieu, but he was not a lackey. His work both affirmed and challenged accepted values.

Shakespeare and Renaissance scripts

Renaissance scripts were not often published. In fact, many playwrights went to great lengths to keep their scripts secret. There was often only one copy of the whole script: 'the prompt book'. Even the actors were not given a whole script, merely their own lines. This was largely because there was no copyright in England at this time. If a company had a great success with a new play (such as *Hamlet*), and a rival company acquired the script, they could simply put on a rival production next door and siphon off half the audience. Rival theatre companies actually sent spies into theatres to copy down the lines of plays, and drew upon the memories of actors. (A 'bad quarto' copy of *Hamlet* was printed in 1603, probably from the memory of the actor who played the very insignificant part of Marcellus.) So, scripts were secret intellectual property, which had to be guarded.

In addition, plays were often seen as a lower form of writing (compared with poetry, for example). They were the short-lived entertainment for that month and were designed to be seen, not read, which was another reason not to print them. For example, Shakespeare's *Complete Works* was never published in his lifetime. Shakespeare had made all his money by being a financial stakeholder in the theatre, so he was not particularly interested in the few paltry pounds he would earn by publishing his plays. It was only after a lesser (although still good) dramatist, Ben Jonson, published his collected works that old associates of Shakespeare thought they should collect up his plays and bind them together. This work became the First Folio, without which many of Shakespeare's plays would be lost.

Activity

Imagine you are Henry Condell, one of the men who attempted to put together the First Folio. Your task is Herculean. Shakespeare did not have definitive versions of his plays. In front of you there are piles of 'foul papers', which are Shakespeare's first drafts. Next to them lies a stack of 'prompt books' from which the actors' lines were written down. Flooding over your desk are towers of individual actors' scripts, which may have been changed by Shakespeare during rehearsal after they were copied from the prompt book. Scattered around the floor are unauthorised printed copies of some plays. You cannot ask Shakespeare's opinion; he died six years earlier.

Work out a policy for how you are going to put these sources together to form a definitive version of the plays for hundreds of future generations. As part of this job, rank your sources from what you think are the most to the least reliable.

Question

Re-read the section about new historicist criticism in Unit 1 (pages 17–18). What does the previous activity tell you about the production and reception of texts? How, if at all, does it affect your reading of Shakespeare's texts in class?

Shakespeare and criticism

In this section, we focus on two different types of criticism and apply them to passages from selected Shakespearean plays. Criticism here does not mean that the critics are criticising Shakespeare's plays. Instead, they are critically applying other strands of thought (such as Marxism) to the plays. (See also the sections about some of these perspectives in Unit 1.)

King Lear and the Marxist perspective

King Lear is about a king who divides up his kingdom among his three daughters on the basis of how much they say they love him. The two eldest, Goneril and Regan, hypocritically shower Lear with praise and are richly rewarded. The 'true' daughter, Cordelia, stays silent (because she disagrees with the test) and is banished. Once Lear loses his power, Goneril and Regan quickly disregard and abuse him. They refuse to let him have more than his basic needs, and will not tolerate his entourage of (loutish) hangers-on. Lear is furious at this, and rather than accept this indignity he expels himself into the wilds and a storm. It is here that he comes to realise the poverty-stricken state of many of his subjects and recognises his foolish choices.

Terry Eagleton is a well-known British Marxist critic. He is concerned with how different economic systems have a prime role in oppressing and liberating masses of people. First, he is very interested in why Lear feels that he requires more than his basic needs. After all, shouldn't everything more than a need be seen as just a desire or a want? Eagleton comes to the sobering conclusion that humans will insist that certain things that are not essential are, in fact, needs. He states:

> There is no reason why human beings should delight in more than is strictly necessary for their physical survival; it is just structural to the human animal that demand should outstrip exact need, that culture should be of its nature.

Second, Eagleton focuses on the way in which an excess of material possessions actually cuts us off from poverty-stricken people so that we no longer feel for them and their condition (and thus do not do anything about it). This he considers to be a real flaw in a consumer society. He sees an example of this being Lear not realising the poverty-stricken state of his subjects until he himself has been struck low. Eagleton states:

> Too many material possessions blunts one's capacity for fellow feeling, swaddling one's senses from exposure to misery of others. If one could truly feel that wretchedness, register it sharply on the senses, then one would be moved to share one's surplus with the poor in a fundamental redistribution of wealth.

KING LEAR: EXTRACT I
Act II, scene IV

Lear says these lines to Regan and Goneril when they ask him what need he has for any of his own servants when they have servants of their own to look after him

O, reason not the need! Our basest beggars
Are in the poorest thing superfluous.
Allow not nature more than nature's needs,
Man's life's as cheap as beast's. Thou art a lady;
If only to go warm were gorgeous,   260
Why, nature needs not what thou gorgeous wear'st,
Which scarcely keeps thee warm.[1]

1 Lear is saying that Regan and Goneril don't need clothes as gorgeous as they are wearing to keep them warm, and, in fact, the clothes are too scanty to keep them warm.

KING LEAR: EXTRACT 2

Act III, scene IV

Lear says the following lines when he finds a hovel in which to shelter from the storm

Poor naked wretches, whereso'er you are,
That bide the pelting of this pitiless storm,   30
How shall your houseless heads and unfed sides,
Your looped and windowed raggedness, defend you
From seasons such as these? O, I have ta'en
Too little care of this! Take physic, pomp;
Expose thyself to feel what wretches feel,   35
That thou mayst shake[1] the superflux[2] to them,
And show the heavens more just.

1 Distribute
2 Surplus

KING LEAR: EXTRACT 3

Act IV, scene I

The following lines are spoken by another older nobleman, named Gloucester, who is also suddenly wandering the wilds, destitute and with his eyes torn out

Heavens, deal so still!   65
Let the superfluous and lust-dieted[1] man,
That slaves your ordinance[2], that will not see
Because he doth not feel, feel your power quickly;
So distribution should undo excess,
And each man have enough.   70

1 Overly self-indulgent
2 Makes your law a mere servant of his own desire

Questions

1 How does extract 1 from *King Lear* (page 77) demonstrate Eagleton's first point? How does it use language to make this point more powerful?

2 How do extracts 2 and 3 from *King Lear* demonstrate Eagleton's second point? How do they use language to make this point more powerful?

»

3 How does the sentiment expressed by Gloucester in extract 2 relate to those expressed by King Lear in extract 2?

4 Compare your own relationship to material possessions with King Lear's. Do you agree with Eagleton's ideas? How does this Marxist perspective of *King Lear* make you consider the cultural messages you receive each day about material possessions?

5 Shakespeare lived 300 years before Marx. What, if any, value do you think there is in applying Marxist thinking to his plays?

The Tempest and the colonial perspective

The Tempest is about the ex-Duke of Milan, Prospero, who is exiled by his evil brother to an island where he uses his magical powers to dominate quickly the few inhabitants: the fairy, Ariel, and the brute, Caliban. Prospero originally attempts to civilise Caliban, but then enslaves him after Caliban tries to rape Prospero's daughter, Miranda. After a time, a shipwreck brings various other Italians, including Prospero's brother, to the island. Prospero uses magic, island fairies and so on to wreak a mild and restorative revenge on them. In the last scene, he frees the native inhabitants before his departure to Milan.

Barry Otto as Prospero in a production of *The Tempest*.

The Tempest was first performed in 1611, only four years after the English colonised the US state of Virginia. In the Elizabethan and post-Elizabethan era there was a real fascination with both the colonising adventure and the exotic lands that were being colonised. The issue of colonial domination over the people native to the colonised area was beginning to be aired, and indeed would be for centuries afterwards. *The Tempest* engages in the issue by presenting a problematic, colonial relationship between Prospero and his deemed 'subjects'. JP Conlin states that Shakespeare was well known as a critic of the colonisation of Virginia. Further, Shakespeare would have known that King James would attend the play and thus it shows us how Shakespeare could have been using the theatre to provide the king with some advice about the colonial enterprise.

THE TEMPEST
Act 1, Scene II

[Caliban has entered and is cursing Prospero]

CALIBAN: As wicked dew as e'er my mother brush'd
    With raven's feather from unwholesome fen
    Drop on you both! a south-west blow on ye   325
    And blister you all o'er!
    »

PROSPERO: For this, be sure, to-night thou shalt have cramps,
    Side-stitches that shall pen thy breath up; urchins
    Shall, for that vast of night that they may work,
    All exercise on thee; thou shalt be pinch'd   330
    As thick as honeycomb, each pinch more stinging
    Than bees that made 'em.

CALIBAN: I must eat my dinner.
    This island's mine, by Sycorax my mother,
    Which thou tak'st from me. When thou cam'st first,
    Thou strok'st me, and made much of me, wouldst give me   335
    Water with berries in 't; and teach me how
    To name the bigger light, and how the less,
    That burn by day and night: and then I lov'd thee,
    And show'd thee all the qualities o' th' isle,
    The fresh springs, brine-pits, barren place and fertile: 340
    Curs'd be I that did so! All the charms
    Of Sycorax, toads, beetles, bats, light on you!
    For I am all the subjects that you have,
    Which first was mine own King: and here you sty me
    In this hard rock, whiles you do keep from me   345
    The rest o' th' island.

PROSPERO: Thou most lying slave,
    Whom stripes may move, not kindness! I have us'd thee,
    Filth as thou art, with human care; and lodg'd thee
    In mine own cell, till thou didst seek to violate
    The honour of my child.   350

CALIBAN: O ho, O ho! would't had been done!
    Thou didst prevent me; I had peopled else
    This isle with Calibans.

PROSPERO: Abhorred slave,
    Which any print of goodness wilt not take,
    Being capable of all ill! I pitied thee,   335
    Took pains to make thee speak, taught thee each hour
    One thing or other: when thou didst not, savage,
    Know thine own meaning, but wouldst gabble like
    A thing most brutish, I endow'd thy purposes
    With words that made them known. But thy vile race,
    Though thou didst learn, had that in't which   360
    good natures
    Could not abide to be with; therefore wast thou
    Deservedly confin'd into this rock,
    Who hadst deserv'd more than a prison.

        »

CALIBAN: You taught me language; and my profit on 't   365
    Is, I know how to curse. The red plague rid you
    For learning me your language!
PROSPERO: Hag-seed, hence!
    Fetch us in fuel; and be quick, thou 'rt best,
    To answer other business. Shrug'st thou, malice?
    If thou neglect'st, or dost unwillingly   370
    What I command, I'll rack thee with old cramps,
    Fill all thy bones with aches, make thee roar,
    That beasts shall tremble at thy din.
CALIBAN: No, 'pray thee.

Questions

1 What arguments are there to claim that Prospero is a benevolent (kind) ruler over the domain? What arguments are there to claim that he is a tyrant? In your view is there justification for him 'taking control' of the island and its inhabitants?

2 Caliban's portrayal reflects conscious (and perhaps unconscious) perceptions of the time about the inhabitants of the new world. Through Caliban's portrayal, what do these passages reveal about:
   a the perceived level of civilisation
   b physical appearance
   c the desire for education?

3 Homi Bhabha has done work on the importance of colonial subjects strategically using the language of the colonial powers (such as Indians taking on English). One of the elements of this is that subjects, by mimicking the colonial power's language, can use the coloniser's language against them. In doing so, the subject can become a type of colonial rebel. How is this idea raised in the exchange between Prospero and Caliban?

4 Re-read the section about postcolonialism in Unit 1 (pages 14–15). What other issues raised in that section do you find in this extract (such as hybridity, language, identity formation and the construction of the other)?

Milton and *Paradise Lost*

John Milton (1608–1674)

Milton was born in 1608, and studied at Cambridge University. He became involved in the republican cause against King Charles during the 1640s. When the republicans defeated the royalists in 1649, Milton became their 'Secretary for Foreign Tongues' and wrote a great deal of political prose for the revolution. However, the republican cause had failed by 1660 and Milton only barely escaped execution when the monarchy was restored.

Milton's personal life was also very difficult during this decade. He went blind in 1651, and in the same year his only son died. His wife died the following year, then his daughter in

An illustration from a nineteenth-century edition of *Paradise Lost*.

1657 and his second wife in 1658. He lived a quiet, blind, gout-ridden, arthritic life for the next sixteen years until his death. However, it was during this time that he dictated his epic poem *Paradise Lost*, the work for which he is now chiefly remembered.

Paradise Lost

Paradise Lost is an epic poem of over 10 000 lines in twelve books. Its scale, seriousness, lack of satire, and view of Christian humanism make it a Renaissance piece. It tells the story of Satan's fall from heaven into hell for rebellion against God. However, Satan breaks out of hell (in the extracted piece) and finds his way to the Garden of Eden where he tempts Eve to eat from the Tree of Knowledge. Adam realises, in horror, what Eve has done, but eats the fruit too, so that he can share in her fall. God's son is sent down to judge them. Sin and Death enter the world. Adam and Eve are expelled from the Garden of Eden.

PARADISE LOST

Hell bounds, high reaching to the horrid roof,	
And thrice threefold the gates; three folds were brass,	645
Three iron, three of adamantine rock,	
Impenetrable, impaled with circling fire,	
Yet unconsumed. Before the gates there sat	
On either side a formidable shape;	
The one seemed woman to the waist, and fair,	650
But ended foul in many a scaly fold	
Voluminous and vast, a serpent armed	
With mortal sting. About her middle round	
A cry of Hell hounds never ceasing barked	
With wide Cerberean mouths full loud, and rung	655
A hideous peal; yet, when they list, would creep,	
If aught disturbed their noise, into her womb,	
And kennel there, yet there still barked and howled	
Within unseen …	

ooooo

The other shape,	
If shape it might be call'd that shape had none	
Distinguishable in member, joint, or limb,	
Or substance might be called that shadow seemed,	
For each seem'd either; black it stood as night,	670
Fierce as ten Furies, terrible as Hell,	
And shook a dreadful dart; what seemed his head	
The likeness of a kingly crown had on.	
Satan was now at hand, and from his seat	
The monster moving onward came as fast,	675

»

With horrid strides, Hell trembled as he strode.
Th' undaunted fiend …

∞∞∞∞∞

with disdainful look thus first began.   680
'Whence and what art thou, execrable shape,
That dar'st, though grim and terrible, advance
Thy miscreated front athwart my way
To yonder gates? Through them I mean to pass,
That be assur'd, without leave asked of thee.   685
Retire, or taste thy folly, and learn by proof,
Hell-born, not to contend with spirits of Heaven' …

∞∞∞∞∞

[Death then] grew tenfold   705
More dreadful and deform. On th' other side
Incensed with indignation Satan stood …

∞∞∞∞∞

Each at the [other's] head   711
Leveled his deadly aim; their fatal hands
No second stroke intend …

∞∞∞∞∞

the snaky sorceress that sat
Fast by Hell-gate, and kept the fatal key,   725
Ris'n, and with hideous outcry rushed between.
'O Father, what intends thy hand,' she cried,
'Against thy only Son? What fury O son,
Possesses thee to bend that mortal dart
Against thy father's head?'   730

It transpires that the 'snaky sorceress' is Sin, Satan's daughter to whom he gave birth out of his head. He then
made love to Sin who gave birth to a son, Death, who is the grisly terror about to kill Satan. Sin and Death
have been sent to guard the gates of Hell.

Questions

1 How are language forms and features used to
make the gates seem unpassable in lines 644–8?

2 What is your personal reaction to the hell
hounds? What is it about Milton's writing that
creates this reaction?

3 Milton's language has been praised for its 'epic
grandeur'. What evidence do you see of this
grandeur from lines 667–80? Closely refer to
language features in your analysis.

4 How is Satan portrayed in this section? Do you
find him noble, courageous or something else?

Activities

1 Make up a storyboard of eight panels for a sequence that films the preceding section of *Paradise Lost*. Your budget is large.

2 What assumptions is Milton making about the status and role of women in his portrayal of 'Sin'? Write Milton a letter challenging these assumptions. (Before attempting this, re-read the section on feminist criticism in Unit 1, pages 15–16.)

3 Your are starting up a new heavy metal concept band called A Hideous Peal (line 656), which will be based on Milton's *Paradise Lost*. Make up the following by using the extract provided

or the whole of *Paradise Lost* (available at the Representative Poetry Online site <rpo.library.utoronto.ca/poet/225.html>) as well as your own experience of popular music:

a an album name

b the titles of ten tracks

c the lyrics to one song

d a concept design for the cover.

4 Read Phillip Pullman's *His Dark Materials* trilogy, and particularly *The Amber Spyglass*. How do these novels subvert or recontextualise the story of the war between God and Satan, and the Fall of Man?

Review Questions & Activities

...RENAISSANCE LITERATURE

1 **Sonnet smorgasbord**

a In groups, use the web (see the site on page 85) to select three sonnets: one from Sidney, one from Wyatt and one from Shakespeare. Write out or photocopy the three sonnets. Cut each sonnet into seven equal pieces (consisting of two lines each). Give the twenty-one pieces to another group and see how accurately they can reconstruct the sonnets. At the same time, take twenty-one pieces from another group and see how well you can reconstruct these.

b Now cut all the pieces in half so that you have forty-two single lines. Use these lines in any combination to make up your very

own 'Frankenstein sonnet'. Then compare Frankenstein sonnets around the class and see which sonnet makes the most sense and, if possible, has the most poetic dignity.

c The rules are as follows:

- No more than six lines can be used from any one sonnet.
- Consecutive lines from the original sonnet cannot be used in the Frankenstein sonnet. However, consecutive lines can be spaced apart.
- The Frankenstein sonnet does not need to rhyme.

d Explain what you think your poem is expressing.

2 Choose two texts from this unit. Show how they are the product of the Renaissance era in which they were produced and explain why they have remained popular to the present day. In your answer look closely at the language forms and features of the texts you have selected.

3 'One view of Renaissance fiction is that it mapped out a terrain that was more hospitable to human hopes and human fears.' What is your response to this statement? What are the features of the terrain that you think Renaissance fiction 'maps out'? In your answer refer closely to two texts as well as the context of the times.

4 It is 1623. You are a courtier of King James I. He is about to have a royal banquet hosting the French king, Louis XIII. In the past, the French king has made some rather rude remarks about the state of culture in Britain. Comments such as 'unoriginal, dull, and centuries behind Europe, all of it spoken in a tongue that is tortured doggerel' have been known to pass his lips. King James wants to be ready with a reply to such remarks. He asks you to write a report for him on the 'fine state of literature in our faire land'. He will learn this report and use it at the dinner to counter any further outrageous remarks made by the French king. Write your report.

5 Imagine Mary Wroth and John Donne meet. Presume that Wroth believes the 'flattering' imagery about women used in men's poems actually makes women sound like objects (such

as treasure and booty) rather than people. She is challenged by John Donne, who says that women should not write poetry because male poets can make women 'sparkle like diamonds' far better than a woman can. Write a dialogue of the argument they have about the representation of women in sonnets. You should refer closely to a number of the sonnets you have studied as well as the section on feminist criticism in Unit 1 (pages 15–16).

In your argument you may also use the following lines from Donne's poems (translations are provided):
- "Th' Indias of spice ... lie here with me'— All the spices of India are his woman lying on his bed (from 'The Sunne Rising').
- 'Let maps to others, worlds on worlds have shown: Let us possess one world; each hath one, and is one'—Let us admit that maps have shown investigators new worlds, but we only need to possess one world: each other (from 'The Good-Morrow').
- 'She is all states, and all princes I'—She is all the nations of the world lying in Donne's bed (from 'The Sunne Rising').
- 'Hope not for mind in women; at their best, Sweetness and wit they are, but mummy, possess'd'—Hope for sweetness, not a mind, in a woman ('Possessed' possibly refers to Donne's possession of the woman.) (from 'Love's Alchemy').

Note: The full texts of poems can be found at the Representative Poetry Online site (rpo. library.utoronto.ca).

Visions, Nature & Tyrants

ROMANTIC LITERATURE

Highlights

¶ *London hellhole exposed!*

¶ *Drug-fuelled fantasyland rises from dream*

¶ *Despotic tyrant falls into ruin*

¶ *Rich man moves into area—women make marriage plans*

Outcomes

By the end of this unit you should have:

¤ developed an understanding of the relationship between the texts and the context of the Romantic era (including the literary, cultural and historical contexts).

¤ gained an appreciation of the way in which the texts can be seen as cultural products of both their authors and their times

¤ engaged in detailed textual interpretation of a number of Romantic pieces and developed an understanding of how language forms and/or techniques shape the meaning of these pieces

¤ challenged and evaluated some of the cultural assumptions that exist in Romantic texts and considered alternative readings of some texts

¤ come to a personal view about valuing the texts and the Romantic period based on your own context and preferences

¤ engaged with the texts in a number of ways, including writing essays and letters, participating in role-plays and writing 'legal' judgments

¤ gained enjoyment through exposure to the texts and their ideas and contexts.

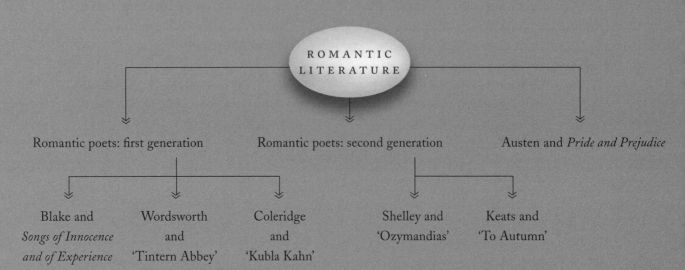

ROMANTIC LITERATURE

Romantic poets: first generation

Romantic poets: second generation

Austen and *Pride and Prejudice*

Blake and
Songs of Innocence and of Experience

Wordsworth and
'Tintern Abbey'

Coleridge and
'Kubla Kahn'

Shelley and
'Ozymandias'

Keats and
'To Autumn'

Context *of* the period

It is important to make clear from the outset that, in a literary context, 'Romantic' does not mean 'love' in the sense of a 'candlelit dinner for two'. The group of writers we identify as the English Romantics hardly wrote about love at all. Instead, Romanticism (which was evident in the period 1780–1830) was concerned with passion, imagination, outlandish landscapes, wondrous journeys and dreams. The neoclassical, or Augustan, period, which preceded the Romantic period, had seen over a century of classical formality. The Romantic writers began to experiment with non-classical genres, themes and settings. Built on top of a neoclassical preoccupation with rhyme and metre there was a flowering of wild images and less restrained speaking voices. Instead of a neoclassical interest in intellectual satire, Romanticism mainly valued and emphasised individual passion and the genres that allowed this to breathe. In short, Romanticism valued subjective imagination over objective observation as the source and inspiration of art.

Romantic is a word that was originally used to link the writing of the late eighteenth century with a medieval genre called 'romance'. The medieval romance (such as the *Morte D'Arthur*, pages 44–9) was typically a lengthy story about a noble quest undertaken by brave knights in exotic places. The word picks up the interest of many Romantic authors in things medieval, as well as settings, themes and narratives that are fanciful and mysterious. To critics it also meant 'excess'. The critics who coined the word 'Romantic' in the nineteenth century preferred the more rational and restrained kinds of writing associated with the neoclassical period.

Historical context

Romanticism developed in an historical period characterised by turbulent change, revolution, conservative counterattack, democratic idealism, dictatorships, improvement in technology and the kinds of suffering caused by rapid and enthusiastic industrialisation.

The Romantics worked in the political and social context of revolutions and change. In the late eighteenth century there were the American (1775–83) and French (1789–99) revolutions. In France, cries of 'liberty, equality and fraternity' rang through the streets. It seemed like a golden age of democracy and it made much of the English aristocracy quite nervous. As young people, the Romantics were interested in rebellious figures and social outsiders rather than community and social cohesion. Romantics also took some of their revolutionary ideals from radical English political writings, such as Thomas Paine's *The Rights of Man* (1791–92) and William Godwin's *Enquiry Concerning Political Justice* (1793). However, the revolutionary spirit unleashed demons of its own, with the revolutionaries in France executing large numbers of people (including each other) in a period called 'the Terror'. The Romantics had to work simultaneously with the problems and the potential benefits of the revolutionary spirit.

Britain stayed politically calm in comparison to France. George III reigned during 1760–1820, almost the entire Romantic era, although he was mad for much of that time. George, Prince of Wales, took over as Prince Regent in 1811 when George III was declared incurably insane. British politics reacted to republican idealism by becoming staunchly conservative.

This conservatism began to fray at the edges in the period 1820–32, with increasing agitation from people of the middle and lower classes.

Literary context

The term 'Romantic' is an umbrella that covers all sorts of different styles, methods and concerns. There are, however, some important threads that can be seen to hold the Romantic group together. These are shown in the figure below.

The Romantics were reacting against the past: in this case the Age of Reason (or Enlightenment), which lasted from approximately 1660 to 1780. During that period, reason and sensibility were valued. The writers of the Age of Reason—the neoclassicists—believed that reason was the key to all understanding and they were constantly inspired by the classics. They emphasised the importance of logic, proportion, balance, restraint and objectivity. Satire was a weapon they used to mock excessive, imaginative and antisocial forces. The Romantics were somewhat fed up with this moderation and wanted something new.

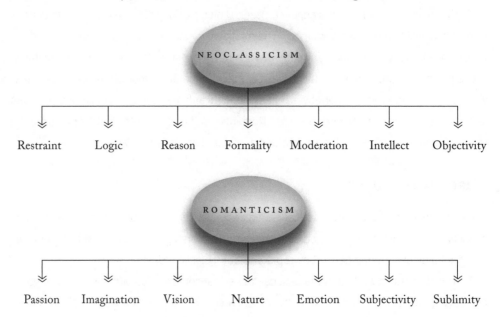

Features of neoclassicism and Romanticism.

The Romantics insisted on the importance of feeling and passion. To a certain extent, imagination had been subservient to reason during the Enlightenment, and they wanted to right this imbalance. They felt that imagination was an amazing and visionary faculty allowing an insight into the truth of things, both natural and supernatural. Dry reason or intellect could not provide this extraordinary insight. Spontaneous feeling and the life of the senses were newly important.

The Romantics focused on the individual (subjective) perspective and not on 'objective' reality. Meditations on landscapes and nature were a stage for the individual appreciation of the picturesque and sublime. The Romantics preferred the natural world, seeing industrialisation as alienating. This attitude is not surprising, for the cities were stinking and crowded with the crush of humanity—not exactly places for subjective, poetic flights of ecstasy.

Lastly, the Romantics were ready to play with language and form. They used new kinds of language so that they could more expressively and widely convey experience, nature and change. They experimented with different genres (such as meditations and verse fragments). When they wrote gothic works, they displayed an interest in extremity and excess. Their settings could be as exotic, medieval or supernatural as they liked.

Questions

1 RECAP: Construct a mind map that outlines what you consider to be the key features of Romanticism. What tended to be the sociopolitical values of the Romantics?

2 Why do you think the various revolutions were important for the Romantic period?

3 What is the importance of imagination and logic in your own life? Which one, ultimately, do you prefer? Which do you find most important?

4 Do you think understanding Romanticism is significant for understanding the present? If so, in what ways?

Romantic poets: *first generation*

The first generation of Romantic poets includes William Blake, William Wordsworth and Samuel Taylor Coleridge.

Blake and *Songs of Innocence and of Experience*

William Blake (1757–1827)

Although Blake was a unique writer, he can also be seen as a quintessential Romantic poet. His life, work and political and religious views speak strongly of the Romantic poet as an independent and rebellious visionary. Blake remained a political, religious and artistic radical all his life. He departed from the concerns of the previous Age of Reason. This is best expressed by the fact that he spent his writing life working towards his own poetic 'mythic system'. This was a whole mythology of his own creation, representing humanity's past, present and future.

Blake was the son of a London stocking-maker, and was the least economically privileged of the first generation of Romantic writers. He grew up in relatively poor circumstances and at age fourteen was apprenticed to an engraver. This working life was broken up for Blake by less typical childhood events, such as seeing God in a tree. He states he saw God 'put his head through the window' and 'a tree filled with angels' bright, angelic wings, bespangling every bough like stars'.

Blake lived almost his whole life in London. Thus, he saw first hand the suffering and exploitations of the emerging industrial revolution; such as child chimneysweeps suffering lung disease due to the soot they had to breathe. To him, much of this seemed like child slavery. Several of his most bitter poems are about the mistreatment of children. Liberty, both economic and spiritual, was of great significance for Blake, as were the curiosity and innocence of childhood, which he regarded as almost holy.

His training as an engraver and his teenage lyrics came together in 1789 with his creation of an engraved, illustrated volume of lyrics called *Songs of Innocence*, and, in 1794, *Songs of Experience*. Other major works Blake produced include *The Marriage of Heaven and Hell* and *Jerusalem*. He died in 1827 at the age of seventy and was buried in an unmarked grave, having profoundly linked Englishness with Christianity.

'Holy Thursday' as it appears in *Songs of Innocence*, written and etched by Blake.

Songs of Innocence and of Experience

At the beginning of Blake's career much poetry was written in the form of satires, which were very specialised and formal. What Blake did in *Songs of Innocence* was introduce a markedly different voice that sounded both lyrical and visionary. The forty-six short poems in the volume are written in a simple style, many of them as if composed by children, but have a strong symbolic content. Other poems comment on the state of infancy.

The poems in *Songs of Experience*, which Blake wrote five years later, are meant to be read in partnership with those in *Songs of Innocence*. Many of the songs have identical titles to the poems in *Innocence*, but the tone is very different. The innocence of childhood is contrasted most often with the corrupting experience and perspective that comes with maturity. *Experience* is about the social effects of industrialisation, including exploitation, enslavement, corruption, materialism and the loss of a rich spiritual life. The poems contained in *Songs of Experience* do not often actually contradict those in *Songs of Innocence*, but they do reply to them in a tone that questions and offsets their simplicities. As Blake suggests in *The Marriage of Heaven and Hell*, 'Without contraries [opposites] there is no progression'.

The best snapshot of the two different volumes can be seen in those poems that echo one another, such as the paired poems entitled 'The Chimney Sweeper' and 'Holy Thursday'. Holy Thursday is the thirty-ninth day after Easter. During Blake's time, on this day the poor and orphaned children of London were marched from the charity schools to St Paul's Cathedral for a church service.

HOLY THURSDAY
From Songs of Innocence

'Twas on a Holy Thursday, their innocent faces clean,
The children walking two and two, in red and blue and green;
Grey headed beadles walkd before with wands as white as snow,
Till into the high dome of Paul's they like Thames' waters flow.

O what a multitude they seemd, these flowers of London town!   5
Seated in companies they sit with radiance all their own.

»

The hum of multitudes was there, but multitudes of lambs,
Thousands of little boys and girls raising their innocent hands.

Now like a mighty wind they raise to heaven the voice of song,
Or like harmonious thunderings the seats of heaven among.   10
Beneath them sit the agèd men, wise guardians of the poor;
Then cherish pity, lest you drive an angel from your door.

Questions

1 What overall idea do you think Blake is
attempting to communicate in this poem?

2 Create a mind map of all the similes and
metaphors that describe the children as powerful.
Explain how they relate to the writer's purpose.
What is your overall impression of the children?

3 What is the effect created by the rhyme?

4 Do you find the use of primary colours
significant? Justify your answer.

Activity

Imagine you are a hungry orphan dragged along to church. You have read to you Blake's 'Holy
Thursday' from *Songs of Innocence*, which tells you about the lovely time you were supposed to
have had in church. Prepare an oral response (after all, you could not write) saying how you
really felt about the day.

HOLY THURSDAY
From Songs of Experience

Is this a holy thing to see,
In a rich and fruitful land,
Babes reduced to misery,
Fed with cold and usurous hand?

Is that trembling cry a song?   5
Can it be a song of joy?
And so many children poor?
It is a land of poverty!

                                                                   »

And their sun does never shine,
And their fields are bleak and bare,   10
And their ways are fill'd with thorns,
It is eternal winter there.

For where-e'er the sun does shine,
And where-e'er the rain does fall,
Babe can never hunger there,   15
Nor poverty the mind appall.

Questions

1 In what ways is 'Holy Thursday' from *Songs of Experience* different from 'Holy Thursday' from *Songs of Innocence*?

2 In the introduction (page 90), you read about the difference between Blake's *Songs of Innocence* and *Songs of Experience*. What evidence of the points made in that section can you find when looking at these two poems?

3 Select two images from the above poem that you feel are significant and effective. What makes them so?

4 Why are there so many questions in this poem? What is the effect of this?

The following poem, 'London', is another from Blake's *Songs of Experience*.

LONDON

I wander thro' each charter'd street,
Near where the charter'd Thames does flow,
A mark in every face I meet,
Marks of weakness, marks of woe.

In every cry of every Man,   5
In every Infant's cry of fear,
In every voice, in every ban,
The mind-forg'd manacles I hear:

How the Chimney-sweeper's cry
Every blackning Church appals,   10
And the hapless Soldier's sigh
Runs in blood down Palace walls.

»

But most, thro' midnight streets I hear
How the youthful Harlot's curse
Blasts the new-born Infant's tear,   15
And blights with plagues the Marriage hearse.

Questions

1 What impressions of London life do you take
from this poem?

2 What do you think 'mind-forg'd manacles'
(line 8) could be?

3 Find two examples of juxtaposition (two
opposite things referred to closely together)
in the last stanza. In what way has this textual
device shaped the overall meaning?

4 What would you describe as the overall tone of
the poem? How is it achieved?

Along with poems such as 'The Tyger' and 'The Lamb', these poems represent the most
accessible of Blake's work and also can be seen as part of the transition from a neoclassical
to a Romantic sensibility in English poetry.

Questions

1 Three of Blake's poems are reproduced in this
section. What evidence can you see in these
poems of:
 a Blake's personal context as a writer
 b the literary context of the time
 c the socioeconomic context of the time?
How do these affect your reading of these
poems?

2 Re-read the section about new historicist
criticism in Unit 1 (pages 17–18). Blake's poetry
makes overt and powerful comments on the
political context from which it emerges. What,
in your view, is Blake's criticism of the prevailing
social values of his period?

3 Re-read the introductory section about Marxist
criticism in Unit 1 (page 16).
     On the basis of what you have read in the
poems and the introduction, do you think Blake
would have become a Marxist if the option had
existed during his lifetime?
 a If you do, justify why he would not simply
     have become a social liberal, which is
     someone with views that are much less
     extreme than those of a Marxist.
 b If you do not, justify what extra views the
     poems would have to demonstrate before
     Blake could be considered Marxist.
     Could you see Blake's poems as offering
a Marxist interpretation of the way in which
economics produces inequality?

Activities

1 Imagine you are a US travel agent in the future. Time travel has been invented and is widely used by holidaymakers. You are organising tours to sunny Jamaica in the early twentieth-century. Your competitor is arranging tours to London during Blake's time (that is, the end of the eighteenth century). All the US clients want to go to eighteenth-century London to view the grandeur and beauty of the old city. The London tours are booking up fast, but no-one has booked your tours to Jamaica. You need to convince your clients that London is a dreadful place, not worthy of their visit. However, all you have to base your views on are these three poems from Blake. Write a speech convincing them not to go to London, making close reference to the poems as an eyewitness report on the city.

2 You are going to draw an animation of London in 1794. The only reference material you have are these three poems from Blake. Do a storyboard of eight panels, showing the major features of your animation. Include quotes from the poems underneath your panels.

3 Many people thought that Blake was mad. The writer John Ruskin found him 'diseased and wild'. Research Blake's views on religion and how his religious context finds expression in his later poetry.

4 Write two poems about students starting at your school. Make one poem optimistic and full of innocence and the other pessimistic and full of experience.

Wordsworth and 'Tintern Abbey'

William Wordsworth (1770–1850)

William Wordsworth is often considered to be the major poetic voice of the Romantic period. His name is synonymous with the power of the imagination in contemplation of the natural world. Like Blake, he was a highly original writer who made significant breaks with the formal traditions of writing that preceded him. When his work appeared in the late eighteenth century, reviewers found the simplicity of his style and subjects both shocking and 'unpoetical'.

Wordsworth was born in Cumbria in 1770, the son of an attorney. His mother died when he was eight and his father when he was thirteen. He lived for much of his childhood in the Lake District. He often spent much of the day and sometimes half the night roaming the countryside of the area. He then spent the early 1790s in France, powered by a youthful and passionate belief in the French Revolution. In 1794, England declared war on France. This shocked Wordsworth. In addition, the French revolutionaries had been decapitating their enemies and even allies at such a startling rate that it was difficult to stay idealistic about the revolution. Wordsworth became disillusioned with the republican cause of his youth.

In 1795, he met Samuel Taylor Coleridge and began a collaboration that is expanded upon below. The late 1790s was a period of intense creativity for both poets, and they produced the *Lyrical Ballads*, published anonymously in 1798. It was a landmark publication for literary Romanticism.

During the nineteenth century, Wordsworth became more financially comfortable and many contemporaries, such as Percy Shelley, found him more poetically conservative. In 1843, he was made England's poet laureate (the post of official poet of the monarch) and he died in 1850. His longest and one of his most famous works, the autobiographical *The Prelude*, was published after his death.

Literary context: *Lyrical Ballads* and 'Tintern Abbey'

The first generation of Romantic poets (Blake, Wordsworth and Coleridge) wanted to revolutionise how poetry was written and what it was about. Instead of following the neat, witty, formal writings of the previous period, they wanted to emphasise wildness and imagination. They wished to stress the *individual*, with all of his or her amazing emotions and experiences. Wordsworth also wanted to show how nature helps create the individual, particularly as a child. Another radical characteristic of Wordsworth's poetry was that although he wrote about visionary experiences, he didn't mention organised religion. A few hundred years earlier this would have placed him at risk of execution.

The Lake District.

Wordsworth and Coleridge worked together on *Lyrical Ballads* when they lived near one another in England in 1797 in the rural region called the Quantock Hills in Somerset. They decided that Wordsworth would work mainly on verse that dealt with the natural world and Coleridge would write about the supernatural world. Both of these were unusual subjects for poetry at the end of the eighteenth century. In addition, they planned to use comparatively more plain language (natural diction in blank verse) or form (ballads).

Of Wordsworth's poems in *Lyrical Ballads*, 'Lines Composed a Few Miles above Tintern Abbey, on Revisiting the Banks of the Wye during a Tour, July 13, 1798' (henceforth 'Tintern Abbey') is one of the most significant. He states that he began writing it at the start of a ramble (walk) when he saw Tintern Abbey in South Wales, and finished it five days later when he got to Bristol. He also states 'Not a line of it was altered, and not any part of it written down till I reached Bristol'. The poem is reproduced on pages 96–100.

Activity

Complete this activity before you read 'Tintern Abbey'.

1 Have the class stand in two circles: an outer circle and an inner circle with an equal number of people in each, as shown in the diagram. There should be a minimum of nine people in each circle. Face the person nearest to you in the other circle.

2 Each person in the outer circle should form a pair with the person facing them in the inner circle. Tell your partner about the most amazing landscape or place to which you have ever been. Explain what it looked like, the reason you were there and what made it so good. (The subject matter of this part of the activity links to part 1 of 'Tintern Abbey'; that is, lines 1–22.) After a minute or two, the inner circle of people should move clockwise by three outer people. »

3 Tell your new partner about what memories you use to cheer yourself up when you are feeling down. Are they memories of a place, or something you did, or something else? (The subject matter of this part of the activity links to part 2 of 'Tintern Abbey'; that is, lines 23–57.) After a minute or two, the inner circle of people should move clockwise by three outer people.

4 Tell your new partner about what made you happy when you were a child. How does it differ from what makes you happy now? (The subject matter of this part of the activity links to part 3 of 'Tintern Abbey'; that is, lines 58–111.) After a minute or two, the inner circle of people should move clockwise by three outer people.

5 When you are old you will probably look back upon some part of your teenage years happily. Tell your new partner about what part of your teenage years you think you will remember fondly. (The subject matter of this part of the activity links to part 4 of 'Tintern Abbey'; that is, lines 112–59.)

TINTERN ABBEY

Five years have past; five summers, with the length
Of five long winters! and again I hear
These waters, rolling from their mountain-springs
With a soft inland murmur.—Once again
Do I behold these steep and lofty cliffs,   5
That on a wild secluded scene impress
Thoughts of more deep seclusion; and connect
The landscape with the quiet of the sky.
The day is come when I again repose
Here, under this dark sycamore, and view   10
These plots of cottage-ground, these orchard-tufts,
Which at this season, with their unripe fruits,
Are clad in one green hue, and lose themselves
'Mid groves and copses. Once again I see
These hedge-rows, hardly hedge-rows, little lines   15
Of sportive wood run wild: these pastoral farms,
Green to the very door; and wreaths of smoke
Sent up, in silence, from among the trees!
With some uncertain notice, as might seem
Of vagrant dwellers in the houseless woods,   20
Or of some Hermit's cave, where by his fire
The Hermit sits alone.

These beauteous forms,
Through a long absence, have not been to me

                                                                 »

As is a landscape to a blind man's eye:
But oft, in lonely rooms, and 'mid the din   25
Of towns and cities, I have owed to them
In hours of weariness, sensations sweet,
Felt in the blood, and felt along the heart;
And passing even into my purer mind,
With tranquil restoration:—feelings too   30
Of unremembered pleasure: such, perhaps,
As have no slight or trivial influence
On that best portion of a good man's life,
His little, nameless, unremembered, acts
Of kindness and of love. Nor less, I trust,   35
To them I may have owed another gift,
Of aspect more sublime; that blessed mood,
In which the burthen of the mystery,
In which the heavy and the weary weight
Of all this unintelligible world,   40
Is lightened:—that serene and blessed mood,
In which the affections gently lead us on,—
Until, the breath of this corporeal frame
And even the motion of our human blood
Almost suspended, we are laid asleep   45
In body, and become a living soul:
While with an eye made quiet by the power
Of harmony, and the deep power of joy,
We see into the life of things

If this
Be but a vain belief, yet, oh! how oft—   50
In darkness and amid the many shapes
Of joyless daylight; when the fretful stir
Unprofitable, and the fever of the world,
Have hung upon the beatings of my heart—
How oft, in spirit, have I turned to thee,   55

O sylvan Wye! thou wanderer thro' the woods,
How often has my spirit turned to thee!
And now, with gleams of half-extinguished thought,
With many recognitions dim and faint,
And somewhat of a sad perplexity,   60
The picture of the mind revives again:
While here I stand, not only with the sense
Of present pleasure, but with pleasing thoughts
That in this moment there is life and food

»

For future years. And so I dare to hope,   65
Though changed, no doubt, from what I was when first
I came among these hills; when like a roe
I bounded o'er the mountains, by the sides
Of the deep rivers, and the lonely streams,
Wherever nature led: more like a man   70
Flying from something that he dreads, than one
Who sought the thing he loved. For nature then
(The coarser pleasures of my boyish days,
And their glad animal movements all gone by)
To me was all in all.—I cannot paint   75
What then I was. The sounding cataract
Haunted me like a passion: the tall rock,
The mountain, and the deep and gloomy wood,
Their colours and their forms, were then to me
An appetite; a feeling and a love,   80
That had no need of a remoter charm,
By thought supplied, nor any interest
Unborrowed from the eye.—That time is past,
And all its aching joys are now no more,
And all its dizzy raptures. Not for this   85
Faint I, nor mourn nor murmur; other gifts
Have followed; for such loss, I would believe,
Abundant recompense. For I have learned
To look on nature, not as in the hour
Of thoughtless youth; but hearing oftentimes   90
The still, sad music of humanity,
Nor harsh nor grating, though of ample power
To chasten and subdue. And I have felt
A presence that disturbs me with the joy
Of elevated thoughts; a sense sublime   95
Of something far more deeply interfused,
Whose dwelling is the light of setting suns,
And the round ocean and the living air,
And the blue sky, and in the mind of man:
A motion and a spirit, that impels   100
All thinking things, all objects of all thought,
And rolls through all things. Therefore am I still
A lover of the meadows and the woods,
And mountains; and of all that we behold
From this green earth; of all the mighty world   105
Of eye, and ear,—both what they half create,

                                                             »

And what perceive; well pleased to recognise
In nature and the language of the sense,
The anchor of my purest thoughts, the nurse,
The guide, the guardian of my heart, and soul   110
Of all my moral being.

Nor perchance,
If I were not thus taught, should I the more
Suffer my genial spirits to decay:
For thou art with me here upon the banks
Of this fair river; thou my dearest Friend,   115
My dear, dear Friend; and in thy voice I catch
The language of my former heart, and read
My former pleasures in the shooting lights
Of thy wild eyes. Oh! yet a little while
May I behold in thee what I was once,   120
My dear, dear Sister! and this prayer I make,
Knowing that Nature never did betray
The heart that loved her; 'tis her privilege,
Through all the years of this our life, to lead
From joy to joy: for she can so inform   125
The mind that is within us, so impress
With quietness and beauty, and so feed
With lofty thoughts, that neither evil tongues,
Rash judgments, nor the sneers of selfish men,
Nor greetings where no kindness is, nor all   130
The dreary intercourse of daily life,
Shall e'er prevail against us, or disturb
Our cheerful faith, that all which we behold
Is full of blessings. Therefore let the moon
Shine on thee in thy solitary walk;   135
And let the misty mountain-winds be free
To blow against thee: and, in after years,
When these wild ecstasies shall be matured
Into a sober pleasure; when thy mind
Shall be a mansion for all lovely forms,   140
Thy memory be as a dwelling-place
For all sweet sounds and harmonies; oh! then,
If solitude, or fear, or pain, or grief,
Should be thy portion, with what healing thoughts
Of tender joy wilt thou remember me,   145
And these my exhortations! Nor, perchance—

»

> If I should be where I no more can hear
> Thy voice, nor catch from thy wild eyes these gleams
> Of past existence—wilt thou then forget
> That on the banks of this delightful stream   150
> We stood together; and that I, so long
> A worshipper of Nature, hither came
> Unwearied in that service: rather say
> With warmer love—oh! with far deeper zeal
> Of holier love. Nor wilt thou then forget,   155
> That after many wanderings, many years
> Of absence, these steep woods and lofty cliffs,
> And this green pastoral landscape, were to me
> More dear, both for themselves and for thy sake!

Brief explanation of 'Tintern Abbey'

PART 1 (LINES 1–22)

This section is like a wide mental photograph in which Wordsworth looks down at the landscape around the Wye River. He tells us that that he has been here five years before, and then goes on to describe it.

Questions

1 What is your overall impression of the landscape? How is it created?

2 Divide a page into two columns. On the left-hand side write in some of the poem's descriptions of the landscape. On the right-hand side fill in what could be the human reactions to these scenes.

3 What sort of life has Wordsworth had in the five years between last being at this spot (1793) and writing this poem (1798)? How do we know? Use the text and also Wordsworth's biography (pages 94–5). Use your knowledge of the political situation in England and France at that time to explain why Wordsworth might be writing about nature.

PART 2 (LINES 23–57)

This section is about how Wordsworth has remembered this rural scene during the five years since he was last there. The memory of it kept him going when he was in towns and it sometimes encouraged him to be a good person. At times it also allowed him to perform a type of meditation; he used the memories to put his body to sleep and become a 'living soul'.

1 How does Wordsworth contrast the town and the countryside? What do you think are the effects and purposes of this comparison?

2 How does Wordsworth contrast the body and the mind? What do you think are the effects and purposes of this comparison?

3 What is your interpretation of lines 40–50?

PART 3 (LINES 58–111)

In this section Wordsworth hopes that looking at the landscape again will provide him with memories to sustain him in the future. He reflects on how innocently and physically he loved nature as a younger man. He feels that now he is mature he cannot have that joy any more; instead, he can have a deeper, more adult love for nature.

1 How would you describe Wordsworth's younger love of nature? What language forms and features are used to shape the expression of this love (lines 67–72 and 75–85)?

2 Explain, in your own words, what inspires Wordsworth now (lines 95–101). Analyse how this is different from the elements that inspired him when he was younger (lines 107–10).

PART 4 (LINES 112–59)

In this section Wordsworth speaks to his sister Dorothy (who was walking with him) and says that he can see part of his younger self in her. He goes on to say that nature protects the minds of those people who value her and makes them cheerful and optimistic. Wordsworth tells his sister that when she is elderly her memories of this day will help drive away any sadness she may feel and that she will be able to remember how much he worshipped nature.

1 How is nature evoked here? How is it contrasted with the everyday lives of people?

2 What do you think the last five lines mean?

3 Critically consider the role of the female in this section. What do you imagine Wordsworth's interpretation of the role of his sister would be? Can you provide an alternative reading that provides a radically different opinion about the status of women?

Questions

Overall questions

1. Wordsworth states that he essentially wrote the poem in his head and copied it down later. What is your reaction to this? How does it shape our impressions of the 'Romantic poet'?

2. Overall, what is your interpretation of what Wordsworth says about:
   a memory
   b time
   c identity
   and the landscape's effect on these?

3. Re-read the introductory section that provides a historical and literary context for Romanticism (pages 87–9). Use it to draw links between this text and its context.

4. Wordsworth reflects on the meaning of life because he has the opportunity for tranquillity. Where, if anywhere, do we have opportunities for tranquillity today? Speculate on what effects there would be on society if there was more Wordsworthian tranquillity.

5. Discuss your introductory circle activity (pages 95–6). How appropriate is it to use that process to help you to understand the poem? Use your study of the poem to reflect on and discuss the answers you gave in that activity.

6. The language form of this poem is blank verse. Wordsworth believed this would make the poem sound more natural and like direct speech. How natural or artificial does this poem sound to you in our contemporary environment? Why?

7. What value is there in reading 'Tintern Abbey' in the early twenty-first century? Identify values that have changed between then and now, and how this may affect your reading.

Activities

1. Pick out what you think are the five best images in this poem. Use a search engine (such as Google) to find copyright-free visual images that match or suggest them. (Use the keywords sublime and landscape.) The visual images you select do not have to be literal, but can evoke the sense of the images in the poem. Collate all the visual images to create a class wall chart of the images with the corresponding lines underneath them. See whether, amongst the class, you can create a visual representation of the whole poem. Make the wall chart as resonant as the poem.

2. Watch the first section of the film *Dead Poets Society* in which the teacher, Keating, talks passionately about carpe diem and the energy of poetry, particularly Walt Whitman's.
   a What links can you make between this sequence and Wordsworth?
   b Imagine you are the screenwriter of *Dead Poets Society*. The director wants to include a scene in which Keating is equally passionate about Wordsworth. What do you get Keating to say, and how do you make Keating present Wordsworth in a way that will arouse the same passion in his students?

Philosophical context and contemporary parallel: the sublime

The sublime is a critical or aesthetic term that is connected to arousing a sense of awe and wonder. 'Tintern Abbey' famously arouses the sublime. The key text that influenced the Romantics' ideas of the sublime was Edmund Burke's *A Philosophical Enquiry into the Sublime and the Beautiful*, published in 1757. In this text, Burke argues that two 'instincts' lay behind human emotions: 'self-propagation' and 'self-preservation'. He linked aesthetically pleasing and calming forms to self-propagation and called this 'the beautiful'. Those forms that inspired fear, pain and astonishment or conveyed a concept of the infinite he linked to self-preservation. He called these 'the sublime'. Burke listed attributes of the sublime as:

A sublime image: a galaxy seen from the Hubble Telescope.

- ¤ terror
- ¤ power
- ¤ privations (vacuity, darkness, solitude and silence)
- ¤ vastness
- ¤ infinity.

More recently, this sense of sublimity has been applied to a much larger landscape: that of the universe. The opening paragraph in Carl Sagan's 1979 book and television series *Cosmos* appears below.

COSMOS

The Cosmos is all that is or ever was or ever will be. Our feeblest contemplations of the Cosmos stir us—there is a tingling in the spine, a catch in the voice, a faint sensation, as if a distant memory, of falling from a height. We know that we are approaching the greatest of mysteries.

The size and age of the Cosmos are beyond ordinary human understanding. Lost somewhere between immensity and eternity is our tiny planetary home. In a cosmic perspective, most human concerns seem insignificant, even petty. And yet our species is young and curious and brave and shows much promise ... I believe our future depends on how well we know this Cosmos in which we float like a mote[1] of dust in the morning sky.

1 Speck

Questions

1 What features of language is Sagan using to evoke the sense of wonder and the sublime?

2 How are the concerns and writing style of this extract similar to and different from those of Wordsworth in 'Tintern Abbey'?

3 What else do you think could be written about in our society in a 'sublime' way (for example, babies or football)? What could not? Explain.

4 Link the philosophical context of the sublime to 'Tintern Abbey'. Where and how does it show itself in the poem?

5 In what ways, if any, does being aware of sublimity allow you to value 'Tintern Abbey' in a twenty-first century context?

Activity

Why do you think the sense of sublimity has expanded to include astronomy over the last fifty years? Look up images of the universe on the NASA website (nix.nasa.gov). Explain how the images do (or do not) create a sense of sublimity.

Coleridge and 'Kubla Khan'

Samuel Taylor Coleridge (1772–1834)

When Samuel Taylor Coleridge was a child his father died and he was sent to a fairly grim boarding school called Christ's Hospital. (This school was set up in London to educate talented students who couldn't afford to go to the traditional 'private' schools of the time.) He was unhappy and lonely there, and then even more unhappy and lonely at Cambridge University. Little did he know that they would be some of the best years of his life. He enrolled in the army, and was, according to *The Norton Anthology of English Literature*, 'the most inept cavalryman in the long history of the British army'.

Shortly after this he became addicted to opium, which made him an emotional and physical wreck until his forties. Many nights he would have nightmares so bad that he would be woken by his own screaming. He was also unhappily married. It wasn't until he moved in with his doctor, James Gillman, in 1816, that he managed to control his opium habit and write with some degree of steadiness. He lived in his doctor's house for the rest of his life, another eighteen years.

Despite all these difficulties, Coleridge produced a great deal of extremely significant writing. As seen earlier, he famously collaborated with Wordsworth on *Lyrical Ballads*. He wrote many newspaper and periodical articles, and a play. He was also a well-known Shakespearian critic.

Coleridge's most well-known poem is 'The Rime of the Ancient Mariner', which he composed during 1797–98 and included in *Lyrical Ballads*. This supernatural poem includes ghost ships, an undead crew and the spectral figures of Life and Death playing dice for the souls of the crew. It contains many of the Romantic preoccupations with wildness, imagination and individual experience.

Questions

1 RECAP: Outline the major challenges of Coleridge's life.

2 What features in common can you see in the lives of Wordsworth, Coleridge and Blake? How can you connect these features to the overriding features of Romanticism?

3 To what extent do you think personal adversity is, or is not, important in shaping the creative impulse? Explain your answer.

'Kubla Kahn'

At about the same time as writing 'The Rime of the Ancient Mariner', Coleridge produced another supernatural work called 'Kubla Khan'. 'Kubla Khan' is famous for being both incomplete and allegedly written by Coleridge under the influence of opium. It was not published until 1816—almost twenty years after it was written.

KUBLA KHAN

In Xanadu did Kubla Khan
A stately pleasure dome decree:
Where Alph, the sacred river, ran
Through caverns measureless to man
Down to a sunless sea.   5

So twice five miles of fertile ground
With walls and towers were girdled round:
And there were gardens bright with sinuous rills,
Where blossomed many an incense-bearing tree;
And here were forests ancient as the hills,   10
Enfolding sunny spots of greenery.

But oh! that deep romantic chasm which slanted
Down the green hill athwart a cedarn cover!
A savage place! as holy and enchanted   »

As e'er beneath a waning moon was haunted   15
By woman wailing for her demon lover!
And from this chasm, with ceaseless turmoil seething,
As if this earth in fast thick pants were breathing,
A mighty fountain momently was forced:
Amid whose swift half-intermitted burst   20
Huge fragments vaulted like rebounding hail,
Or chaffy grain beneath the thresher's flail:
And 'mid these dancing rocks at once and ever
It flung up momently the sacred river.
Five miles meandering with a mazy motion   25
Through wood and dale the sacred river ran,
Then reached the caverns measureless to man,
And sank in tumult to a lifeless ocean:
And 'mid this tumult Kubla heard from far
Ancestral voices prophesying war!   30
The shadow of the dome of pleasure
Floated midway on the waves;
Where was heard the mingled measure
From the fountain and the caves.
It was a miracle of rare device,   35
A sunny pleasure dome with caves of ice!

A damsel with a dulcimer
In a vision once I saw:
It was an Abyssinian maid,
And on her dulcimer she played,   40
Singing of Mount Abora.
Could I revive within me
Her symphony and song,
To such a deep delight 'twould win me,
That with music loud and long   45
I would build that dome in air,
That sunny dome! those caves of ice!
And all who heard should see them there,
And all should cry, Beware! Beware!
His flashing eyes, his floating hair!   50
Weave a circle round him thrice,
And close your eyes with holy dread,
For he on honeydew hath fed
And drunk the milk of Paradise.

BRIEF EXPLANATION OF 'KUBLA KAHN'

Stanza 1 (lines 1–11): Underpinning the man-made 'pleasure dome' of the first two lines runs the river Alph. It is a natural force that the Khan's artistry cannot control or contain. This means that, from the start, the poem has an opposition between the created world and the natural, untamed world.

Questions

1 How does Coleridge evoke these created and natural worlds in this first stanza?

2 Do you think there is an opposition between the two worlds or do they go together in harmony? Justify your view.

Stanza 2 (lines 12–30): In this stanza we read about the environment on which the pleasure dome is going to be built, including chasms, waterfalls and caverns. The stanza celebrates the mountainous and natural world that the Khan's artistry seeks, but fails, to tame. The Khan, who had a wartime reputation for being a tyrant, hears prophecies of war.

Question

What impressions do you get of the images of the natural world in this stanza? How are language features used to shape these impressions?

Stanza 3 (lines 31–6): This stanza combines the opposite landscapes in a way that links them as a 'mingled measure' (line 33). For example, the created artistic fountains and the natural caves are connected.

Questions

1 Why do you think the poem depicts an image of the *shadow* of the pleasure dome (line 31) instead of the real dome?

2 Which do you personally find more evocative: the images of the natural world in stanza 2 or the images of the 'mingling' here? Justify your answer. Link this to your own personal preference for outdoor and built environments.

Stanza 4 (lines 37–54): Here Coleridge suggests that if he could effectively revive the song of an Abyssinian maid singing about Mount Abora accompanied by her dulcimer, he could create his very own pleasure dome. The poet's 'dome' would be a sublime musical pattern or order. This pattern would convey the poet's vision clearly to the listener. If the poet could only revive or remember the song of the maid, then he could create a work of art so powerful that he would be revered—perhaps like Kubla Khan himself.

Questions

1 Why would listeners cry 'Beware! Beware!' (line 49) when they see or hear the poet's dome?

2 What do you think is the effect of the punctuation in this section (lines 46–9)?

3 What is the significance of the Abyssinian maid? What is interesting about her singing?

4 The ancient Greek philosopher Plato wrote of inspired poets who are like 'Bacchic maidens who draw milk and honey from the rivers when they are under the influence of Dionysus, but not when they are in their right mind'. How do the last few lines of 'Kubla Khan' relate to this description? (For this task it would be helpful to research Bacchus and Dionysus, gods of ancient mythology.) Also link this last stanza to the overall cultural and literary context of Romantic poets.

Questions

Overall questions

1 a Draw a horizontal line across the middle of a page.

b Choose four images or phrases from 'Kubla Khan' that describe the world above the surface and write them above the horizontal line.

c Choose four images or phrases from the poem that describe the world below the surface and write them below the line.

What conclusions can you draw about the worlds that Coleridge creates in the poem?

2 Coleridge stated in a letter to his friend John Thelwall that he wanted to convey the impossible sense of grandeur and majesty of the natural world in supernatural terms. Do you think he succeeded? How have language forms and features been used in Coleridge's attempt?

3 What features do you think are shared by 'Kubla Khan' and 'Tintern Abbey'?

4 In concentrating on the natural and supernatural worlds, what aspects of late eighteenth-century life are Coleridge and Wordsworth leaving out? Why do you think they are ignoring them and what conclusions can you draw from this about Romanticism? Re-read the introduction about Romanticism (pages 87–9) to assist you.

5 Re-read the section on psychoanalytic criticism in Unit 1 (pages 16–17). What sexual symbolism can you find in the poem? (To begin with, look at the dome, and the mighty fountain that 'momently was forced' in line 19.) In what ways does this psychoanalytic reading affect your overall interpretation of the poem?

6 The Khan's act of civilising the area doesn't really tame the environment. Can you make links between this and the attempt of the poet to use language to capture the landscape?

1 Write a short mythical history of Xanadu and of how Kubla Khan came to power. Use the images and mood from 'Kubla Khan' to guide your tone.

2 Find images using search engines (such as Google) in order to make a montage of what you think Xanadu could look like.

3 Imagine that you are either:
   • a property developer who wants to build a sumptuous tourist resort over some inhospitable forest
   • a committed environmental activist who wants to stop a tacky tourist development of a pristine natural environment.

Undertake an alternative reading of the poem from the perspective of your chosen character.

   a What can you see in 'Kubla Khan' to enjoy that supports your already existing view of the world? Justify your answer.

   b Rewrite excerpts from the poem so that it more closely fits your vision.

You be the judge: drug-induced genius or hard-working cover-up?

4 Imagine you are presiding over a case in which you are in a position to decide whether Coleridge's 'Kubla Khan' is a hallucinatory account of a drug trip or a carefully thought out and closely crafted romantic poem.

   Read the pointers below and then compose a carefully written judgment.

Case for the drug-induced genius

Evidence A: The whole poem, according to Coleridge, was written under the effects of a drug that gave him hallucinations. This drug was probably laudanum, an opiate. In Coleridge's time, opiates were legal medicines used as painkillers for various ailments—from headaches to tuberculosis.

Evidence B: Coleridge states that he wrote the whole poem while in a dream. (The poem has the subtitle 'A Vision in a Dream'.) As is stated in the preface to his poem: 'During [the dream] he had the most vivid confidence that he could not have composed less than two to three hundred lines, if that indeed can be called composition, in which all the images rose up before him as things ... without any sensation or consciousness of effort'.

Evidence C: When Coleridge wrote the poem, it was in a fit of passion, straight from his brain to the paper.

Evidence D: The poem is merely a fragment and only about fifty of the original 200 lines remain. Coleridge was interrupted in the peak of passion by a local man from Porlock knocking on his door on business. Coleridge then couldn't bring himself to finish the poem. As is stated in the preface to the poem: 'Yet, with the exception of some eight or ten scattered lines and images, all the rest had passed away like the images on the surface of a stream into which a stone has been cast'.

Case for the hard-working cover-up

Evidence A: On 14 October 1797, at about the time that he was composing 'Kubla Khan', Coleridge wrote a letter to his friend John Thelwall. In it he stated: 'My mind feels as if it ached to behold and know something great—something one and indivisible [unable to be divided]—and it is only in the faith of this that rocks or waterfalls, mountains or caverns give me the sense of sublimity or majesty'.

Evidence B: In 1934, an 1810 manuscript version of the poem was discovered (the Crewe manuscript). This is of a poem that was supposed to have been written in 1797 in half an hour and then hidden away for twenty years.

≫

Evidence C: There was actually a Romantic form called the 'fragment' being composed and discussed in Germany at the same time. Coleridge read German and had visited Germany. A fragment or unfinished poem could be seen as a complete literary entity. Fragments allowed the poet to hint at something about the sublime experience because they are improvised and open-ended at the same time as being technically accomplished.

Conclusion

You be the judge. Write a 'summing up' statement in which you sift through the evidence and decide whether Coleridge was a drug-induced genius or a hard-working cover-up. In your judgment include why the 'drug-induced genius' characterisation fits the 'image' of Romanticism and Romantic poets.

Cultural and contemporary context

There seems to be a longstanding tradition of society admiring those people, particularly creative people, who apparently produce things through inspiration rather than effort. This 'Romantic cult of genius' was particularly apparent during the early part of the nineteenth century, and poets such as Coleridge and Byron were certainly examples of it. (Byron was a Romantic poet whose life in the early nineteenth century was as prominent as his poetry.) This inspiration was often connected with heightened emotional feelings, sensitivity and often instability. Flamboyant lives, excess (often drug related) and dramatic early deaths also overlapped quite a lot with the Romantic cult of genius.

Kurt Cobain.

More recently, Beat poets such as Alan Ginsberg and rock musicians such as Jim Morrison have had this Romantic genius tag placed on them. One of the most notable recent examples is the lead singer and songwriter of Nirvana: Kurt Cobain. He and his band's first album, 'Bleach', were well-received. Nirvana's second album, 'Nevermind', was an outstanding success, establishing Cobain as a major rock figure. Yet the follow-up album, 'In Utero' (originally titled, rather less ambiguously, as 'I Hate Myself and I Want to Die'), was equivocally received on its release in 1993.

Some critics began to wonder if Cobain was a bit of a 'one-album wonder'. In 1994, Cobain shot himself in a room above his garage. He had been drug-dependent and depressed for years before this. In the decade after his death, Cobain's reputation, already well established during his lifetime, soared further. He took his place amongst other musical geniuses, such as Jimi Hendrix and Janis Joplin. Every note he may have sung to a mixing desk, live audience or tape recorder was posthumously lapped up by an avid public. In 2004, one of the guitars he played was sold for $117 500. The Romantic cult of genius is certainly alive and well in contemporary society.

Questions

1 Compare the lives of Coleridge and Cobain. What similarities and differences do you notice? (Further research into both figures will strengthen your answer.)

2 What societal values have stayed the same since the nineteenth century, allowing a version of the 'Romantic cult of genius' to continue to exist? What aspects of society have changed so that the cult of genius today differs from the nineteenth-century version? (Consider the growth in media exposure and the paparazzi, for example.)

3 Imagine you have read a particular poem and found it to be brilliant. Would you admire the poet more if you learnt that the poem had been written in half an hour or had been slaved away at for two years? What does this say about your personal values and attitude towards the 'Romantic cult of genius'?

4 Is our brief biography of Cobain unfair? Based only on the biography, do you think we should respect him as a 'rock god' who really did write some of the best songs of the late twentieth century?

Romantic poets: second generation

The younger generation of Romantic poets includes Shelley and Keats. They wrote diversely about individual experience, idealism and vision. Because they both died young, neither of them had their vision 'dimmed' by increasing age, compromise and conservatism. (This is in contrast to Wordsworth, who lived a very long time and was very 'establishment' by the end.) These younger poets, unlike Wordsworth and Coleridge, died in Europe, estranged from their native England.

The social responsibility of the poet was a major concern of young Romantics, such as Shelley in the years 1814–24. They remained true to the original French radical spirit throughout the period of conservatism in England; that is, during the early nineteenth century. They felt that Wordsworth offered an unattractive instance of the poet turning away in selfish solitude from his obligations to the community at large.

For Keats and Shelley (but not Byron), Wordsworth was nevertheless the most significant figure among the living and recent poets because of his treatment of nature. They copied his intimacy of natural description. They used images of nature to show what 'subjective consciousness' (the amazing place deep inside a person's mind) could look like.

Shelley and 'Ozymandias'

Percy Byssche Shelley (1792–1822)

Shelley was born into an aristocratic family in Sussex and was an heir to a baronetcy. Educated at Eton and Oxford, he was a political radical despite his aristocratic upbringing. He was called 'Mad Shelley' or 'Shelley the Atheist' at Eton, and his graffiti in a classroom is cut so deep that it is still there. (He wrote 'Shelley', so he was caught.) Shelley was thrown out of Oxford for circulating a pamphlet he had written called 'The Necessity of

Atheism'. This indicates some of his early non-conformism, as well as his emerging political and social questioning, which later became explicit aspects of his writing.

His short adult life was tempestuous. He married twice. His first wife committed suicide. His second wife (Mary Shelley, author of *Frankenstein*) had a nervous breakdown. Two of his children died during his lifetime and eventually he was hounded out of England to live in Italy. Shelley's death was as dramatic as his life. He drowned at twenty-nine when a boat he was sailing in (on the way back from visiting the poet Byron) hit a violent squall and sank. He was found with a volume of Keats in his coat pocket.

Shelley's poetry is sometimes ethereal and abstract, but nevertheless demonstrates his interest in a range of concrete topics, including science. He was interested in the way the world is driven by natural forces, such as wind, tide, electricity and volcanic eruptions. He thought the function of poetry was to restore the imaginative power that the overly rational Enlightenment had destroyed. Shelley's work also displays the idealism of a frustrated radical in a time of English political conservatism. It is little wonder Shelley had to spend much of his life in self-imposed exile and that he often had trouble finding publishers in Britain.

The ruins of a statue of Ozymandias.

'Ozymandias'

Ozymandias was one of the names for the Egyptian pharaoh Ramses II in the thirteenth century BC. Not a modest man, he was reputed to have had the largest statue in Egypt built of him. It had the following inscription underneath it: 'I am Ozymandias, King of Kings; if anyone wishes to know what I am and where I lie, let him surpass me in some of my exploits'. This poem tells the story of a traveller who finds the ruins of this statue in the desert.

OZYMANDIAS

I met a traveller from an antique land,
Who said—'Two vast and trunkless legs of stone
Stand in the desert ... Near them, on the sand,
Half sunk a shattered visage lies, whose frown,
And wrinkled lip, and sneer of cold command,   5
Tell that its sculptor well those passions read
Which yet survive, stamped on these lifeless things,
The hand that mocked them, and the heart that fed;
And on the pedestal, these words appear:
My name is Ozymandias, King of Kings: 10
Look on my Works, ye Mighty, and despair!
Nothing beside remains. Round the decay
Of that colossal Wreck, boundless and bare
The lone and level sands stretch far away.'

Questions

1 What is your initial view of this poem?

2 Explore how juxtaposition is used to contrast the ambitions of Ozymandias and his fate.

3 What understanding do you take from this poem about time, fate and human nature?

4 Link the overall theme of the poem to Shelley's political views and historical context. (Refer to the introduction to Shelley as well as the context section at the start of this unit, pages 87–9.)

5 What features of Romanticism do you find in this poem? How does this poem differ from the other Romantic poems you have read?

6 Ironically, could Ozymandias's wish for immortality have been granted through Shelley's poem humiliating him?

7 Explore the links between the following image, taken in 2003, and 'Ozymandias'. How does the technology and medium of production of each piece (that is, a poem and a photo) affect its meaning?

A statue of Saddam Hussein is toppled by US troops when they entered Baghdad during the invasion of Iraq in 2003.

Keats and 'To Autumn'

John Keats (1795–1821)

The son of a stable keeper in Moorfields, John Keats was apprenticed to an apothecary and for a time intended to be a surgeon. However, he abandoned that career path in 1815 in his determination to be a poet. Unlike the aristocrats Shelley and Byron, Keats was of lower middle class origin. He produced the book *Poems* in 1817, helped by Shelley, who was an admirer of his. 1818 is known as the 'Great Year' of his poetic production, but throughout the year he experienced persistent sore throats and was tormented by his love for Fanny Brawne. He wrote 'Endymion' during this year as well as 'The Eve of St Agnes', a medieval Romance fragment. During 1819, Keats wrote his now famous odes, such as 'Ode to a Nightingale'. In 1820, Keats coughed up blood and believed that soon he would be struck down by tuberculosis, as had his brother and mother before him. He was right. Keats died of tuberculosis in Italy in 1821 at the age of twenty-five.

Keats believed that the deepest meaning of life lay in the appreciation of material beauty (aestheticism). This beauty could be found in a woman, a nightingale, a season or a terracotta pot. He wanted to revel in this beauty by turning it into the form of something abstract: a poem. As a result, much of Keats's poetry is a strong evocation of human senses experiencing what he perceived as the sensuous wonder of the physical world.

Keats's odes

The origins of the ode form lie in the victory songs of ancient Greece. Keats's odes offer a new way of looking at the major Romantic theme of subjective imagination and objective reality. They represent the most complex expression of Keats's aesthetic approach to life. In each poem a description of beauty of the material world is made poignant by the knowledge that this beauty will fade and die. Keats's odes can be divided into two groups. The first group includes 'Ode to Psyche', 'Ode on a Grecian Urn' and 'Ode to a Nightingale'. These attempt to bring images of perfection into focus, and present a struggle with the effects of time and mortality on art. They also show states of trance and rapture. The second group includes 'To Autumn' and 'Ode on Melancholy', which display a greater acceptance of impermanence.

How to spot a Romantic ode

. . .

- ¤ It takes the form of an intricately rhymed, highly structured lyric.
- ¤ It uses apostrophe; that is, a direct address to dead people, things or abstract ideas as if they are alive and present.
- ¤ An altered mood or deepened insight is achieved through the sustained dialogue with the object of the address.
- ¤ The subject matter is serious. There is no satire or lightheartedness.
- ¤ The feeling and style are generally dignified or exalted.
- ¤ It aims at sublimity, from a mind 'transported by enthusiasm and fervour'.

'To Autumn'

'To Autumn' suggests an evolution in Keats's poetic thinking. Previously, Keats had struggled with the idea of mortality. In 'To Autumn' he accepts it. Through its presentation of changing seasons, the poem suggests that we can live with instability and transience (lack of permanence). In 'To Autumn', the speaker does not attempt to arrest time, but to prolong the passing moment as a form of serene acceptance.

'To Autumn' begins with a personification of the season as the enabler of harvest-time abundance. This moves to a personification of the season as an autumn worker, engaged in various harvest tasks. The third stanza, foreshadowing winter, picks up on the fact that songs about seasons have typically been for Spring. In this section, Autumn's sounds are foregrounded and celebrated in the form of 'singing', 'mourning', 'bleating' and 'twittering'.

TO AUTUMN

1

Season of mists and mellow fruitfulness,
Close bosom-friend of the maturing sun;
Conspiring with him how to load and bless
With fruit the vines that round the thatch-eves run;
To bend with apples the moss'd cottage-trees,   5
And fill all fruit with ripeness to the core;
To swell the gourd, and plump the hazel shells
With a sweet kernel; to set budding more,
And still more, later flowers for the bees,
Until they think warm days will never cease,   10
For summer has o'er-brimm'd their clammy cells.

2

Who hath not seen thee oft amid thy store?
Sometimes whoever seeks abroad may find
Thee sitting careless on a granary floor,
Thy hair soft-lifted by the winnowing wind;   15
Or on a half-reap'd furrow sound asleep,
Drows'd with the fume of poppies, while thy hook
Spares the next swath and all its twined flowers:
And sometimes like a gleaner thou dost keep
Steady thy laden head across a brook;   20
Or by a cyder-press, with patient look,
Thou watchest the last oozings hours by hours.

3

Where are the songs of spring? Ay, where are they?
Think not of them, thou hast thy music too,—
While barred clouds bloom the soft-dying day,   25
And touch the stubble-plains with rosy hue;
Then in a wailful choir the small gnats mourn
Among the river sallows, borne aloft
Or sinking as the light wind lives or dies;
And full-grown lambs loud bleat from hilly bourn;   30
Hedge-crickets sing; and now with treble soft
The red-breast whistles from a garden-croft;
And gathering swallows twitter in the skies.

Questions

1 What is your overall impression of this poem? What mood does it evoke and what point do you think it is making to you?

2 How are language forms and features used in stanzas 1 and 2 to make autumn sound warm and inviting?

3 Divide a page into two. List the images of abundance on the left-hand side. List the images of fading and transience on the right-hand side. What is the effect of having these images together in the poem? How does this relate to Keats's overall points and concerns?

4 Many of the images, particularly in stanza 3, are ones that are similar to 'spring' images. How has Keats altered them so that they sound autumnal (such as the 'full-grown lambs' in line 30)?

5 Link the concerns in the poem with Keats's personal context and life.

Activity

Write your own poem that uses landscape as a springboard to explore some other personal, emotional or conceptual issue (such as fear, grief or change). Reflect afterwards on how the landscape helped you or restricted you in your exploration of the issue.

Alternative readings: the pastoral, English landscape and imperialism

Many Romantic poems evoke a lush sense of the specifically English countryside. These poems are known as pastorals; although pastoral as a form of literature has a much longer and older history than this. These images can make people yearn for the English countryside as a perfect, ideal landscape. The unofficial national anthem of England goes so far as to say, 'We will build Jerusalem (heaven) in England's green and pleasant land'. Now this is very pleasant if you live in England. But what if you live in another country (such as Australia or India) and your natural landscape is completely different from that of England? Could you yearn for England as the ideal even if you have never been there? Would the Romantic poems make you feel as if England was your 'true' home? Can these poems have the effect of alienating you from your own country and landscape?

Critics who claim that the English canon is imperialistic point to this effect. They say that these poems colonise the reader's imagination. The poems may not intend to do this, these critics say, but it is simply inevitable that they do so.

Questions

Re-read the section about postcolonialism in Unit 1 (pages 14–15) before completing these questions.

1 How does postcolonial theory relate to the importance of landscape?

»

2 How does reading 'To Autumn' or 'Tintern Abbey' make you feel about your own landscape? How does it make you feel about the English landscape by comparison? Link this to any nationalistic sentiments you may have. Do you think these poems can have an imperialistic effect? To what extent do you think these texts are conveying English values?

3 Do you think that English children's books (such as the *Harry Potter* series) affect non-English readers in the way described above? Justify your answer.

4 Look at Australian poet Dorothea Mackellar's evocation of the Australian landscape in opposition to the English pastoral vision in 'My Country' (page 203).

a What different feelings does Mackellar's poem create? (Note: The first stanza is about the English countryside that she cannot love.)

b Write a dialogue in which Keats is challenged by a nationalistic (and angry) Dorothea Mackellar. She uses his poems to make her point that the Australian imagination has been colonised by poems such as 'To Autumn'.

Alongside Romanticism: Austen

The distinctive voice of domestic realism

The eighteenth century heralded the birth of the novel. Daniel Defoe, Jonathon Swift, Henry Fielding and Samuel Richardson all began to work with the young novel form in the 1700s. However, one of the lesser-known histories of the eighteenth century is the number of women writers who successfully composed and sold works of 'sentiment and sensation'. The gothic novel of terror and horror also became hugely popular, written increasingly by accomplished women, such as Ann Radcliffe, Maria Edgeworth and, later, Mary Shelley (author of *Frankenstein*).

It was the nineteenth-century novelist George Eliot (the pseudonym of Mary Anne Evans) who later pointed out that the novel form offered opportunities for women to work in a society that otherwise constrained their activity. However, there is a gloomy side to this. To many men, novels were seen as less accomplished than poetry or philosophy. Thus, genteel women could safely write them between their needlepoint and piano playing, without disturbing the literary dominance of men. It was not until Sir Walter Scott's success as a novelist in the early 1800s that novels became a reasonable genre for male writers to produce, which they did with increasing frequency in the nineteenth century.

The leading writers and critics in the eighteenth-century neoclassical period had placed special value upon moderation, good taste and social decorousness in literature. If someone wanted to write a 'good' novel they wrote realistically, without the sensationalism of popular journalism. If someone wanted to write a trashy novel, then they wrote 'romances' of gothic exaggeration. The literary market is not hugely different in the way it treats various genres today. Horror, science fiction and science fantasy are often considered by the literary market to be B-grade genres written by B-grade writers.

In order to understand Jane Austen it is important to see that she inherited both neo-classical and Romantic traditions, and that her work strikes an interesting balance between her literary influences. Certainly, the distinctiveness of Austen's voice and style significantly changed forever the way in which the realistic novel was written.

Austen is certainly a novelist whom people almost automatically associate with the word 'classics'. Despite the narrowness and conventionality of her interest, and because of the economy of her plots and sentences, she is held up in the early twenty-first century as the producer of several 'classics'.

A portrait of
Jane Austen.

Jane Austen (1775–1817)

Jane Austen was born in Steventon, Hampshire, in 1775. Her father, George Austen, was a clergyman who had married Cassandra Leigh in 1764. The couple had seven children, of which Jane was the sixth. Her sister, Cassandra, (to whom she remained very close) was born two years earlier and the other children were boys. The Austen family was financially secure and close-knit. They belonged to the gentry: the social class below the nobility. In Austen's experience, family relationships were important and valuable—actually liking or respecting one's family was of great importance. Austen's formal education was limited but she had access to her father's substantial library of over 500 books.

The family moved from their quiet country parish in 1801 to Bath, which Jane hated. In 1805, her father died, leaving his wife and two daughters a small annual sum. In 1809, they moved again: this time to a cottage on one of Jane's brother's estates. Austen's life was not brimming with external eventfulness. She did not marry; although she did accept one suitor only to withdraw her acceptance the next morning.

Her novels were all published in the last five years of her life, after a long history of failing to get them into print. For example, *Pride and Prejudice*, published in 1813, was first rejected by the publisher Cadell sixteen years earlier in 1797. *Northanger Abbey* was sold to Crosby and Sons (for ten pounds) in 1803, but the company never published it. Jane Austen finally got back the rights to it a year before she died.

Questions

1 Look at the biographies of Shelley, Coleridge and the other Romantic writers discussed in this unit. Then re-read Austen's biography. What differences are there? How do you explain this?

2 Very few portraits of Austen were completed in her lifetime. What does this tell you about her society?

Austen's works

So, in the midst of a relatively short life of genteel restraint, Jane Austen produced a powerful set of works: *Sense and Sensibility* (published in 1811), *Pride and Prejudice* (1813), *Mansfield Park* (1814) and *Emma* (1816). Both *Northanger Abbey* and *Persuasion* were published in 1818, although *Northanger Abbey* was the first full novel she wrote. Austen's wit, workmanship and background were not obviously Romantic but more neoclassical. She mocked the Romantic excesses of the gothic novel in *Northanger Abbey*. While she clearly favoured the clarity and structure of a neoclassical approach, she also drew emotional power and energy from the Romantics of her own period. Her heroines acquire wisdom by the counterbalancing of the two forces of passion and reason. Her last novel, *Persuasion*, shows some signs of a writing style and plot that leans towards expressiveness and liberation of feeling.

It is intriguing that Austen achieved all this while writing about an extraordinarily small world. She restricted her material to a narrow range of society and events: the gentry and their surrounding circle and related provincial houses. She was interested in family affairs, love affairs and social manners. What Austen did more successfully than any previous author was to apply the techniques of the novel to the acute observation of society in microcosm. 'Three or four families in a country village is the very thing to work on', she advised her niece, Anna, who was thinking of trying her hand at writing.

Austen avoided simplistically virtuous heroines, sensational plots and supernatural interventions. Instead, her fiction put the dynamics of human relationships in families and villages into a sharp focus. Indeed, her books are sometimes set during tumultuous international events, such as the Napoleonic Wars, yet we never hear directly about these events from any of the characters. We could say that what she lacked in breadth she more than made up for in depth. One of Austen's most famous statements was likening her books to a 'little bit (two inches wide) of ivory on which I work with so fine a brush as produces little effect after much labour'. Her favourite fictional scenario followed the fortunes of young women (usually aged 19–21) teetering on the threshold of married adult life. She followed their behaviour and prudential choices about love and marriage with sharp irony as well as witty compassion.

Upper middle class women of Austen's time were generally allowed only limited education, were unable to attend university, lacked widespread rights of inheritance and had no real means of financial independence. If these women wanted money they often had to marry it. This was not 'gold digging', but simply finding a way of supporting oneself. It is for these reasons that good judgment, self-control and a prudent marriage were such significant themes in Austen's work.

Resistant reading of Austen's work

You could take the position that Austen was a fusty old conservative desperately ignoring her wider social and political context in order to support the gentry's status quo. Although Austen speaks of love in a marriage, she is just as concerned that everyone is married sensibly. All her characters' choices (particularly marital choices) take place within the terms of conservative gentry ideology: an ideology that puts social and economic concerns before personal ones.

Austen's work is often discussed as a showcase for 'the novel of manners', which demonstrates that the formal and hierarchical manners of the time were not just a series of pointless gestures. Instead, they involved an important moral code that women attempting to avoid matrimonial disaster needed to be able to understand. A person's manners revealed a great deal about the person's character, respectability, integrity and judgment as well as position in the social hierarchy. Austen, who loved good manners and good judgment equally, could have criticised this code much more strongly than she does. During her youth, writers such as Mary Wollstonecraft were strongly and bravely agitating for women's equality, so Austen would have at least known about more radical ideas. At best she satirically scratched at the side of the conservative ideology.

Wit and irony

If you ask most Austen fans what they love about her, one immediate reply will be her wit, which is based on her supreme control of verbal irony. Irony occurs when the *apparently* stated meaning is different from (often opposite to) the *actual* meaning of the author. Possibly the most famous line in English literature is the ironic opening to *Pride and Prejudice*: 'It is a truth universally acknowledged, that a single man in possession of a good fortune, must be in want of a wife'. This is both hilarious and satirical, but it is difficult to explain why in simple terms.

Sir Walter Scott praised Austen's 'exquisite touch, which renders ordinary, commonplace things and characters interesting from the truth of description and the sentiment' and nineteenth-century critics saw in her work a gentle, domestic female focus. In fact, Austen's humour is quite sharp in its exposure of human weaknesses and follies, especially around the decadent aristocracy and self-promoting nouveau riche. Many Austen heroines endure painful lessons in self-knowledge and moral self-discipline, often delivered in ironic portraits both gentle and harsh, but never dull.

The following extract is the opening section of *Pride and Prejudice*.

PRIDE AND PREJUDICE

It is a truth universally acknowledged, that a single man in possession of a good fortune, must be in want of a wife.

However little known the feelings or views of such a man may be on his first entering a neighbourhood, this truth is so well fixed in the minds of the surrounding families, that he is considered as the rightful property of some one or other of their daughters.

'My dear Mr Bennet,' said his lady to him one day, 'have you heard that Netherfield Park is let at last?'

Mr Bennet replied that he had not.

'But it is', returned she; 'for Mrs Long has just been here, and she told me all about it'.

Mr Bennet made no answer.

'Do not you want to know who has taken it?' cried his wife impatiently.

'*You* want to tell me, and I have no objection to hearing it.'

»

This was invitation enough.

'Why, my dear, you must know, Mrs Long says that Netherfield is taken by a young man of large fortune from the north of England; that he came down on Monday in a chaise and four to see the place, and was so much delighted with it that he agreed with Mr Morris immediately; that he is to take possession before Michaelmas, and some of his servants are to be in the house by the end of next week.'

'What is his name?'

'Bingley.'

'Is he married or single?'

'Oh! single, my dear, to be sure! A single man of large fortune; four or five thousand a year. What a fine thing for our girls!'

'How so? how can it affect them?'

'My dear Mr Bennet,' replied his wife, 'how can you be so tiresome! You must know that I am thinking of his marrying one of them'.

'Is that his design in settling here?'

'Design! nonsense, how can you talk so! But it is very likely that he *may* fall in love with one of them, and therefore you must visit him as soon as he comes.'

'I see no occasion for that. You and the girls may go, or you may send them by themselves, which perhaps will be still better, for as you are as handsome as any of them, Mr Bingley may like you the best of the party.'

'My dear, you flatter me. I certainly *have* had my share of beauty, but I do not pretend to be any thing extraordinary now. When a woman has five grown up daughters, she ought to give over thinking of her own beauty.'

'In such cases, a woman has not often much beauty to think of.'

'But, my dear, you must indeed go and see Mr Bingley when he comes into the neighbourhood.'

'It is more than I engage for, I assure you.'

'But consider your daughters. Only think what an establishment it would be for one of them. Sir William and Lady Lucas are determined to go, merely on that account, for in general, you know they visit no new comers. Indeed you must go, for it will be impossible for us to visit him, if you do not.'

'You are over scrupulous, surely. I dare say Mr Bingley will be very glad to see you; and I will send a few lines by you to assure him of my hearty consent to his marrying which ever he chooses of the girls; though I must throw in a good word for my little Lizzy.'

'I desire you will do no such thing. Lizzy is not a bit better than the others; and I am sure she is not half so handsome as Jane, nor half so good humoured as Lydia. But you are always giving *her* the preference.'

'They have none of them much to recommend them,' replied he; 'they are all silly and ignorant like other girls; but Lizzy has something more of quickness than her sisters'.

»

'Mr Bennet, how *can* you abuse your own children in such a way? You take delight in vexing me. You have no compassion on my poor nerves.'

'You mistake me, my dear. I have a high respect for your nerves. They are my old friends. I have heard you mention them with consideration these last twenty years at least.'

Questions

1 Explore what is being satirised in the first two paragraphs of the *Pride and Prejudice* extract. How is language used to make the tone appear lighthearted?

2 What is your view of Mrs Bennet? How has Austen built up an impression of her character? How might a feminist reading understand the characterisation of Mrs Bennet? Re-read the section about feminist criticism in Unit 1 (pages 15–16) before you complete this question. In particular, go through each of the dot points about what feminist critics do when they read a text.

3 What do Mr and Mrs Bennet's contrasting opinions of their daughters reveal about their own characters?

4 Identify the sections in which Mr Bennet refuses to be serious. Of those sections, identify those in which is he being ironic. What is the cumulative effect of this irony and refusal to be serious? What impression do you gain of his character?

5 What is your overall impression of this passage?

6 Marxist critics seek to point out the economic struggles and conditions that lie underneath other sorts of activities and behaviours (such as those concerning 'love'). Re-read the section on Marxist criticism in Unit 1 (page 16), and then discuss how some of the key ideas of Marxism can be linked to issues in Jane Austen's works.

Activities

1 Watch the opening episode of the 1995 BBC miniseries *Pride and Prejudice* directed by Simon Langton. How does it present Austen's society? How does it represent the scene extracted above (particularly the opening lines)? What is the effect of this?

2 Read a sample chapter of *Pride and Prejudice*. Extract some of the sections that you find particularly witty and explain what makes them so humorous.

3 Read a summary of Austen's novel *Emma* (or read the whole of *Emma*) then watch the film *Clueless*, which is an adaptation of *Emma*'s plot to the 'valley girls' of contemporary Los Angeles. What are the similarities in the plot structure? What similar areas are being satirised? How effective do you find this satire? What, if anything, did the film-maker of *Clueless* gain by adapting a Jane Austen plot, instead of writing an original satire of LA teenage girls?

Review Questions & Activities

1 Write a letter that is to be sent back in time to William Wordsworth in 1840. In this letter, tell Wordsworth what assumptions about the world he and his fellow Romantics carried into their works. Explain to him how and why we in the early twenty-first century resist some of these assumptions. Also explain to him how and why we value these Romantic texts today. Closely refer to three Romantic texts in your answer.

2 Compare the very different tone of 'London' with either 'To Autumn' or 'Tintern Abbey'. Explore the relationship between these two texts and how they can both be considered 'Romantic'. Closely refer to language forms and features in your answer.

3 Imagine that John Keats has gone to heaven and, a decade after exploring the delights of the afterlife, he applies to join the Dead Poets' Society. The poet William Blake supports his membership. However, other existing members, including John Donne and Alexander Pope (an eighteenth-century poet), oppose it. They say that Keats is a disgrace to poetry, that his self-obsessed, syrupy writings are an embarrassment to style and taste. Such riff raff should not be allowed anywhere near the Dead Poets' Society, they say.

The issue is taken to the President of the Society, William Shakespeare. A hearing is set down. At the hearing:

- William Blake will speak for Keats.
- John Donne will speak against him.
- Donne and Blake will both get an opportunity to question Keats about his poetry.
- William Shakespeare will then make his decision to let Keats into the Society.

Choose people to be Donne, Blake, Keats and Shakespeare. Then enact the hearing in class. (The chosen people will need to do some preparation, perhaps with the help of legal assistants drawn from the class.)

Some hints:

- Use knowledge of each poet's background and era to make sense of why he holds his particular views about poetry. (To do this, read the relevant introductory sections and biographies in this unit and do further research.) For example, Blake might want to show that Donne's attack is 'blinded' by his late Renaissance mind-set.
- Use Keats's, Donne's and Blake's poetry to convince William Shakespeare what 'good' poetry should be. Any other poet you have researched can also be brought into evidence here. You should extend your search more widely than this book.
- Be ready with questions that Donne and Blake can use to examine Keats.

4 Take a sample stanza of 'Tintern Abbey' or 'To Autumn'. Select the images that evoke the English countryside. Then change the language and the images so that they are instead evoking one of the following landscapes:

a the Australian bush (such as 'paddock' instead of 'field')

b the Amazon (such as 'jungle' instead of 'forest')

c the African savannah

Read your new poem out to the class. How has the tone changed? Have the values of the poem changed as a result of its new context? Explain your answer.

Harpies, Goblins & Handbags

VICTORIAN LITERATURE

Highlights

¶ *Lady shatters mirror, invokes curse and dies*

¶ *Mad wife attacks new bride*

¶ *Goblins attack girl with fruit*

¶ *Abandoned baby found in handbag at railway station*

Outcomes

By the end of this unit you should have:

¤ developed an understanding of the relationship between the texts and the context of the Victorian era (including the cultural and historical contexts)

¤ gained an appreciation of the way in which the texts can be seen as cultural products of both their authors and their times

¤ engaged in detailed textual interpretation of a number of Victorian pieces and developed an understanding of how language forms and/or techniques shape the meaning of these pieces

¤ challenged and evaluated some of the cultural assumptions that exist in Victorian texts and considered alternative readings of some texts

¤ come to a personal view about valuing the texts and the Victorian period based on your own context and preferences

¤ engaged with the texts in a number of ways, including writing essays, scripts and diary entries and engaging in creative writing

¤ gained enjoyment through exposure to the texts and their ideas and contexts.

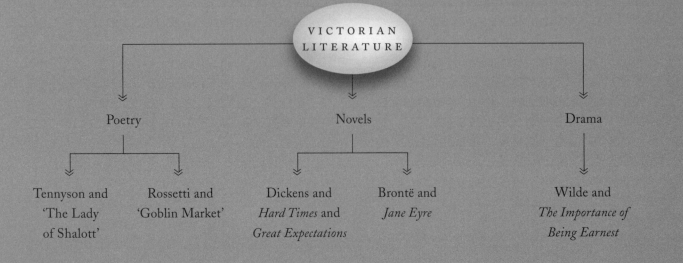

VICTORIAN LITERATURE

Poetry

Tennyson and 'The Lady of Shalott'

Rossetti and 'Goblin Market'

Novels

Dickens and *Hard Times* and *Great Expectations*

Brontë and *Jane Eyre*

Drama

Wilde and *The Importance of Being Earnest*

Context of the period

Many people's view of the Victorian era is of a society that was staid and conservative, with lots of restrained tea parties and minor family scandals all conducted in stiff, uncomfortable clothing. However, the Victorian era was also one of great change and vitality. The rise of industrialisation and the factory forever altered how and where people lived. The study of fossils and the theory of evolution shook the Victorians' most profound and central beliefs. Underneath a frequently repressive social code was something far less austere and genteel; in London alone there were 8000 prostitutes. This kind of contradiction was typical of the Victorian period: Victorian values were proudly enshrined, but extraordinary social unrest was ignored; national success was boasted about, but not the colonial and working class exploitation upon which it was based. No wonder the literature of the period is so rich.

The Victorian era can be broken up into three broad periods. The early Victorian period (1830–48) saw significant social turmoil and the movement of people from rural to urban centres. The middle period (1848–70) was characterised by greater economic confidence, but religious uncertainty. The late period (1870–1901), particularly the 1890s, marked a decay of Victorian values and apprehension about what would come next. Writers of the time termed this period the fin-de-siècle (end of the century).

Towering over the period is the figure of Queen Victoria. She became queen in 1837 and then reigned until her death in 1901. A key event in her life was the early death of her beloved husband, Prince Albert. Upon his death she entered into several decades of mourning, to the eventual bemusement of many of her people. Indeed, much of the surface austerity of the period can be symbolised by the remote, forbidding figure in black that was Queen Victoria for much of her life.

Many people in Victorian London had to endure appalling working and housing conditions.

Socioeconomic context

The shift from rural to urban work accelerated with the rise of mechanisation and factories. Conditions for the mass of workers were appalling. Indeed, many workers were treated less like humans and more like biological cogs in the machine. Adults and children worked side by side for sixteen hours per day on repetitive, arduous and dangerous tasks. The housing was little better: giant, unsanitary, rat-infested, crowded slums grew up in the major cities and towns, particularly in the north of England.

Such conditions were fertile ground for literary works; Charles Dickens's *Hard Times* (extracted on pages 141–2), Elizabeth Gaskell's *North and South* and John Ruskin's *Unto this Last* all dealt with this phenomenon. An extract from Elizabeth Barrett Browning's poem 'Cry of the Children' (1844) is provided on page 126. The poem was thought by many of her contemporaries to be overstatement, but it was based on factual reporting of five-year-old children who worked sixteen hours a day moving coal carts.

CRY OF THE CHILDREN

'True,' say the children, 'it may happen
That we die before our time!
Little Alice died last year—her grave is shapen
Like a snowball, in the rime ...'   40
'It is good when it happens', say the children,
'That we die before our time!' ...

                          ∞∞∞

'For, all day, we drag our burden tiring,   51
Through the coal-dark, underground—
Or, all day, we drive the wheels of iron
In the factories, round and round ...

                          ∞∞∞

'How long,' they say 'how long, O cruel nation,   75
Will you stand to move the world, on a child's heart.' ...

Economic–philosophical context

The way industrialists justified these conditions was by applying two philosophies that were reasonable in theory but can be seen as harmful in their effects. These philosophies came to embody much of the Victorian era. The first was Jeremy Bentham's utilitarianism, which advocated 'the greatest happiness for the greatest number' and judged an act on the basis of how much 'pleasure' and how much 'pain' it caused. If an act created more pleasure than pain, then it was justified. The theory was mathematical, reasonable and unemotional. It allowed individual misery to be subsumed into the greater good of (economic) progress. The other theory was laissez-faire, which stated that economic progress was best attained by unregulated working conditions. It presumed that economic progress of the entire society ultimately benefited everyone, including the workers, because the wealth would trickle down to them.

Legislation and social activism throughout the Victorian period slowly improved the lot of many people. The franchise (right to vote) was extended in the 1832 Reform Bill to the middle class, but not the working class. The price of bread and corn were reduced when the Corn Laws were repealed in 1846. (These laws had made it very difficult to import cheap grain.) The 1848 Public Health Act, passed in response to a cholera outbreak that killed 53 000 people, instituted a Central Board of Health to improve sanitation, water supplies and sewage. In 1890, the Housing of the Working Classes Act allowed for public housing. However, none of these measures solved the entire problem. For example, at the end of the Victorian era 30 per cent of Londoners were still living in terrible slums.

1 RECAP: Draw a mind map diagram that outlines the following aspects of Victorian Britain: the period divisions, the nature of work and the philosophical underpinnings of the economic society.

2 How does Barrett Browning attempt to create sympathy for the children in her poem? Look at the subject matter and the poetic techniques.

Do you find this extract stark or sentimental (or something else)? Explain your answer.

3 Imagine a hypothetical society formed with utilitarianism and laissez-faire economics as its base. Do you think in such a society it would be possible to avoid the abuses of Victorian England?

Religious context

The middle Victorian period was also a time of theological difficulties. Geologists were putting together an increasingly comprehensive fossil record that suggested that the world was far older than the Bible suggested. This caused disquiet enough, as evidenced in a number of Alfred Tennyson's stanzas in his long elegy *In Memoriam* (1850).

> **118**
>
> They [geologists] say,
> The solid earth whereon we tread
> In tracts of fluent heat began,
> And grew to seeming-random forms,   10
> The seeming prey of cyclic storms,
> Till at last arose the man …

This is a cold vision indeed for a culture brought up to believe in the Garden of Eden. The poet Matthew Arnold went further, as shown in the following extract from his poem 'Dover Beach' (1867).

> **DOVER BEACH**
>
> The Sea of Faith
> Was once, too, at the full, and round earth's shore
> Lay like the folds of a bright girdle furled.
> But now I only hear
> Its melancholy, long, withdrawing roar …   25

Seven prominent Anglicans released a book titled *Essays and Reviews*, which expressed doubts about a literal interpretation of accounts in the Bible and suggested that the Bible contained inconsistencies. This caused a storm of protest. However, all this was the calm before the storm. In 1859, Charles Darwin published *On the Origin of Species*, and in 1871 *The Descent of Man*, which suggested that humans had evolved from simpler animals. The mental transition from fallen angels to risen apes was possibly one of the most profound collective shocks humanity has ever undergone. Darwin's theories were famously promoted by men such as Thomas Huxley, who coined the term 'agnostic': one who believes that the existence or non-existence of God cannot be demonstrated rationally. Darwin's work was instrumental in leading to the sense of alienation of much modernist writing in the early twentieth century. In the nineteenth century it helped usher in what we have already seen as the uncertainty of the late Victorian period and the fin-de-siècle work of writers such as Thomas Hardy, who wrote the novel *Jude the Obscure*. Other writers, such as Oscar Wilde, wrote of a decadent society that reflected a world in decline.

Social context

Social life wasn't all gloomy. Many saw London as the most vibrant and cultured city in Europe, and Britain as the most civilised nation in the world. In 1851, Prince Albert (Queen Victoria's husband) organised and opened The Great Exhibition in Hyde Park, which showed off the marvels of Victorian technology. This inspired a great deal of confidence and pride in all things British. The Empire expanded until, by the end of the century, it covered almost a quarter of the globe. Many people were raised into the ranks of the prosperous, or at least comfortable, middle class. Britain was also, relatively speaking, a haven of freedom, particularly freedom of speech. All through Europe, revolutionaries (including Karl Marx) fled to England.

However, in the midst of all this nationalism and legal freedom came a tightening of moral codes. This was due to the evangelical pressure of a number of religious groups, such as Low Church Anglicans, Baptists, Methodists and Congregationalists. Part of this was a reaction against the hedonistic lifestyles promoted by decadent Romantics, such as Lord Byron. This new morality looked back to the Old Testament for its guidance, and also complemented the capitalist idea that frugality and hard work were the basis of success. This code was enthusiastically embraced by much of the emerging (but anxious) middle class because it created and codified for them a covert set of signs to show the world that they were no longer the working class. Sobriety, hard work and moral uprightness all led to that joyless Victorian nirvana: respectability. This was particularly evident in attitudes to female sexuality and the preoccupation with the innocence of young girls. The flipside of this was the figure of the tragic 'fallen woman', whose moments of indiscretion would lead to a lifetime of ruin and disgrace.

Thus, Victorian fiction makes almost no mention of sex. One would believe that couples spent their wedding night having cups of tea, holding hands and gazing mildly at each other. The absence of sex is as telling as its presence, for it shows what is being repressed in the society. Indeed, Victorian society did have its seamy side. The pornography industry was rife and, as we have seen, London had many thousand prostitutes (often middle-class 'fallen' women who could not climb back to respectability).

The emerging financial power of the middle class also presented a problem for the increasingly penniless upper class. To the enduring shock of the aristocracy, it appeared that working hard in Victorian England was often a better way of making money than lounging about. When they realised this, many of the aristocracy set about marrying the middle class, while simultaneously disparaging the middle class for being so bold as to spend what they earned. (These members of the middle class were decried as nouveau riche, which literally means 'new rich'.) By playing this double game much of the upper class both remained in credit and kept the middle class in their place.

There were some advances in the position of women in the society, but there was still considerable inequity at the end of the century. Whereas in 1837 none of England's three universities were open to women, by the end of the century they could take degrees in twelve universities or university colleges. Married women were allowed for the first time to own property (under the Married Women's Property Acts 1870–1908). However, they were not allowed to vote until 1918.

Cultural context

The major forms of literature in the period were poetry, non-fiction prose and novels. Poetry was particularly popular; Tennyson's volume *In Memoriam* sold 60 000 copies in a year. (The rise of the novel is discussed later in this unit.) The other major form of entertainment was drama. Theatregoing was incredibly popular; some estimates have 150 000 people attending the theatre each day in London in the 1860s. Although the period produced the musicals of Gilbert and Sullivan (1880s), the comedies of Oscar Wilde (1890s) and the fin-de-siècle satires of George Bernard Shaw (1890s), few plays of the Victorian period have maintained a critical reputation. In that era, theatre filled the entertainment void that television does today. Much of the work was melodrama. The following extract from the very popular *Black-Ey'd Susan*, written by Douglas Jerrold in 1829, perhaps indicates why many of these works are not studied in the manner of Shakespeare today.

BLACK-EY'D SUSAN
From Act II

CAPTAIN CROSSLEE: Passion hurries me—the wine fires me—your eyes dart lightning into me, and you shall be mine.

[Seizes Susan.]

SUSAN: Let me go! in mercy! William William!
CROSSLEE: Your cries are vain! resistance useless!
SUSAN: Monster! William, William.

[William rushes in L., with his drawn cutlass] »

> WILLIAM: Susan! And attacked by the buccaneers! die!
>
> *[William strikes at the CAPTAIN whose back is turned towards him—he falls]*
>
> CROSSLEE: I deserve my fate.

Questions

1 RECAP: How was traditional religious faith challenged in the nineteenth century? Explain, in your own words, some of the moral and social issues of the period.

2 Re-read the Tennyson and Arnold extracts (page 127). How have physical elements been manipulated to shape the mood in each of them? What differences do you find between them?

Activity

Research melodrama. Then, in script form, write one page of the most extreme melodrama that you think would appeal to Victorian theatre audiences. Include in it a pirate, a red rose, a noose and a block of cheese.

Tennyson and 'The Lady of Shalott'

Alfred Tennyson (1809–1892)

Alfred Tennyson was born in 1809, the fourth of twelve children, to Elizabeth and Reverend George Tennyson, the rector of Somersby. Tennyson's father, despite being a rector, was a violent and depressed drunkard. The lack of serenity in the home rubbed off onto the children. Two of them went insane, one became an opium addict and another an alcoholic. Tennyson eventually left this domestic disaster zone for the solace of Cambridge, where he became a member of a poetic society called 'the Apostles' and the closest friend of its leader, Arthur Hallam. During the 1830s and 1840s Tennyson's career wavered under lukewarm reviews, and poverty. However, the publication in 1850 of his volume of poetry *In Memoriam* turned his fortunes around. It was an exploration of time and mortality based on the early death of Arthur Hallam and it sold an extraordinary 60 000 copies in a year. The following year he was made poet laureate, which is the post of official poet of the monarch. (Tennyson went on to hold this position for the next forty years.)

Suddenly Tennyson was wealthy, famous and feted. So, perhaps oddly, he and his new wife moved to the remote Isle of Wight, where they stayed for the rest of their lives. Tennyson's other works include 'Maude: A Monodrama', which is a poetic drama about the narrator's tragic love and is full of duels, death, insanity and war. He also wrote *The Idylls of the King* (1859), which is the story of the Arthurian legends in verse.

After Tennyson died, his reputation wavered. He was seen as representative of the Victorian era to a later age that was trying hard to break away from it. WH Auden called Tennyson the 'stupidest' of English poets. However, later critics, such as FR Leavis, resuscitated him for the latter part of the twentieth century.

'The Lady of Shalott'

'The Lady of Shalott' is an early poem of Tennyson's, written in 1832 and revised in 1842. It is an Arthurian piece. In it, the eponymous Lady is trapped in her riverside castle room by a curse that says she may not look at the real world, but only its reflection in a mirror. One day she sees a reflection of Sir Lancelot in her mirror, tires of the curse and goes downstairs to directly watch Sir Lancelot riding to Camelot. In doing so, the curse is activated. As she knows she must die, she places herself in a boat and sings her death song as she glides down the river towards Camelot. Tennyson's retreat into an idyllic and chivalric past in this poem can be seen as reflecting an uncertainty that the Victorian age felt towards the brute force of industrialisation. The poem has an elegiac tone, not just for the Lady, but for the entire rose-tinted medieval past as well. Tennyson's trademark tones of melancholy and regret seem strongly in evidence.

The Lady of Shalott.

THE LADY OF SHALOTT

PART I

On either side the river lie
Long fields of barley and of rye,
That clothe the wold and meet the sky;
And through the field the road runs by
To many-towered Camelot;   5
And up and down the people go,
Gazing where the lilies blow
Round an island there below,
The island of Shalott.

Willows whiten, aspens quiver,   10
Little breezes dusk and shiver
Through the wave that runs forever
By the island in the river
Flowing down to Camelot.
Four gray walls, and four gray towers,   15

»

Overlook a space of flowers,
And the silent isle imbowers
The Lady of Shalott.

By the margin, willow-veiled,
Slide the heavy barges trailed   20
By slow horses; and unhailed
The shallop flitteth silken-sailed
Skimming down to Camelot:
But who hath seen her wave her hand?
Or at the casement seen her stand?   25
Or is she known in all the land,
The Lady of Shalott?

Only reapers, reaping early
In among the bearded barley,
Hear a song that echoes cheerly   30
From the river winding clearly,
Down to towered Camelot;
And by the moon the reaper weary,
Piling sheaves in uplands airy,
Listening, whispers 'Tis the fairy   35
Lady of Shalott'.

PART 2
There she weaves by night and day
A magic web with colours gay.
She has heard a whisper say,
A curse is on her if she stay   40
To look down to Camelot.
She knows not what the curse may be,
And so she weaveth steadily,
And little other care hath she,
The Lady of Shalott.   45

And moving through a mirror clear
That hangs before her all the year,
Shadows of the world appear.
There she sees the highway near
Winding down to Camelot;   50
There the river eddy whirls,
And there the surly village churls,
And the red cloaks of market girls,
Pass onward from Shalott.

》

Sometimes a troop of damsels glad,   55
An abbot on an ambling pad,
Sometimes a curly shepherd lad,
Or long-haired page in crimson clad,
Goes by to towered Camelot;
And sometimes through the mirror blue   60
The knights come riding two and two:
She hath no loyal knight and true,
The Lady of Shalott.

But in her web she still delights
To weave the mirror's magic sights,   65
For often through the silent nights
A funeral, with plumes and lights,
And music, went to Camelot;
Or when the moon was overhead,
Came two young lovers lately wed: 70
'I am half sick of shadows', said
The Lady of Shalott.

PART 3
A bow shot from her bower eaves,
He rode between the barley sheaves,
The sun came dazzling through the leaves,   75
And flamed upon the brazen greaves
Of bold Sir Lancelot.
A red-cross knight forever kneeled
To a lady in his shield,
That sparkled on the yellow field,   80
Beside remote Shalott.

The gemmy bridle glittered free,
Like to some branch of stars we see
Hung in the golden Galaxy.
The bridle bells rang merrily
As he rode down to Camelot,   85
And from his blazoned baldric slung
A mighty silver bugle hung,
And as he rode his armour rung,
Beside remote Shalott.   90

All in the blue unclouded weather
Thick-jewelled shone the saddle leather,
The helmet and the helmet-feather
                                                                      »

Burned like one burning flame together,
As he rode down to Camelot. 95
As often through the purple night,
Below the starry clusters bright,
Some bearded meteor, trailing light,
Moves over still Shalott.

His broad clear brow in sunlight glowed; 100
On burnished hooves his war horse trode;
From underneath his helmet flowed
His coal-black curls as on he rode,
As he rode down to Camelot.
From the bank and from the river 105
He flashed into the crystal mirror,
'Tirra lirra', by the river
Sang Sir Lancelot.

She left the web, she left the loom,
She made three paces through the room, 110
She saw the water lily bloom,
She saw the helmet and the plume,
She looked down to Camelot.
Out flew the web and floated wide;
The mirror cracked from side to side; 115
'The curse is come upon me!' cried
The Lady of Shalott.

PART 4
In the stormy east-wind straining,
The pale yellow woods were waning,
The broad stream in his banks complaining, 120
Heavily the low sky raining
Over towered Camelot;

Down she came and found a boat
Beneath a willow left afloat,
And round about the prow she wrote 125
The Lady of Shalott.

And down the river's dim expanse
Like some bold seer in a trance,
Seeing all his own mischance—
With a glassy countenance 130

»

Did she look to Camelot.
And at the closing of the day
She loosed the chain, and down she lay;
The broad stream bore her far away,
The Lady of Shalott.   135

Lying, robed in snowy white
That loosely flew to left and right—
The leaves upon her falling light—
Through the noises of the night
She floated down to Camelot;   140
And as the boat-head wound along
The willowy hills and fields among,
They heard her singing her last song,
The Lady of Shalott.

Heard a carol, mournful, holy,   145
Chanted loudly, chanted lowly,
Till her blood was frozen slowly,
And her eyes were darkened wholly,
Turned to towered Camelot;
For ere she reached upon the tide   150
The first house by the water side,
Singing in her song she died,
The Lady of Shalott.

Under tower and balcony,
By garden wall and gallery,   155
A gleaming shape she floated by,
Dead-pale between the houses high,
Silent into Camelot.
Out upon the wharfs they came,
Knight and burgher, lord and dame,   160
And round the prow they read her name,
The Lady of Shalott.

Who is this? and what is here?
And in the lighted palace near
Died the sound of royal cheer;   165
And they crossed themselves for fear,
All the knights at Camelot:
But Lancelot mused a little space;
He said, 'She has a lovely face;
God in His mercy lend her grace,   170
The Lady of Shalott'.

Brief explanation of 'The Lady of Shalott'

PART 1 (LINES 1–36)

This section describes the countryside and introduces the Lady of Shalott to the reader.

Questions

1 What mood do you think is created in the opening stanzas?

2 Look at the rhythm and rhyme scheme of each stanza. What are they, and how does this form help create this mood? Also explore the images used to create this mood.

3 What is unusual in the word choice 'dusk and shiver' in line 11? What connotations do the words have?

4 How is a sense of mystery created about the Lady of Shalott?

PART 2 (LINES 37–72)

This section explains some of the sights that the Lady of Shalott sees through the mirror in her room. It also explains why she cannot look out of the window.

Questions

1 What do we find out about the curse in this part?

2 How are the sights out of her window made to seem vibrant?

3 What prompts the Lady to say that she is 'half sick of shadows' (line 71)?

PART 3 (LINES 73–117)

In this section the Lady of Shalott sees Sir Lancelot through the mirror and then looks down directly towards Camelot. The curse is activated.

Questions

1 How does Tennyson use language features to make Lancelot sound gallant? You might like to look at imagery, simile, word choice and alliteration.

2 How is a sense of drama and climax created in the final stanza of this part?

PART 4 (LINES 118–71)

In this section the Lady of Shalott finds a boat by the river, and places herself in it to die. The boat drifts to Camelot, where Sir Lancelot looks down at the Lady.

1 How is weather used here to capture the changing mood of the poem?

2 Describe, in your own words, what happens in the final hour of the Lady of Shallot's life.

3 How is language used to create a sense of lyrical melancholy in the final stanzas?

4 What is your response to Lancelot's reaction?

Feminist reading of 'The Lady of Shalott'

A central cultural assumption of the early Victorian era was that women of the middle and upper classes kept the home fires burning while the men went out and battled with the day-to-day world. The women were thought by men to have the better end of this arrangement for they did not have to deal with the corruption of the world. Instead, they were safe and cocooned, unlike their working-class counterparts who endured sixteen-hour working days in factories. (This belief was eventually exemplified in Coventry Patmore's poem *The Angel in the House*, which dates from 1854–63.)

A feminist reading of 'The Lady of Shalott' would highlight that this ideal of femininity is problematic; in the poem the Lady's removal from society is a 'curse'. Similarly, the Lady's looking at the world through her mirror leaves her 'half sick' of her 'shadows' world. It may also be seen that the poem suggests something about the way in which direct experiences of the world (and especially experiences of sexuality and desire) are lethal for women in general and female artists in particular.

Overall questions

1 How does this poem evoke the age of chivalry to you? (See pages 44–45 for a discussion of chivalry.)

2 What is your overall impression of the poem? How is your response linked to your pre-existing interests and preferences, for example?

3 In what ways can this poem be regarded as a product of its times? Use the introductory section, the notes opposite and the poem itself in your answer.

4 Explore a resistant reading of the poem in which you view the romanticising of the Lady's story as a way of oppressing her and all women. In order to do this, re-read the section about feminist criticism in Unit 1 (pages 15–16) and also the introduction to the poem. Use specific lines from the poem to support your reading. For example, account for Lancelot's closing comments about the Lady.

»

5 If you could go back and live as a knight or lady in this 'ideal' age of chivalry, would you? Why or why not?

6 Re-read the section on deconstructive criticism in Unit 1 (page 18). Then complete the following task. Make a list of four binary oppositions that you find in the poem. (An example is art and the real world.) Which term in each pair appears to be the more attractive to you? (For instance, using the previous example, are the reflections that she weaves in the mirror more attractive than Camelot?) What does this tell you about what is valued in the poem?

7 One of the main changes in poetry during the nineteenth century was the shift from writing about 'subjective' experience inside the mind (the Romantics) to a more 'objective' portrayal of the world as it is (the Victorians). The critic Sophie Gilmartin writes that the story of 'The Lady of Shalott' can be seen to represent that transfer from a subjective world of the mind to the harsher, more objective 'real' world. What evidence do you think she takes from the poem to make this theory?

Activities

1 a Imagine you are the Lady of Shalott. Rewrite the poem in the form of three diary entries. Use this form to show us the thoughts and feelings of the Lady in a way that the poem cannot.

 b Compare your diary with the poem. Reflect on how the two different forms and tones affect the meaning for a reader.

2 Research the story of Plato's 'Cave Shadows', in which humanity is likened to a group of people tied up facing the back wall of a cave and who mistake the shadows on the wall of the cave for the whole of reality. What links can you see between this story and 'The Lady of Shalott'? How, if at all, is the comparison useful?

3 Obtain a copy of Loreena McKennitt's setting of this poem to music on her album *Live in Paris and Toronto*. How do the musical and word choices complement each other? Does listening to McKennitt's interpretation help or hinder your appreciation of the poem? What view do you think McKennitt had of the poem, on the basis of her musical arrangement?

4 This poem inspired a number of paintings during the Victorian period. The artists include John Waterhouse and William Hunt. Use a search engine (such as Google Images <images.google.com>) to look at these paintings. Search using the keywords 'Waterhouse' and 'Lady of Shalott'.

 a How have visual techniques been used to generate the atmosphere?

 b Do these pictures enhance your appreciation of the poem? If so, how? Can they make you more critical of the poem? Explain your answer.

 c Imagine you are an artist of today and you cannot bear the chivalric sentimentality of the images. How would you paint the poem to explore what you see as its oppressive ideology? You could attempt to paint one of these images.

The rise of the novel

Today novels are seen as such an established and robust form of literature that it can be hard to believe that the novel form is really only twice as old as film. Before the mid-1700s there were plays galore, poetry aplenty, but novels almost none. Novels began tentatively with practitioners such as Daniel Defoe, Samuel Richardson and Henry Fielding, but it was the increased literacy in England in the nineteenth century that helped to fuel their rise. It may also be that the novel turned out to be the most useful and adaptable literary form for conveying the texture of life and social dynamism in the nineteenth century.

The serialisation of novels also had a huge impact on their popularity. A single novel was too expensive for most people. (In the mid-1800s a well-bound novel cost thirty-one shillings and sixpence a week, whereas a good weekly working class wage was thirty shillings a week.) Thus, many novels were serialised in monthly magazines. This serialisation also made Victorian novels more like the modern-day soap opera than the modern-day work of literature. Many mid-century novels (including Dickens's *Bleak House*, *Our Mutual Friend* and *Little Dorrit*) run to over 1000 pages each. This is because each of these was published in twenty monthly instalments. A Victorian began reading a serialised novel and didn't finish it for over a year and a half. This serialisation meant that, just as in contemporary television serials, cliffhangers were needed in order to ensure that people bought the next copy. To a later audience these can seem melodramatic or sentimental.

Sales figures of these novels in Victorian times were like ratings figures and could vary wildly. Dickens's *The Old Curiosity Shop* in 1840–41 sold up to 100 000 copies per instalment, whereas his later novel, *Martin Chuzzlewit*, in 1843–44, was seen as a relative flop, for some instalments sold only 23 000 copies. A novelist could even see his or her (sales) ratings failing and make adjustments, mid-story, to arrest the decline.

People's tastes were generally fairly fixed. In novels, readers wanted to see their own society reflected or exaggerated. Plot was vital. A moral tone (either overt or covert) was preferable until the very late nineteenth century. Other genres began creeping in as the century progressed. Wilkie Collins pioneered the English detective novel with *The Moonstone* in 1868. Science fiction did not really appear until 1895 with the release of HG Wells's *The Time Machine*, about a man who travels to the earth's far future. However, social realism was the order of the day until the twentieth century.

If you want a good idea of the breadth of the Victorian realist novel in English, the list on page 140 should help. (This is the authors' personal and subjective list.)

Questions

Refer to the list on page 140 before answering the following questions.

1 If you want to 'resist' society, should you pin up this list somewhere and promise to yourself never to read any of them? Why or why not?

»

2 Should there be a list such as this in any book without further notes explaining the cultural and/or historical context of each book? Did we, as the authors, have a right to 'choose' these books?

3 What do you think would be the political and/or cultural effect on you if you read all these books? Do you think this would be a positive effect overall?

Top twenty nineteenth-century English novels

Jane Austen	*Emma*
	Pride and Prejudice
	Sense and Sensibility
Charlotte Brontë	*Jane Eyre*
Emily Brontë	*Wuthering Heights*
Wilkie Collins	*The Moonstone*
Charles Dickens	*Bleak House*
	David Copperfield
	Great Expectations
Arthur Conan Doyle	*The Adventures of Sherlock Holmes*
George Eliot	*Middlemarch*
Elizabeth Gaskell	*North and South*
Thomas Hardy	*Jude the Obscure*
	Tess of the D'Urbervilles
Henry James	*Portrait of a Lady*
Robert Louis Stevenson	*The Strange Case of Dr Jekyll and Mr Hyde*
William Thackeray	*Vanity Fair*
Anthony Trollope	*Phineas Finn*
HG Wells	*The Time Machine*
Oscar Wilde	*The Picture of Dorian Gray*

Dickens and *Hard Times* and *Great Expectations*

Charles Dickens (1812–1870) was the most popular Victorian novelist and remains the most read. He endured an itinerant early life (moving from Portsmouth to Chatham to London) and when he was twelve his father was imprisoned for not being able to pay his debts. Dickens at this time had to leave school, work in a factory for twelve hours each day sticking labels on bottles and then walk home for miles to the prison to be with his family at night.

However, over the next few years, Dickens clambered his way into white-collar work as an office boy and then a court reporter. His first novel was *Pickwick Papers*, which was published when he was twenty-five and extended his earlier comic sketches. He enjoyed almost uninterrupted success, fame and wealth for the next thirty years. His most popular novels include *Oliver Twist*, *A Christmas Carol*, *Great Expectations* and *A Tale of Two Cities*.

As his work matured, it became more serious in tone and theme. In his later life Dickens also went on enormously profitable, but gruelling, reading tours of his own works. He was warned by his doctors not to embark on what became his final tour for health reasons. He ignored them, brought home twenty thousand pounds, and died.

Dickens is most praised for the way in which he brought places and people to life. His popular wit, his satire of people and institutions, his dramatic plots (necessitated by the serial form that required cliffhangers) and his overt emotionalism made him popular both then and now. Diana Neill states that his depictions of the cruelties of Victorian life in novels such as *Oliver Twist*, *Hard Times* and *David Copperfield* also had the great public benefit of awakening the social conscience of his fellow English citizens.

Traditional criticism of Dickens centres on how he tended to only paint women as caricatures: either as sweet angels or as something quite grotesque. (This is an example of the Eve/Virgin Mary issue that was discussed in the *Noah's Flood* section of Unit 2.) Sometimes he reverts to tear-jerking sentimentality. The dark side of his 'dramatic' plots is that he could be sensationalist. Dickens, who had a passion for amateur theatricals, stated that 'Every writer of fiction … writes in effect for the stage', which may help explain why some of his novels can appear stagey.

Two selections from Charles Dickens

Below is one of Dickens's most famous descriptions of place (Coketown in *Hard Times*) and of character (Miss Havisham in *Great Expectations*).

Hard Times

Hard Times is a satire of brutal northern English industry towns. (Coketown is modelled on the real-life Preston.) It also satirises the heartless 'self-made' men who ran those towns.

HARD TIMES
From Chapter 5

It was a town of red brick, or of brick that would have been red if the smoke and ashes had allowed it; but as matters stood, it was a town of unnatural red and black like the painted face of a savage. It was a town of machinery and tall chimneys, out of which interminable serpents of smoke trailed themselves forever and ever, and never got uncoiled. It had a black canal in it, and a river that ran purple with ill-smelling dye, and vast piles of buildings full of windows where there was a rattling and a trembling all day long, and where the piston of the steam engine worked monotonously up and down like the head of an elephant in a state of melancholy madness. It contained several large streets all very like one another, and many small streets still more like one another, inhabited by people equally like one another, who all went in and out at the same

»

hours, with the same sound upon the same pavements, to do the same work, and to whom every day was the same as yesterday and tomorrow, and every year the counterpart of the last and the next.

These attributes of Coketown were in the main inseparable from the work by which it was sustained; against them were to be set off, comforts of life which found their way all over the world, and elegancies of life which made, we will not ask how much of the fine lady, who could scarcely bear to hear the place mentioned. The rest of its features were voluntary, and they were these.

You saw nothing in Coketown but what was severely workful. If the members of a religious persuasion built a chapel there—as the members of eighteen religious persuasions had done—they made it a pious warehouse of red brick, with sometimes (but this is only in highly ornamental examples) a bell in a birdcage on the top of it. The solitary exception was the New Church; a stuccoed edifice with a square steeple over the door, terminating in four short pinnacles like florid wooden legs. All the public inscriptions in the town were painted alike, in severe characters of black and white. The jail might have been the infirmary, the infirmary might have been the jail, the town hall might have been either, or both, or anything else, for anything that appeared to the contrary in the graces of their construction. Fact, fact, fact, everywhere in the material aspect of the town; fact, fact, fact, everywhere in the immaterial. The M'Choakumchild school was all fact, and the school of design was all fact, and the relations between master and man were all fact, and everything was fact between the lying-in hospital and the cemetery, and what you couldn't state in figures, or show to be purchasable in the cheapest market and salable in the dearest, was not, and never should be, world without end, Amen.

Questions

1 What overall impression of a northern town is given in this extract?

2 The first paragraph uses animal similes quite extensively. How are they used and what is their cumulative effect?

3 How does Dickens stress the uniformity and blandness of the buildings in the town?

4 The last sentence is quite a bitter criticism of 'facts'. How does Dickens use language forms and features to convey this bitterness and why do you think he is so opposed to 'facts'?

5 Comment on the name of the 'M'Choakumchild' school.

6 Do you find this passage effective or too caricatured (or both)?

Activities

1 Do some research (for example, by using a search engine) on one of the slums of the twenty-first century. Write a creative piece describing it. Use language to make your description as evocative as you can.

2 Imagine you are a nineteenth-century Marxist ready to convert the citizens of Coketown to your cause. (Re-read the section on Marxist criticism in Unit 1, page 16, to establish what it is that you believe.) You are going to convert the citizens by publishing a pamphlet that will be distributed to all the houses in the town. In your pamphlet you should:

a Point out the features of the town that the people should object to. (Use the Dickens extract for this.)

b Educate them on Marxist principles. (Use the notes from Unit 1 for this.)

Where possible, these two elements should be combined into persuasive and telling points that will have the citizens rushing to the next meeting of the Marxist society in their town.

Great Expectations

Great Expectations is about the development of the child Pip who is brought up simply, but is then left a mysterious income that allows him to rise and have the 'great expectations' of the title. Pip presumes the income comes from the very strange Miss Havisham, described here. Miss Havisham was left at the altar many decades previously and has not changed out of her wedding dress since.

GREAT EXPECTATIONS

From Chapter 8

In an arm-chair, with an elbow resting on the table and her head leaning on that hand, sat the strangest lady I have ever seen, or shall ever see.

She was dressed in rich materials—satins, and lace, and silks—all of white. Her shoes were white. And she had a long white veil dependent from her hair, and she had bridal flowers in her hair, but her hair was white. Some bright jewels sparkled on her neck and on her hands, and some other jewels lay sparkling on the table. Dresses, less splendid than the dress she wore, and half-packed trunks, were scattered about. She had not quite finished dressing, for she had but one shoe on—the other was on the table near her hand—her veil was but half arranged, her watch and chain were not put on, and some lace for her bosom lay with those trinkets, and with her handkerchief, and gloves, and some flowers, and a prayer-book, all confusedly heaped about the looking-glass.

It was not in the first few moments that I saw all these things, though I saw more of them in the first moments than might be supposed. But, I saw that everything within my view which ought to be white, had

»

been white long ago, and had lost its lustre, and was faded and yellow.
I saw that the bride within the bridal dress had withered like the dress,
and like the flowers, and had no brightness left but the brightness of her
sunken eyes. I saw that the dress had been put upon the rounded figure
of a young woman, and that the figure upon which it now hung loose,
had shrunk to skin and bone. Once, I had been taken to see some ghastly
waxwork at the Fair, representing I know not what impossible personage
lying in state. Once, I had been taken to one of our old marsh churches to
see a skeleton in the ashes of a rich dress, that had been dug out of a vault
under the church pavement. Now, waxwork and skeleton seemed to have
dark eyes that moved and looked at me. I should have cried out, if I could.

'Who is it?' said the lady at the table.

'Pip, ma'am.'

'Pip?'

'Mr Pumblechook's boy, ma'am. Come—to play.'

'Come nearer; let me look at you. Come close.'

It was when I stood before her, avoiding her eyes, that I took note
of the surrounding objects in detail, and saw that her watch had stopped
at twenty minutes to nine, and that a clock in the room had stopped at
twenty minutes to nine.

'Look at me', said Miss Havisham. 'You are not afraid of a woman
who has never seen the sun since you were born?'

Questions

1 What is your first impression of Miss Havisham
in this passage?

2 What is the contrast between the first and the
second paragraph of the extract?

3 How are language features used to give a sense of
death and decay in this passage?

4 We have seen that Charles Dickens has been
criticised for caricatured portraits of women.
Do you find the portrait of Miss Havisham
caricatured? Do you find it unsympathetic?
Explain your response.

5 On the basis of your readings, why do you
think Dickens has remained popular today?
(Your reading needs to explain the appeal of the
writing, but does not need to praise it.)

Activity

Imagine you are directing a film version of *Great Expectations*. You have a meeting with the
film's costume designer, set designer and props assistant. Explain to them your vision for this
scene and what you will need them to do and/or create in order to achieve this vision.

The Brontë sisters and *Jane Eyre*

The Brontë sisters

There were three Brontë sisters—Charlotte, Emily and Anne—all of whom became important nineteenth-century novelists. Their father, Patrick Brontë, a rector in the town of Haworth, outlived his wife and all six of his children. The school the girls were sent to was so bad that the two eldest girls died there. The only son, Branwell, died in September 1848 of drug and alcohol addiction. Of the three remaining daughters (who all lived together in the Parsonage at Haworth), Emily died in December 1848 of consumption at the age of thirty, and Anne died of consumption in May 1849 at the age of twenty-nine. After losing three siblings in nine months, the last remaining child, Charlotte, (and the father) held on for another six years. However, in 1855 Charlotte caught a chill after being caught in the rain and died of consumption, at the relatively old age of thirty-nine. Notwithstanding this gruelling account of family life, the Brontë children (and especially the girls) were encouraged by their father to lead very rich, imaginative lives.

Emily Brontë wrote *Wuthering Heights*, Charlotte Brontë wrote *Jane Eyre*, *Shirley* and *Villette* and Anne Brontë wrote *Agnes Grey* and *The Tenant of Wildfell Hall*. *Jane Eyre* and *Wuthering Heights* were published within two months of each other in October and December 1847 (both under male pseudonyms). *Jane Eyre* was an immediate success. *Wuthering Heights*, on the other hand, was met with either incomprehension or hostility. It is now considered one of the Victorian era's most original books. In the nineteenth century, Emily was better regarded for her lyric poetry.

Jane Eyre

Jane Eyre is about a plain-looking, spirited and intelligent governess who goes to work for the moody Mr Rochester at Thornfield Hall. She is employed to teach Mr Rochester's daughter, Adèle. Jane and Mr Rochester are soon attracted to each other—despite the ominous sounds coming from the ceiling. Just as she is about to marry Mr Rochester, Jane's wedding dress is attacked by a mad woman. Jane finds out at the altar, to her horror, that the mad woman is Mr Rochester's Creole (Afro-Caribbean/French) wife, Bertha, whom Mr Rochester exiled to the remote third floor years ago because she was insane (although there may be a chicken and egg element here).

Norton Conyers, in North Yorkshire, the house on which Thornfield Hall is based.

Jane flees Thornfield Hall and eventually stumbles upon some upstanding relatives who take her in. She almost marries one of them but then has an intense supernatural communication telling her that Mr Rochester is in desperate need of her. Jane returns to Thornfield Hall to find the house burnt down by Mrs Rochester (who dies in the fire). Mr Rochester is alive, but both badly burned and blinded. Jane stays with him, tends to his wounds, marries him, has a child by him, and they all live happily ever after.

In the following extract from *Jane Eyre*, Rochester has admitted to Jane that he already has a wife, explaining 'Bertha Mason is mad; and she came of a mad family; idiots and maniacs through three generations. Her mother, the Creole, was both a madwoman and a drunkard!—as I found out after I had wed the daughter'. He has taken Jane and several others to the high-up room in Thornfield Hall where his wife is kept.

JANE EYRE
From Chapter 26

He lifted the hangings from the wall, uncovering the second door: this, too, he opened. In a room without a window, there burnt a fire, guarded by a high and strong fender, and a lamp suspended from the ceiling by a chain. Grace Poole [his wife's nurse] bent over the fire, apparently cooking something in a saucepan. In the deep shade, at the farther end of the room, a figure ran backwards and forwards. What it was, whether beast or human being, one could not, at first sight, tell: it grovelled, seemingly, on all fours; it snatched and growled like some strange wild animal: but it was covered with clothing, and a quantity of dark, grizzled hair, wild as a mane, hid its head and face.

'Good-morrow, Mrs Poole!' said Mr Rochester. 'How are you? And how is your charge to-day?'

'We're tolerable, sir, I thank you', replied Grace, lifting the boiling mess carefully on to the hob: 'rather snappish, but not 'rageous'.

A fierce cry seemed to give the lie to her favourable report: the clothed hyena rose up, and stood tall on its hind-feet.

'Ah! sir, she sees you!' exclaimed Grace: 'you'd better not stay'.

'Only a few moments, Grace: you must allow me a few moments.'

'Take care then, sir!—for God's sake, take care!'

The maniac bellowed: she parted her shaggy locks from her visage, and gazed wildly at her visitors … Mrs Poole advanced.

'Keep out of the way,' said Mr Rochester, thrusting her aside: 'she has no knife now, I suppose? and I'm on my guard'.

'One never knows what she has, sir: she is so cunning: it is not in mortal discretion to fathom her craft.'

'We had better leave her', whispered Mason.

'Go to the devil!' was his brother-in-law's recommendation.

''Ware!' cried Grace. The three gentlemen retreated simultaneously. Mr Rochester flung me behind him: the lunatic sprang and grappled his throat viciously, and laid her teeth to his cheek: they struggled. She was a big woman, in stature almost equalling her husband, and corpulent besides: she showed virile force in the contest—more than once she almost throttled him, athletic as he was. He could have settled her with a well-planted blow; but he would not strike: he would only wrestle. At last he mastered her arms; Grace Poole gave him a cord, and he pinioned them

»

behind her: with more rope, which was at hand, he bound her to a chair. The operation was performed amidst the fiercest yells and the most convulsive plunges. Mr Rochester then turned to the spectators: he looked at them with a smile both acrid and desolate.

'That is *my wife*', said he. 'Such is the sole conjugal embrace I am ever to know—such are the endearments which are to solace my leisure hours! And *this* is what I wished to have' (laying his hand on my shoulder) 'this young girl, who stands so grave and quiet at the mouth of hell, looking collectedly at the gambols of a demon … Wood and Briggs, look at the difference! Compare these clear eyes with the red balls yonder—this face with that mask—this form with that bulk; then judge me, priest of the gospel and man of the law, and remember with what judgement ye judge ye shall be judged!

Postcolonial and feminist readings of *Jane Eyre*

Alternative readings of *Jane Eyre* suggest that Rochester's taking of a Creole heiress (for her money, quite possibly) out of her own society and into the restrictive, cosseted world of Victorian England was always going to be fraught with difficulty. Furthermore, throwing her into an attic for fifteen years when she didn't act like a demure English woman was an unforgivable act of domination that was destined to eventually produce the woman we see before us in this extract from *Jane Eyre*. Jean Rhys's *Wide Sargasso Sea*, written in 1966, offers a postcolonial rewriting of the story of *Jane Eyre*. It does this by sympathetically narrating the story from Bertha's perspective and therefore bringing to light the colonialist and imperialist assumptions of Brontë's text.

The critic Erica Jong argues that the two women Jane Eyre and Bertha Rochester represent different types of ways that women were entrapped in Victorian society. She believes that Jane Eyre represented the way in which women's freedom was denied. She believes that Bertha's wild, animalistic nature shows the way that women's sexuality was also denied. Of course, no writer in Victorian times would write overtly about sex in a middle-class novel. Instead, this more primal subject matter would be reshaped (sublimated) into animal ferocity.

In 1979, Sandra Gilbert and Susan Gubar published an important work of feminist criticism called *The Madwoman in the Attic*. The title of their publication is a direct reference to Bertha Rochester. Their work suggested that the kinds of feminist criticism that had been popular hitherto had involved the analysis of 'images of women' in work by mostly male writers. *The Madwoman in the Attic* sought to establish that there was a hidden line of women writers, and that female authorship both conformed to and subverted male authorship. In the case of Charlotte Brontë, the metaphor of female madness was one of repressed creativity. A wider application of this metaphor indicates that female artists had been figures in the attic, hidden and ferocious. There is an interesting parallel here between *Jane Eyre* (female authored) and 'The Lady of Shalott' (male authored).

Questions

1 How is Mr Rochester's speech given a strident tone here?

2 Explore the resources of language that Brontë has used to make Bertha Rochester sound animalistic and debased.

3 In the last paragraph, how does Mr Rochester use contrast to make us sympathise with him?

4 What is your overall impression of this passage?

5 How persuasive do you find the postcolonial reading described at the start of the section on page 147.

6 What is your opinion of Jong's and Gilbert and Gubar's feminist readings, explained on page 147?

Activities

1 Elizabeth Rigby reviewed *Jane Eyre* in 1848 for *The Quarterly Review*. She wrote, '*Jane Eyre* is throughout the personification of an unregenerate and undisciplined spirit ... she has inherited in fullest measure the worst sin of our fallen nature—the sin of pride'. She says that the author commits the 'highest moral offence a novel writer can commit; that of making an unworthy character interesting in the eyes of the reader ... The tone of the mind and thought which has overthrown authority and violated every code human and divine abroad, and fostered Chartism and rebellion at home, is the same which has also written *Jane Eyre*'. She concludes about *Jane Eyre* that she is one 'whom we should not care for as an acquaintance, whom we should not seek as a friend, whom we should not desire as a relation and whom we should scrupulously avoid as a governess'.

a What does this review tell us about the reviewer and her time? Does it help our understanding of *Jane Eyre*?

b Script a scene in which Elizabeth Rigby comes to your house and watches *Lara Croft: Tomb Raider* or *Bridget Jones's Diary* (or another film of your choice that is set in the present day or the future and has a strong female lead) on DVD. What does Rigby think of the film? Make sure Rigby explains her reaction on the basis of her own cultural context.

2 Read *Jane Eyre* and Jasper Fforde's *The Eyre Affair*. (In *The Eyre Affair* the character of Jane Eyre is kidnapped out of the book and held to ransom. The detective, Thursday Next, has to deal with alternative endings to *Jane Eyre*.) How is the text of *Jane Eyre* subverted or played with in this book?

3 Write the scene after the 'Mad Bertha' one extracted earlier, in which Jane confronts Rochester about his planned bigamous union with her.

Rossetti, the Pre-Raphaelite brotherhood and 'Goblin Market'

Christina Rossetti (1830–1894) and the Pre-Raphaelites

The Pre-Raphaelites were a group of artists and writers, formed in 1848, who wanted to revive the artistic sentiment of the Italians in the time before Raphael (1483–1520). They felt that this period had a sincerity that the ugly, contemporary Victorian era lacked. The Pre-Raphaelites' love of nature, brightness and morality laid it open to the charge that it was a nostalgic group, longing for a saccharine version of the medieval past. It could be said that pining for nature and morality against the chimney stacks and laissez-faire capitalism of much of Victorian society was understandable. Christina Rossetti and her brothers Dante and William were at the core of this group (although Christina was not formally a member).

The Dantes were the children of an exiled Italian radical. Their house was filled with interesting visitors and stirring conversation. Christina thrived in this environment; she had her first volume of poetry published when she was twelve. The Pre-Raphaelites also made the Rossetti's house their base after 1848.

Christina's life was relatively static and she rarely moved from the family hearth. She rejected two marriage proposals: one because her suitor converted to Catholicism, and the other because he was not religious enough. She was always deeply religious herself and as part of this she gave up the sinful pleasures of theatre, opera and chess. She did, however, spend ten years working voluntarily at a penitentiary for prostitutes. As she grew older she became an invalid and concentrated more exclusively on writing a series of devotional poems.

Christina Rossetti was aware of the ways in which poetry objectified women. She wrote (in her sonnet sequence *Monna Innominata*) that because the ladies in poetry are idealised they cannot be real and were thus 'scant of [limited in] attractiveness'. She wonders what the effect would be if these women were actually allowed to speak for themselves rather than simply being the object of the poetic gaze.

'Goblin Market'

Christina Rossetti's best-known poem is 'Goblin Market' (1862). In the poem, two sisters—Laura and Lizzie—meet a party of malevolent goblins in a glen. The goblins tempt the sisters with free fruit. Laura eats, but Lizzie resists. In return for this feast the goblins ask for and receive a lock of Laura's hair. Laura gives up this lock but is soon enchanted, and she begins wasting away in her home, pining for the taste of the goblins' fruit. Lizzie eventually resolves to purchase some more fruit for her sister, but when she finds the goblins, they insist she eat as well. She steadfastly refuses the temptation (see the following extract) and so breaks the spell on her sister.

An etching of a scene from Rossetti's 'Goblin Market'.

On the face of it, 'Goblin Market' is a children's fable. However, the temptation story is as old as Adam and Eve. Even the object of temptation—fruit—is the same. Unlike the Bible story, however, women play the role of both weak-willed temptee and strong-willed resistor.

GOBLIN MARKET

'Look at our apples
Russet and dun,
Bob at our cherries,
Bite at our peaches,   355
Citrons and dates,
Grapes for the asking,
Pears red with basking
Out in the sun,
Plums on their twigs;   360
Pluck them and suck them,
Pomegranates, figs.'—

'Good folk,' said Lizzie,
Mindful of Jeanie:
'Give me much and many:'—   365
Held out her apron,
Tossed them her penny.
'Nay, take a seat with us,
Honour and eat with us,'
They answered grinning;   370
'Our feast is but beginning.
Night yet is early,
Warm and dew-pearly,
Wakeful and starry:
Such fruits as these   375
No man can carry;
Half their bloom would fly,
Half their dew would dry,
Half their flavour would pass by.
Sit down and feast with us,   380
Be welcome guest with us,
Cheer you and rest with us.'—
'Thank you,' said Lizzie: 'But one waits
At home alone for me:
So without further parleying,   385
If you will not sell me any
Of your fruits tho' much and many,

»

Give me back my silver penny
I tossed you for a fee.'—
They began to scratch their pates,   390
No longer wagging, purring,
But visibly demurring,
Grunting and snarling.
One called her proud,
Cross-grained, uncivil;   395
Their tones waxed loud,
Their looks were evil.
Lashing their tails
They trod and hustled her,
Elbowed and jostled her,   400
Clawed with their nails,
Barking, mewing, hissing, mocking,
Tore her gown and soiled her stocking,
Twitched her hair out by the roots,
Stamped upon her tender feet,   405
Held her hands and squeezed their fruits
Against her mouth to make her eat.

White and golden Lizzie stood,
Like a lily in a flood,—
Like a rock of blue-veined stone   410
Lashed by tides obstreperously,—
Like a beacon left alone
In a hoary roaring sea,
Sending up a golden fire,—
Like a fruit-crowned orange-tree   415
White with blossoms honey-sweet
Sore beset by wasp and bee,—
Like a royal virgin town
Topped with gilded dome and spire
Close beleaguered by a fleet   420
Mad to tug her standard down.

One may lead a horse to water,
Twenty cannot make him drink.
Though the goblins cuffed and caught her,
Coaxed and fought her,   425
Bullied and besought her,
Scratched her, pinched her black as ink,
Kicked and knocked her,

                                                        »

Mauled and mocked her,
Lizzie uttered not a word;   430
Would not open lip from lip
Lest they should cram a mouthful in:
But laughed in heart to feel the drip
Of juice that syruped all her face,
And lodged in dimples of her chin,   435
And streaked her neck which quaked like curd.
At last the evil people,
Worn out by her resistance,
Flung back her penny, kicked their fruit
Along whichever road they took,   440
Not leaving root or stone or shoot;
Some writhed into the ground,
Some dived into the brook
With ring and ripple,
Some scudded on the gale without a sound,   445
Some vanished in the distance ...

Questions

1 What is your initial impression of this poem?

2 How do the rhythm and rhyme of this extract
give the sense of a child's fable?

3 How does Rossetti make the fruit sound alluring?

4 Analyse the effectiveness of the similes used in
lines 408–20 to describe Lizzie being attacked by
the goblins.

5 How is cumulation used as a language technique
in this extract? How successful do you find it?

6 Does Lizzie's inaction (in letting the goblins
assault her) make her a more admirable female
hero or a less admirable one?

7 Virginia Woolf has commented on Rossetti that
she seemed to be both sensuous and severe;
'no sooner have you feasted on beauty with your
eyes that your mind tells you that beauty is vain
and beauty passes'. Explore the contrast you can
find between the sensuous and the severe in this
extract.

Activities

1 Re-read the section on psychoanalytic criticism
in Unit 1 (pages 16–17). Also revise the section on

sexuality and repression in the introduction to
Victorian literature (page 128).

»

a Do you think that there is a sexual subtext to the sequence between the goblins and Laura? If so, what aspects of the language of this section provide evidence for your view?

b Explore how some aspects of Rossetti's own constrained Victorian experience could have led to this piece of writing.

2 Carry out research so that you can compare and contrast the ways in which temptation is handled and symbolised in the Book of Genesis, 'Goblin Market' and JRR Tolkien's *Return of the King*.

3 Re-read Rossetti's criticism of love poetry. Make links between this criticism and the Mary Wroth and John Donne activity in Unit 3 (activity 5, page 85).

4 a Write your own fable for children aged 6–8 years in which one character is tempted and the other character resists. You can set it in the current world or in a mythical time. Remember that your audience should not be your peers but young people. You can write in prose or rhyming verse.

b Use the fable you have written and turn it into a picture book. Your pictures can be your own illustrations or collages constructed of copyright-free images from the Internet. Then, as a class group, have an excursion to a class of seven-year-olds to read your stories to them. (You can do this in groups of four of five seven-year-olds to four or five people from your class.) After this, reflect on what they enjoyed and what they didn't enjoy. Whose story seemed to be the most popular and why?

Wilde and *The Importance of Being Earnest*

Oscar Wilde (1854–1900)

Oscar Wilde was born in Ireland in 1854 but moved to England and studied at Oxford University. He became a disciple of the 'aesthetic' theories of John Ruskin and Walter Pater, which promoted 'art for art's sake'. This theory spurned art that may try to teach a moral lesson, or politically educate. Instead, it claimed art was simply an end in itself; if it is beautiful and perfect that is all that matters.

Wilde moved to London in 1878 and was set up in the most fashionable circles. His conversation was known as the most dazzling in the city. Even the poet Yeats said 'I never before heard a man talking in such perfect sentences, as if he had written them all overnight'. Wilde said of himself: 'I put all my genius into my life; I put only my talent into my works'.

Professionally, Wilde wrote in a number of forms. He worked as a critic and a poet. He wrote several famous children's stories, including *The Happy Prince*. His novel, *The Picture of Dorian Gray*, was met with widespread acclaim. However, Wilde is best known as the writer of mannered theatrical comedies. The play *The Importance of Being Earnest* is generally considered to be his masterpiece.

A sculpture of
Oscar Wilde.

However, the opening of this play in 1895 also led to his downfall, disgrace and, eventually, death. Since 1891 Wilde had been in a relationship with the young poet Lord Alfred Douglas. Douglas's father, the Marquis of Queensbury, was furious at this. The Marquis went to the opening of *The Importance of Being Earnest* with the aim of creating a scene. Wilde knew this in advance, and so the Marquis was ejected from the theatre. Soon afterwards the Marquis left a calling card at Wilde's club: 'To Oscar Wilde posing Somdomite' [sic]. Wilde had the Marquis arrested for libel—always a dangerous thing to do when the claim is, in fact, true. Wilde lost the case; his cause was not helped by a list of ten boys whom the defence claimed Wilde had solicited. Wilde was subsequently imprisoned for two years on the charge of 'gross indecency between males'.

Wilde was released in 1897, but he was bankrupt, and a social and literary outsider. He exiled himself to Paris, where he died in 1900 in a hotel room, apparently pronouncing on his deathbed: 'Either the wallpaper goes, or I do'.

The Importance of Being Earnest

In *The Importance of Being Earnest* the central characters Jack Worthing and Algernon Moncrieff both lead double lives. Algernon has invented an invalid relative called Bunbury to whom he always needs to tend when there are social obligations he wishes to avoid. Jack has invented a whole character called Ernest, a character he exists as when in the city. He uses this to get away with a dandyish lifestyle in the city, while remaining respectable 'Jack' in the country.

However, this double act gets in the way of Jack marrying Algernon's cousin, Gwendolen Fairfax, whom he meets in the country. This is because Gwendolen has a rather odd fetish for the name Ernest, and will only marry someone with that name. Also standing in his way is Gwendolen's mother, Lady Bracknell, who is appalled to find out that Jack has no parents, and was found in a handbag at a railway station. Many complications later, it transpires that Jack has always been a member of the Bracknell clan and his name has always really been Ernest—and so all impediments to the marriage between Jack and Gwendolen are overcome.

The following scene comes from Act 1, where the formidable Lady Bracknell interviews Jack to see whether he is an appropriate suitor for Gwendolen.

THE IMPORTANCE OF BEING EARNEST

LADY BRACKNELL: Do you smoke?
JACK: Well, yes, I must admit I smoke.
LADY BRACKNELL: I am glad to hear it. A man should always have an occupation of some kind. There are far too many idle men in London as it is … »

LADY BRACKNELL: ... Now to minor matters. Are your parents living?

JACK: I have lost both my parents.

LADY BRACKNELL: Both? To lose one parent may be regarded as a misfortune—to lose *both* seems like carelessness. Who was your father? He was evidently a man of some wealth. Was he born in what the Radical papers call the purple of commerce, or did he rise from the ranks of the aristocracy?

JACK: I am afraid I really don't know. The fact is, Lady Bracknell, I said I had lost my parents. It would be nearer the truth to say that my parents seem to have lost me ... I don't actually know who I am by birth. I was ... well, I was found.

LADY BRACKNELL: Found!

JACK: The late Mr Thomas Cardew, an old gentleman of a very charitable and kindly disposition, found me, and gave me the name of Worthing, because he happened to have a first-class ticket for Worthing in his pocket at the time. Worthing is a place in Sussex. It is a seaside resort.

LADY BRACKNELL: Where did the charitable gentleman who had a first-class ticket for this seaside resort find you?

JACK: [*gravely*] In a handbag.

LADY BRACKNELL: A handbag?

JACK: [*very seriously*] Yes, Lady Bracknell. I was in a handbag—a somewhat large, black leather handbag, with handles to it—an ordinary handbag, in fact.

LADY BRACKNELL: In what locality did this Mr James, or Thomas, Cardew come across this ordinary handbag?

JACK: In the cloak room at Victoria Station. It was given to him in mistake for his own.

LADY BRACKNELL: The cloak room at Victoria Station?

JACK: Yes. The Brighton line.

LADY BRACKNELL: The line is immaterial. Mr Worthing, I confess I feel somewhat bewildered by what you have just told me. To be born, or at any rate bred, in a handbag, whether it had handles or not, seems to me to display a contempt for the ordinary decencies of family life that reminds one of the worst excesses of the French Revolution. And I presume you know what that unfortunate movement led to? As for the particular locality in which the handbag was found, a cloak room at a railway station might serve to conceal a social indiscretion—has probably, indeed, been used for that purpose before now—but it could hardly be regarded as an assured basis for a recognized position in good society.

JACK: May I ask you then what you would advise me to do? I need hardly say I would do anything in the world to ensure Gwendolen's happiness.

LADY BRACKNELL: I would strongly advise you, Mr Worthing, to try and acquire some relations as soon as possible, and to make a definite

»

effort to produce at any rate one parent, of either sex, before the season is quite over.

JACK: Well, I don't see how I could possibly manage to do that. I can produce the handbag at any moment. It is in my dressing room at home. I really think that should satisfy you, Lady Bracknell.

LADY BRACKNELL: Me, sir! What has it to do with me? You can hardly imagine that I and Lord Bracknell would dream of allowing our only daughter—a girl brought up with the utmost care—to marry into a cloak room, and form an alliance with a parcel? Good morning, Mr Worthing!

[*Lady Bracknell sweeps out in majestic indignation.*]

Questions

1 Explain Wilde's wit in Lady Bracknell's comments about smoking.

2 What elements of humour does the exchange about the handbag provide for audiences?

3 How are Jack's responses unusual?

4 Closely analyse the wit in Lady Bracknell's closing statement before she majestically sweeps from the room.

5 The above passage is regarded by a number of people as one of the funniest sections of the wittiest play in the English language. Do you agree? If not, why not?

6 a What would late nineteenth-century audiences enjoy in this extract that an early twenty-first century audience would not?

b Are there aspects of this extract that an early twenty-first century audience would enjoy that a late nineteenth-century audience would not?

c Why do you think this play is still so popular?

7 Explore further the following readings (some traditional, some resistant) that have been made of this play. Use the introductory notes about Wilde, the synopsis of the play and the extract above to help you discuss them.

a It is an aesthetic play. It focuses on the 'pure art' in which the story hardly matters, the realism of the characters is irrelevant and any moral point is crushed under the wittiness and the word play. The critic Arthur Ransome said of Wilde that he took 'extraordinary liberties with [his plots] and amused himself with quips, bon mots, epigrams and repartee that had really nothing to do with the business in hand'.

b The play is a clever social satire that lampoons the upper class from the perspective of someone who paradoxically is both inside and outside the Victorian power structure. Wilde was renowned, loved and respected. Yet he knew that he was also outside the power structure because he was Irish.

c The play is actually a reflection of Wilde's own double life as a homosexual man in Victorian society. Re-read the section on queer criticism in Unit 1 (page 19) before you complete this task.

Monty Python satire of Oscar Wilde

The British comedy troupe Monty Python performed a satire on Oscar Wilde in 1972 as part of their 'Flying Circus' programme of skits. Part of the script appears below.

OSCAR WILDE

THE PRINCE OF WALES: Ah, my congratulations, Wilde. Your play is a great success. The whole of London's talking about you.

OSCAR WILDE: Your highness, there is only one thing in the world worse than being talked about, and that is not being talked about.

(There follows fifteen seconds of restrained and sycophantic laughter)

THE PRINCE OF WALES: Oh, very witty, Wilde … very, very witty.

JAMES MCNEILL WHISTLER: There is only one thing in the world worse than being witty, and that is not being witty.

(Fifteen more seconds of the same)…

OSCAR WILDE: Your Highness, do you know James McNeill Whistler?

THE PRINCE OF WALES: Yes, we've played squash together.

OSCAR WILDE: There is only one thing worse than playing squash together, and that is playing it by yourself.

(Silence)

OSCAR WILDE: I wish I hadn't said that …

THE PRINCE OF WALES: Well, you must forgive me, Wilde, but I must get back up the Palace.

OSCAR WILDE: Your Majesty, you're like a big jam doughnut with cream on the top.

THE PRINCE OF WALES: I beg your pardon?

OSCAR WILDE: Um … It was one of Whistler's.

JAMES MCNEILL WHISTLER: I didn't say that.

OSCAR WILDE: You did, James, you did.

THE PRINCE OF WALES: Well, Mr Whistler?

JAMES MCNEILL WHISTLER: I—I meant, Your Majesty, that, uh, like a doughnut your arrival gives us pleasure and your departure merely makes us hungry for more.

(Laughter and congratulations)

»

JAMES MCNEILL WHISTLER: Yes, thank you. Right, Your Majesty is like a stream of bat's piss.

(Gasps)

THE PRINCE OF WALES: What?

JAMES MCNEILL WHISTLER: It was one of Wilde's.

OSCAR WILDE: It sodding was not! It was Shaw!

THE PRINCE OF WALES: Well, Mr Shaw?

GEORGE BERNARD SHAW: I, um, I, ah, I merely meant, Your Majesty, that, ah, you shine out like a shaft of gold when all around is dark …

Questions

1 What elements of Wilde's life and style of writing can you see evidenced in this piece?

2 Wilde is well-known for his use of rhetorical balance, such as the line 'There is only one thing worse than being talked about and that is not being talked about' from his novel, *The Picture of Dorian Gray*. How is his use of rhetorical balance satirised in this piece?

3 How does Monty Python subvert Wilde's wit into a new, late twentieth century direction? How effective is it?

4 Which piece do you prefer: this or *The Importance of Being Earnest*? Explain your response.

Activities

1 Write the next fifteen lines of this script.

2 Source the rest of the actual script. What additional elements of humour have been included that have not been extracted above?

Review Questions & Activities

1 In what ways can three of the Victorian texts be seen as products of their time? Demonstrate with close reference to the texts and their context. Explain why you think these texts may have remained popular over time.

2 If only one of the texts you have studied in this unit could be preserved for future generations, which one would you pick? Explain your choice and why you value the text you chose.

3 Forge a poet

In this activity/game you will forge a Victorian poet. The aims of the game are to spot other people's forgeries and to make your own undetectable forgery. The procedure to follow is outlined in the box below.

How does this activity make you reflect on Victorian poetry, writing poetry and learning how to read and appreciate poetry?

Forge a poet: lesson 1

1 In groups of three, form your detection agency. Give your agency a name.

2 Have a Victorian poet allocated to you. Examples are Thomas Hardy, Robert Browning, Elizabeth Barrett Browning, Gerald Manley Hopkins, Matthew Arnold, Algernon Charles Swinburne, Dante Rossetti and Rudyard Kipling.

3 Find a collection of poems by your poet. Peruse the collection and select one poem. (Hint: It would be useful to choose a slightly more obscure poem.) The Victorian Web website (www.victorianweb.org) has a selection of poems by each of the poets listed above.

4 Select eight lines from the poem.

5 Forge another eight lines from it. This is the hard part. You have to write something completely new, but its style and subject matter should match those of the selected eight lines. Show your teacher as you go. *Do not show anyone else.*

6 Carry out research so that you can prepare a brief biography of your poet as well as a summary of the main concerns and styles of his or her poetry.

Forge a poet: lesson 2

1 Read the following to the other detection groups:
   a the name of your poet
   b the biography and summary of your poet
   c the title of the poem
   d the real eight lines and your forged eight lines. (*Do not tell the detection groups which one is which.*)

2 The other groups then have to guess which eight lines are real and which are forged.

3 You will then take your place as a detector trying to spot the forgeries of the other groups.

4 Each person will be given a marking sheet. The marking sheet on page 160 can be used as a template. You will receive marks in two ways:
   a Each forgery you correctly spot will gain you one mark.
   b Each person who thinks your poem is the real one (and the real one the forgery) will result in one mark for you.

---

4 Explore the cultural assumptions that were being:

a challenged by two of the Victorian texts you have studied

b made by two of the Victorian texts you have studied.

Show the way in which language was used to challenge or make these cultural assumptions.

5 Use multimedia presentation software (such as PowerPoint or Flash) to create and present a visual montage of ten to twenty images that best represent the Victorian era. Your images do not always need to be literal. Explain to the class the reasons for your choices.

Forge a poet: marking sheet for _____ of _____ detection group

i Other people's forgeries:

Group name	Which 8 lines are forged: the 1st or 2nd?	Why? (10 words or less)

ii How many people thought your 8 lines were real not forged? _____

Total mark: _____

Anxieties, Rebellions & Mermaids

MODERN LITERATURE

Highlights

¶ *Crazed man becomes cannibal in Africa*

¶ *Dozens killed in Irish freedom uprising*

¶ *Beast slouches towards Bethlehem*

¶ *Lady lies in bed and dreams of special love*

¶ *Lonely man ignored by mermaids*

Outcomes

By the end of this unit you should have:

¤ developed an understanding of the relationship between the texts and the context of the modern era (including the literary, cultural and historical contexts)

¤ gained an appreciation of the way in which the texts can be seen as cultural products of both their authors and their times

¤ engaged in detailed textual interpretation of a number of modern pieces and developed an understanding of how language forms and/ or techniques shape the meaning of these pieces

¤ challenged and evaluated some of the cultural assumptions that exist in modern texts and considered alternative readings of some texts

¤ come to a personal view about valuing the texts and the modern period based on your own context and preferences

¤ engaged with the texts in a number of ways, including writing essays, dialogues and discussions and participating in drama presentations

¤ gained enjoyment through exposure to the texts and their ideas and contexts.

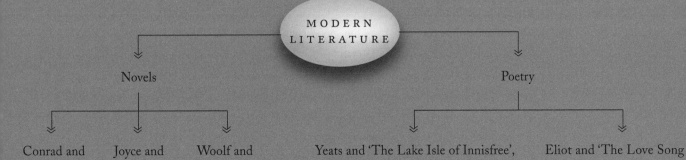

MODERN LITERATURE

Novels

Poetry

Conrad and *Heart of Darkness*

Joyce and *Ulysses*

Woolf and *To the Lighthouse*

Yeats and 'The Lake Isle of Innisfree', 'The Wild Swans at Coole', 'Easter 1916' and 'The Second Coming'

Eliot and 'The Love Song of J Alfred Prufrock'

Context of the period

A curious point about modernism is that the 'modern' part of this name tag is confusing. How could literature that began to flourish over a century ago be understood as modern? From a twenty-first century perspective shouldn't this movement in literature be called 'oldism'? The Model T Ford was not even on the road when European writers began to break away from their Victorian predecessors and create art that recorded something of what it was like to live in the 'modern' age (the first half of the twentieth century). Nevertheless, there is a strong connection between the methods and concerns of modernist literature and the philosophy, politics and art of the early twentieth century. It was these methods and concerns that provoked a rethinking of cultural and social values.

Commentators in the 1950s and 1960s agreed that in the period between 1890 and 1940 (with a high point in the 1920s) the work of a range of writers shared distinctive forms and features. It was also obvious in hindsight that modernist literature in English participated in a much wider movement towards change and experimentation in European art at that time. The cutting-edge (avant-garde) rejection of 'stuffy' Victorian realism and, as poet and critic Ezra Pound put it, the urge to 'make it new', were responses to what people saw as the strangeness and urgency of the new twentieth century. And what newness there was: new machines, new industrialisation, new capitalism and a whole new world order. Society felt as if it had disembarked from the quaint old horse and buggy and re-embarked on the hurtling steam train of progress. This may have been exhilarating, but it was also frightening and alienating.

Questions

1 What does the word 'modern' mean to you? What are its associations? Is it a positive or negative term? Why?

2 What kind of images does the word 'modern' suggest? Find three images using a search engine and explain why you chose them.

Literary context

The modernists made a conscious break with the developmental cause-and-effect narratives of Victorian realist novels. Novels began to be organised in different ways: sometimes discontinuous, fragmented or structured through symbols, allusions, unreliable memories and parallels with stories from mythology.

By experimenting with form the modernists produced the 'new'. In poetry, this meant rejecting traditional forms and metre in favour of imagism, free verse, fragmentation, frequent allusions to other texts and a strong emphasis on symbolism (often at the expense of accessibility). Fiction shared the emphasis on allusion and symbol and there was the emergence of unreliable narrators or at least individual narrators with highly individual points of view.

The interest in 'external reality' obvious in nineteenth-century realist fiction was replaced by an emphasis on internal reality—the experience inside the mind. Sometimes this resulted in quite impressionistic writing with a focus on the individual's perception or perspective. It could also lead to an emphasis on the strange mechanism of memory and the individual experience of time passing.

Modernists were interested in really facing up to the 'new'. They wanted to show what they saw as being the truly 'real' experience. The modernists were concerned with considering a world without an 'old-fashioned' God. They criticised traditional values about culture and individual behaviour and wanted to face the loss of innocence caused by the horror of World War I.

Questions

1 RECAP: If you had to explain modernism in fifty words or less to your parent or guardian, what would your explaination be?

2 Look back over novels, short stories and/or films that you have studied in English over the last few years. Select two that contain features of modernism. With the class, explain and explore the features you find.

3 Write a piece about your previous lesson that contains elements of the following: symbolism, memory, the experience of the inside of your mind, mythic parallels, discontinuity, fragmentation and imagism. See who in the class can write the piece that appears the most alienating and strange.

Philosophical, cultural and historical context

To really see the origins of many aspects of modernism in literature it is necessary to trace the influence of the work of three philosophers from the nineteenth century: Nietzsche, Marx and Freud.

Friedrich Nietzsche felt that humankind was being held back by values that had been learnt from religious beliefs. Humankind had progressed as far as it had through the strong conquering the weak (Darwinism) and yet our moral philosophies held that people should be equal; that is, the feeble should have the same rights as the strong. Nietzsche felt that people should instead develop their maximum life potential, untrammelled by the 'slave morality' of conscience. Only then, by using their 'will to power', would they become fulfilled 'supermen'.

Friedrich Nietzsche.

Karl Marx worked on looking at history scientifically, which meant he believed he could predict future stages of history. He studied the 'current' stage, in which a small number of capitalists held most of the means of production (such as factories), and said that it was inevitable that this would be overthrown in revolution by the exploited but numerically larger working class. This would result in a conflict-free, communist society.

Sigmund Freud explored the application of scientific principles to the sphere of the mind. He believed that all behaviour had causes and explanations. If these causes could not be found in the conscious mind, then one had to go looking in the 'unconscious' mind. The unconscious mind was like the section of an iceberg hidden underneath the water, and it manifested itself in areas such as dreams. This theory put rational humans at the mercy of unconscious drives (such as sexual urges) and emotions (such as a child's envy of his or her parent) that humans are not even aware of themselves.

The groundbreaking work delivered by these three (as well as parallel developments in science, sociology and the study of language) led to the kinds of writing experiments that were famous in literature from the early twentieth century. It is important to note here the importance of Darwin's work to the dismantling of Victorian certainties. The post-Darwinian world questioned all the stabilisers of Victorian society: religion, social structures and ethics.

Not everybody was enthusiastically modernist. For example, Georg Lukács, an influential Marxist critic working after the Russian Revolution of 1917, saw the modernist movement as a typical example of a waste of bourgeois leisure time. He thought that a focus on oneself and one's linguistic experiments led to a lack of commitment to political reality and revolution. Why waste time being radical about a novel, he thought, when you could spend it being radical about bringing down the bourgeoisie? He had no taste for the chaotic and difficult writing of western modernism, seeing it as essentially elitist.

There was a great deal of fuss about the turn from the nineteenth century into the twentieth century. After all, society wasn't merely clicking over from one century to another, but from one millennium to another. The twentieth century was also very much associated with the 'new' because of the enormous acceleration in technology. This growth spurt also brought with it the arms race, and the kind of military technology that caused such unprecedented slaughter in World Wars I and II. The expansion of urban life, as opposed to traditional rural life, was also a feature of this period.

Some writers were making forays into modernist styles as early as the late nineteenth century. Henry James became more and more interested in psychological realism in books such as *Portrait of a Lady* (1881). Thomas Hardy was writing increasingly bleak portrayals of the loss of community in novels such as *Tess of the D'Urbervilles* (1891). This novel actually refers to the 'ache of modernism'. Novels such as these were the trailblazers for the fully developed modern pieces. Writers were also beginning to record aspects of England's colonialist endeavours. This made for a very different theme than that of the social and moral experience of the English. Such writers included Rudyard Kipling, Joseph Conrad and EM Forster. Kipling very much wrote from an imperialist perspective. However, others, such as Conrad (see page 165), engaged with and criticised the colonial project.

Questions

1 RECAP: Create a mind map diagram that shows the societal context within which modern writers worked.

2 On the basis of your knowledge of colonial attitudes (such as Australians in the nineteenth

»

century), what do you think the imperialist attitude of Kipling would have been? How do you think it would have found expression in his writing?

3 Do you think that a change in century really can alter people's thinking about politics, history and/or literature? If you do, does this mean that we would tend to find the most avant-garde (or new) literature occurring in the first decades of each new century?

Activity

Imagine you are a writer at the beginning of the century and have just heard about the theories of Marx, Freud and Nietzsche. You are very excited at the literary possibilities these theories provide, and decide to write three short stories, each influenced (both in style and content) by one of these three theorists. Write a one-paragraph summary of each short story.

Conrad and *Heart of Darkness*

Joseph Conrad (1857–1924)

A colonial trading place for rubber and other goods in the Congo.

Joseph Conrad's work demonstrates the way in which English-language modernism was really an international and cross-cultural movement, pioneered by Americans, Europeans and Irish as much as the English. Born Teodor Jozef Konrad Korzeniowski, Conrad was the son and grandson of Polish gentlemen who dedicated their lives to resisting the Russian rule of the Ukraine. His mother died in exile in northern Russia when he was seven, his father when he was eleven. At sixteen he went to sea, joining a French ship at Marseilles. He became a master mariner and a British subject and, after twenty years at sea, he settled in England and married an English woman. English was his third language, after French and Polish. In 1895, Conrad published *Almayer's Folly*. He explained in his preface to *The Nigger of the Narcissus* (1897) that 'My task ... is, by the power of the written word, to make you hear, to make you feel—it is, before all, to make you see'. He seemed like a pre-modernist realist writer in the sense that he wanted to explore moral issues. However, his way of doing it was quite different from the realists—it was 'modern'.

Heart of Darkness is Conrad's most famous work. It is a novella based on his own trip up the Congo in 1890 to become a river pilot for the Belgians who ran the trade on the river. To reach the heart of the Dark Continent had been his boyhood dream. However, despite the fact that he was well travelled, the Congo experience was exceptional. It both seriously undermined his health and completely affected his political and social views. He was astounded and appalled at the way in which a 'civilised' country could treat indigenous peoples so brutally. *Heart of Darkness* was first serialised in *Blackwood's Magazine* in 1899. It was first published in book form in 1902.

As Andrew Roberts has surmised:

> This work epitomises many features of modernist fiction: the need to confront violence, nihilism and despair; the fascination with, but fear of, the unconscious; the centrality of a dramatised narrator who is not omniscient [all knowing] but rather himself searching for understanding; a symbolic richness which invites multiple interpretations.

Heart of Darkness

In *Heart of Darkness*, Marlow tells of his journey up the Congo River in Africa, in the employment of a Belgian trading company. This supposedly benevolent organisation is, in fact, ruthlessly enslaving the Africans and stripping the area of ivory, and what Marlow sees when he arrives disgusts him. At the company's Central Station he hears much about Kurtz, their most successful agent, who is lying ill at the Inner Station up the river, in the heart of ivory country. Marlow sets off after him. He experiences a sense of dread as his steamer carries him deeper into the primitive jungle, but this is combined with a strong desire to meet the mysterious Kurtz. After being attacked from the bank by natives, they reach the Inner Station where an eccentric young Russian adventurer, who idolises Kurtz, tells Marlow of Kurtz's power over local inhabitants and the fluency and fascination of his ideas. But Kurtz's hut is surrounded by heads on poles; he has become addicted to unspecified barbaric practices, presumably involving human sacrifice, and has an African mistress. Marlow gets Kurtz away down river, but Kurtz dies, his last words being, famously, 'the horror, the horror'. Marlow returns to Europe and lies to Kurtz's beloved, saying that the last thing he uttered was her name. Kurtz also leaves a report for the Society for the Suppression of Savage Customs that includes the sentence: 'Exterminate all the Brutes'.

At the turn of the twentieth century, Conrad's tale gave an important and unpopular account of the actual impact of European imperialism and colonialism. In fact, far from acting as a 'civilising' force, the West (like Kurtz, and even potentially Marlow) is the murderer and the cannibal. The dark vision of the effects of European colonialism anticipates the general collapse of values that happened during World War I. European culture could produce violence, murder and destruction on an unheard-of scale, it seemed. Didn't that make Europe far worse than the 'natives' it was attempting to 'civilise'? Kurtz's conduct suggests that civilisation may just be a veneer, and when you go behind it there is only darkness—a heart of darkness. Even worse, at the centre of things is just 'the horror'. This is a bleak modern vision indeed for a new century.

Uncertainty is laced all the way through this text, which is another modern feature. Marlow himself describes the meaning of the tale as a 'mist' around the story instead of the 'kernel' (inner part of a nut) at the centre of the tale. All this would have been very confronting for people used to the omniscient narrators of the nineteenth century. Conrad's presentation of the partial and fallible perspective of just one observer means that we don't have 'real' access to what that observer is reporting on. As a result, we are obliged to think about *how* he reports it. We are thus forced to think about how language does and doesn't work. All in all, this is a lot of ground to cover in a novella that barely scrapes 100 pages.

HEART OF DARKNESS: EXTRACT 1

In this extract, the narrator, Marlow, is on the steamboat heading inland, up the river towards where Kurtz is living.

'Going up that river was like travelling back to the earliest beginnings of the world, when vegetation rioted on the earth and the big trees were kings. An empty stream, a great silence, an impenetrable forest. The air was warm, thick, heavy, sluggish. There was no joy in the brilliance of sunshine. The long stretches of the waterway ran on, deserted, into the gloom of overshadowed distances. On silvery sandbanks hippos and alligators sunned themselves side by side. The broadening waters flowed through a mob of wooded islands; you lost your way on that river as you would in a desert, and butted all day long against shoals, trying to find the channel, till you thought yourself bewitched and cut off for ever from everything you had known once—somewhere—far away—in another existence perhaps. There were moments when one's past came back to one, as it will sometimes when you have not a moment to spare to yourself; but it came in the shape of an unrestful and noisy dream, remembered with wonder amongst the overwhelming realities of this strange world of plants, and water, and silence. And this stillness of life did not in the least resemble a peace. It was the stillness of an implacable force brooding over an inscrutable intention. It looked at you with a vengeful aspect ...'

Trees, trees, millions of trees, massive, immense, running up high; and at their foot, hugging the bank against the stream, crept the little begrimed steamboat, like a sluggish beetle crawling on the floor of a lofty portico. It made you feel very small, very lost, and yet it was not altogether depressing, that feeling. After all, if you were small, the grimy beetle crawled on—which was just what you wanted it to do. Where the pilgrims imagined it crawled to I don't know. To some place where they expected to get something, I bet! For me it crawled towards Kurtz—exclusively; but when the steam-pipes started leaking we crawled very slow. The reaches opened before us and closed behind, as if the forest had stepped leisurely across the water to bar the way for our return. We penetrated deeper and deeper into the heart of darkness.

Questions

1 How is personification manipulated throughout the extract? What is its effect?

2 Explore the effect of the use of magic, imagery and dreams throughout this passage.

3 What do you think is meant by the phrase 'an implacable force brooding over an inscrutable intention'? What is the effect of this phrase?

4 What do you think the 'heart of darkness' represents here?

5 The extract provides a European description of African forest. This can account for why the narrator sees it as so unfamiliar. Where can you find evidence of respect for the forest? Explore where you can find evidence of a 'colonial' mind-set about Africa influencing his writing (such as 'travelling back to the earliest beginnings of the world'). Before answering this, read the section about postcolonialism in Unit 1 (pages 14–15), particularly the 'construction of the other' and the 'construction of the margin from the centre'.

HEART OF DARKNESS: EXTRACT 2

In this extract, Marlow is at the beginning of his story. He is speaking to a group of sailors on the Thames River while waiting for the tide to turn.

'You know I hate, detest, and can't bear a lie, not because I am straighter than the rest of us, but simply because it appals me. There is a taint of death, a flavour of mortality in lies,—which is exactly what I hate and detest in the world—what I want to forget. It makes me miserable and sick, like biting something rotten would do. Temperament, I suppose. Well, I went near enough to it by letting the young fool there believe anything he liked to imagine as to my influence in Europe. I became in an instant as much of a pretense as the rest of the bewitched pilgrims. This simply because I had a notion it somehow would be of help to that Kurtz whom at the time I did not see—you understand. He was just a word for me. I did not see the man in the name any more than you do. Do you see him? Do you see the story? Do you see anything? It seems to me I am trying to tell you a dream—making a vain attempt, because no relation of a dream can convey the dream-sensation, that commingling of absurdity, surprise, and bewilderment in a tremor of struggling revolt, that notion of being captured by the incredible which is of the very essence of dreams …'

    He was silent for a while.

    '… No, it is impossible; it is impossible to convey the life-sensation of any given epoch of one's existence—that which makes its truth, its meaning—its subtle and penetrating essence. It is impossible. We live, as we dream—alone …'

1 Given that Marlow lies to Kurtz's beloved at the end, what do you think happened to his high moral ground about lying?

2 Can you think of an experience that was surreal and dreamlike in the way that Marlow describes? How would you narrate this experience?

3 Why do you think that Marlow finds it so hard to tell his story?

4 The work was originally entitled 'The Heart of Darkness'. What is the effect of taking out the 'the'?

Activity

There have been some significant postcolonial criticisms of Conrad's work, pointing out the way in which his novel simultaneously condemns European imperialism and also upholds some of its central assumptions. Research these criticisms. You should read the section on postcolonialism in Unit 1 (pages 14–15) as a starting point for your investigation.

WB Yeats (1865–1939)

Born in Dublin, William Butler Yeats spent much of his boyhood travelling between school in London and his mother's native Irish county of Sligo, a wild and beautiful county in north-western Ireland. This county provided a background to much of his poetry. He later studied at the School of Art in Dublin, where he became interested in mystical religions and the supernatural. At twenty-one he abandoned art in favour of a profession in literature, editing *The Poems of William Blake* in 1893.

His youth was passed during the upsurge of Irish political nationalism as represented by the Home Rule movement. Yeats shared the general Romantic dislike of the urban and industrial harshness and materialism of contemporary English culture. He sought to resist it by using Irish peasant folk traditions and ancient Celtic myths. His first work was on a theme from this mythology: *The Wanderings of Oisin*. So, Yeats's early career could not have looked less modernist. His early verse reads like a continuation of Romantic interests in the natural world and childhood, all wrapped up in various Irish mystical and nationalist elements.

Yeats's early inclination for mysticism, cultural nationalism and all things Celtic found its erotic expression in a longstanding obsession with a beautiful revolutionary Irish woman, Maud Gonne. Maud felt that her greatest duty to Ireland would not be served by accepting any of his many offers of marriage over a fifteen-year period. He often begged and she always refused, and indeed his unrequited passion for her did inspire furious creativity from him.

The advent of the violent realities of World War I, with the parallel political events in Ireland, made a serious and sustained impact on his verse and politics. His style altered, already affected by the American imagist Ezra Pound, who worked briefly as his secretary. Slowly he transformed into a modern poet. His diction became tougher and stronger; he energised his often trance-like rhythms. At the same time he became less interested in the mystical and personal vision and more interested in concrete language and the political role of the poet. (He was an Irish Nationalist.) However, some characteristics of Yeats's work never changed. His interest in symbolism and the non-naturalistic (including an elaborate mythical scheme of history) remained a constant.

In 1917, he married Georgie Hyde-Lees and in the same year moved into an old stone tower in County Galway. He won the Nobel Prize for Literature in 1923, and became a senator of the Irish Free State at about the same time.

Question

RECAP: Make a mind map diagram of what you see as Yeats's cultural, political and personal influences during his life. Refer to this when analysing his poetry.

Activity

Research the Home Rule movement and the political situation in Ireland around the turn of the century. How do you think this may have affected Yeats's poetry?

'The Lake Isle of Innisfree' and 'The Wild Swans at Coole'

Yeats's style moved from the kind used in his poem 'The Lake Isle of Innisfree' (1892) to the quite different 'The Wild Swans at Coole' in 1917.

THE LAKE ISLE OF INNISFREE

I will arise and go now, and go to Innisfree,
And a small cabin build there, of clay and wattles made;
Nine bean-rows will I have there, a hive for the honey-bee,
And live alone in the bee-loud glade.

And I shall have some peace there, for peace comes dropping slow,   5
Dropping from the veils of the morning to where the cricket sings;
There midnight's all a glimmer, and noon a purple glow,
And evening full of the linnet's wings.

»

I will arise and go now, for always night and day
I hear lake water lapping with low sounds by the shore;
While I stand on the roadway, or on the pavements grey,
I hear it in the deep heart's core.

10

Questions

1 What is your first impression of this poem? Justify your response.

2 What do you notice about the rhythm and metre of the stanzas?

3 How is nature being used in this poem? What images are there of flora and fauna, and what is their effect?

4 How does the poem end? What is significant about this?

5 If you have not studied the Romantics, have a look at the features of their poems on pages 88–9. How and to what extent do you find these features in this poem?

THE WILD SWANS AT COOLE

I have looked upon those brilliant creatures,
And now my heart is sore.
All's changed since I, hearing at twilight,
The first time on this shore,
The bell-beat of their wings above my head,
Trod with a lighter tread

15

Unwearied still, lover by lover,
They paddle in the cold
Companionable streams or climb the air;
Their hearts have not grown old;
Passion or conquest, wander where they will,
Attend upon them still …

20

Questions

1 What does the speaker value about the swans?

2 What does this poem represent about Yeats's feelings and state of mind?

»

3 Draw up a table in which you list the similarities and differences you can find between 'The Lake Isle of Innisfree' and this excerpt from 'The Wild Swans at Coole'. (You could begin by looking at the disillusionment of the poet and the importance of symbols.)

4 How does comparing these poems give you insights into the contrast between Romanticism and modernism?

'Easter 1916' and 'The Second Coming'

Ruins in Dublin after the Easter 1916 revolt.

During Easter in 1916 there was an uprising in Dublin; Ireland was still under direct British control. The entire centre of town was occupied by 700 members of the Irish Republican Brotherhood (IRB) who held out until 29 April before being captured and a number executed. This act of defiance is known as the Easter Rising. It was a moment in Irish history that set in train a series of events leading to the establishment of the Irish Free State in 1922. Yeats wrote the poem 'Easter 1916' between May and September 1916. The Irish commentator Declan Kiberd remarked:

'Easter 1916' brought Yeats's wavering in the role of the national bard to a crisis point. It enacts the quarrel within his own mind between his public duty (to name and praise the warrior dead) and his more personal urge (to question the wisdom of their sacrifice). The poem speaks, correspondingly, with two voices, and sometimes it enacts in single phrases ('terrible beauty') their contestation.

'Easter 1916' was published in Yeats's volume of poetry *Michael Robartes and the Dancer* in 1921 when Yeats was fifty-six. This poem and book represent a further turning point in Yeats's work.

EASTER 1916

I have met them at close of day
Coming with vivid faces
From counter or desk among grey
Eighteenth-century houses.
I have passed with a nod of the head   5
Or polite meaningless words,
Or have lingered awhile and said
Polite meaningless words,

》

And thought before I had done
Of a mocking tale or a gibe   10
To please a companion
Around the fire at the club,
Being certain that they and I
But lived where motley is worn:
All changed, changed utterly: 15
A terrible beauty is born.

That woman's days were spent
In ignorant good-will,
Her nights in argument
Until her voice grew shrill.   20
What voice more sweet than hers
When, young and beautiful,
She rode to harriers?
This man had kept a school
And rode our wingèd horse.   25
This other his helper and friend
Was coming into his force;
He might have won fame in the end,
So sensitive his nature seemed,
So daring and sweet his thought.   30
This other man I had dreamed
A drunken, vainglorious lout.
He had done most bitter wrong
To some who are near my heart,
Yet I number him in the song;   35
He, too, has resigned his part
In the casual comedy;
He, too, has been changed in his turn,
Transformed utterly:
A terrible beauty is born.   40

Hearts with one purpose alone
Through summer and winter seem
Enchanted to a stone
To trouble the living stream.
The horse that comes from the road,   45
The rider, the birds that range
From cloud to tumbling cloud,
Minute by minute they change;
A shadow of cloud on the stream

》

Changes minute by minute;   50
A horse-hoof slides on the brim;
And a horse plashes within it;
The long-legged moor-hens dive,
And hens to moor-cocks call;
Minute by minute they live: 55
The stone's in the midst of all.

Too long a sacrifice
Can make a stone of the heart.
O when may it suffice?
That is Heaven's part, our part   60
To murmur name upon name,
As a mother names her child
When sleep at last has come
On limbs that had run wild.
What is it but nightfall?   65
No, no, not night but death.
Was it needless death after all?
For England may keep faith
For all that is done and said.
We know their dream; enough   70
To know they dreamed and are dead;
And what if excess of love
Bewildered them till they died?
I write it out in a verse—
MacDonagh and MacBride   75
And Connolly and Pearse
Now and in time to be,
Wherever green is worn,
Are changed, changed utterly:
A terrible beauty is born.   80

Questions

1 What are your initial thoughts about this poem?
Look, for example, at its mood and its message.

2 The second stanza describes the three
revolutionaries who are only named at the very end
of the poem. For example, 'this man' (line 24)

is Patrick Pearse and 'this other' (line 26) is
Thomas MacDonagh. How does Yeats describe
them? How is language used to shape this
impression? Do they sound like revolutionary
heroes or something else? Why does he do this?

»

3 What is your explanation of the extended metaphor of the stone in stanza 3? Think about the political passions of the people in the poem to guide your response.

4 There are a number of rhetorical questions in this poem. What effect do they create?

5 'A terrible beauty' is a famous phrase that has echoed through the last hundred years as a way of describing the twentieth century. Why do you think it has had this impact? How can the terrible be beautiful and vice versa?

6 Yeats's attitude towards the Easter Rising is complex. Draw up a mind map diagram in which you present some of the views that you think he had. (Courage, and horror at violence would be good places to start.) Do you think Yeats believed that the deaths at Easter were ultimately worth it?

7 Re-read the section on new historicist criticism in Unit 1 (pages 17–18) and also the political context of 'Easter 1916'. If you were to pursue a new historicist reading of this poem, what would be your three main points?

8 Do you think political activism is an appropriate subject for poetry? Why or why not?

9 The people in this poem died violently for a political cause. What are our society's conflicting positions about such people in the early twenty-first century? How do our contemporary views affect our reading of the poem?

Activities

1 Read some of the lyrics of the rock group Midnight Oil, such as 'Beds Are Burning' and 'The Dead Heart' (Aboriginal issues), 'Blue Sky Mine' (asbestos poisoning) and 'US Forces' and 'Read About It' (US and Australian relations). The lyrics can be found at the LyricsDownload site (www.lyricsdownload.com). What do the lyrics say about each issue and how effectively do they make their point?

2 Choose a major political event (either national or international) that has occurred over the last decade. Research it. Establish the conflicting feelings that you could have about the event. Then write a serious poem about this event and the conflicting feelings.

Yeats's horror at violence reappears in the poem 'The Second Coming', also published in *Michael Robartes and the Dancer* (1921).

THE SECOND COMING

Turning and turning in the widening gyre
The falcon cannot hear the falconer;

»

Things fall apart; the centre cannot hold;
Mere anarchy is loosed upon the world,
The blood-dimmed tide is loosed, and everywhere   5
The ceremony of innocence is drowned;
The best lack all convictions while the worst
Are full of passionate intensity.

Surely some revelation is at hand;
Surely the Second Coming is at hand.   10
The Second Coming! Hardly are those words out
When a vast image out of *Spiritus Mundi*
Troubles my sight: somewhere in sands of the desert
A shape with lion body and the head of a man,
A gaze blank and pitiless as the sun,   15
Is moving its slow thighs, while all about it
Reel shadows of the indignant desert birds.
The darkness drops again; but now I know
That twenty centuries of stony sleep
Were vexed to nightmare by a rocking cradle,   20
And what rough beast, its hour come round at last,
Slouches towards Bethlehem to be born?

Questions

1 What is your emotional reaction to this poem?

2 Why do you think Yeats has chosen a falcon
rather than another bird? What is the falcon's
relationship to the falconer? Why, then, is it
significant that the falcon has moved out of
hearing?

3 Explore why the line 'Things fall apart; the
centre cannot hold' (line 3) could be a powerful
line in the years after the horror of World War I.

4 The second coming of Christ is prophesised in
the Bible in Matthew 24:1–31. St John described
the beast of the Apocalypse in the Book of
Revelation. How are these prophecies used in
this poem? How is the beast described in this
poem?

5 Look at diction, imagery and symbols to discuss
the effect of the last line on the poem as a whole.

'The Second Coming': an alternative reading

According to Edward Malins, in his *A Preface to Yeats*, there are two ways of reading this
poem:

¤ without knowledge of Yeats's personal system of belief

¤ with some knowledge of it.

The preceding questions presumed no knowledge of Yeats's system of belief. Below we have included some elements of his personal belief or imagery system so that the poem can be analysed further. Yeats published a prose work called *A Vision* in 1925 that contained an explanation of many of these personal symbols and ideas:

¤ The gyres (line 1) are two spirals in the form of cones, one the mirror of the other. Yeats used these figures to illustrate this theory of cyclical patterns in history, where time winds and unwinds. If Yeats's account of the cycles of history—the 'gyres'—is followed through, then the twentieth century was going to be a crucial stage in history. It would probably be anarchic, but ultimately would be followed by an age in which order, joy and beauty will be restored, if we follow the logic of cycles.

¤ The falcon (line 2) is associated with intellect and logic in Yeats's symbolism. The departure of the falcon demonstrates the break-up of the present historical cycle, which has been 'vexed to nightmare' (line 20).

¤ When the outward gyre reaches its termination ('the centre cannot hold'), the Christian phase (ushered in by the nativity—the 'rocking cradle' in line 20) will be replaced by a contrary movement.

¤ A 'rough beast' (line 21)—the anti-Christ—will be born. In the poem the reference to Bethlehem as the beast's destination parodies Christian hope. The end of one phase of culture marks the beginning of another phase. The new phase will be the opposite, or reversal, of the preceding phase.

¤ A new age is ushered in by a birth; for example, Helen of Troy, Christ and now a 'rough beast'.

There is a sense in this work that an apocalypse (end of the world) is approaching for western culture. The innocence and holiness of the nativity is replaced by the image of a savage god born out of a hallucinatory desert at that focal point in time when, in Yeats's gyres, one cycle intersects with another. This beast-God heralds and echoes the irrational destructiveness of all wars.

Questions

1 Now that you have read the explanation of Yeats's personal symbols and visions:

a What aspects of your analysis of 'The Second Coming' stay the same?

b What changes or becomes more sophisticated?

2 Contrast your two readings of the text. Which do you prefer?

Activity

Find out more about the prophecies about 'the beast' and 'the second coming'.

a Read the opening section of the Book of Revelation. This can be found at the »

University of Virginia Library's Electronic Text Center (etext.lib.virginia.edu/ebooks/ subjects/subjects-bible.html). What imagery and resources of language does it use to reinforce its message? In what ways does the author (St John) maximise the likelihood that his audience will be affected by the message that he brings them?

b With this knowledge, what further analysis can you make of Yeats's poem?

c What cultural and/or personal values and beliefs would someone need to hold in order to take these writings very seriously? What cultural and/ or personal values and beliefs would someone hold who did not?

d How has contemporary culture used and exploited these prophecies in the Book of Revelation? You could begin by pooling your knowledge of films such as *End of Days*, *The Seventh Seal*, *The Omen*, *Constantine* and *The Second Coming*.

Joyce and *Ulysses*

James Joyce (1882–1941)

Yeats, being an elitist, was interested in the heroic, folkloric and nationalistic. On the other hand, James Joyce, his fellow Irish modernist, believed that literature should relentlessly represent the exact opposite: the experiences of ordinary life. He did not do this by simply listing all the banal experiences like a shopping list. Instead, he found radical new ways of expressing the consciousness and experience of ordinary life, which turned out to be anything but ordinary.

James Joyce was born in Dublin in 1882 and attended school in county Kildare. He was raised Catholic, educated by Jesuits and seemed destined for the priesthood. However, he renounced Catholicism, despite attending University College, Dublin, where he earned his degree in modern languages in 1902. At about this time he fell in love with the fetchingly named Nora Barnacle and they married. In 1904, they left Dublin to live and work abroad for the rest of their lives. Nevertheless, Dublin remained the setting for all Joyce's fiction, and it really does operate as the heart of his work. His main works before *Ulysses* (1922) were *Dubliners* (1914) and *A Portrait of the Artist as a Young Man* (1914–15), both of which tried to use language to stress the importance (or 'privilege') of ordinary experience.

The US journal *The Little Review* started publishing instalments of *Ulysses* in 1918. However, the Society for the Suppression of Vice charged the magazine in 1920 with publishing pornography. The pornographic sections in question included Joyce's frank accounts of the *Ulysses* character Bloom masturbating and going to the toilet. *The Little Review* stopped the serialisation. This made Joyce even more determined to continue to introduce radical innovations in style. No publisher in Britain or the USA would go near the novel, fearing legal action. Finally, Sylvia Beach of the Paris bookshop Shakespeare and Co. agreed to publish the book, and did so in 1922. In 1933, the ban on *Ulysses* was overturned and Random House in the USA proceeded to publish the notorious, scandalous book.

Joyce dedicated the next seventeen years to what was to become *Finnegans Wake*. This difficult novel is based on one night in the life of a character who, because he never quite wakes up, isn't bound by the linguistic and sense rules of usual daytime consciousness. During all this time, Joyce was concerned about his failing eyesight, which was not arrested by twenty-seven operations on his eyes. The worsening mental health of his daughter, Lucia, was also a great concern to him. When *Finnegans Wake* was published in 1939 it received a lot of negative criticism, which affected him deeply. He died in 1941 in Zurich.

A photo taken on Bloomsday, an annual celebration held in honour of Joyce's *Ulysses*.

Ulysses

Ulysses (all 600-odd pages of it) is about a single, ordinary day in the lives of Stephen Dedalus and Leopold Bloom. Molly and Leopold Bloom are a middle-aged married couple without children. Leopold, an earthy Jewish advertising agent, carries on with ordinary business during the day. After a morning routine of bath, toilet and breakfast, he wanders through Dublin, spending time at a funeral, a pub and a newspaper office, having lunch and so on. Molly stays at home in bed. The younger and better-educated Stephen Dedalus (the schoolteacher from *A Portrait of the Artist as a Young Man*) has returned to Dublin for his mother's funeral and is in the process of rejecting his faith and his father. He begins his day at his Martello tower home and then goes to the school, the seaside, the library, the pub and a brothel. Stephen and Leopold meet in the evening after not quite bumping into each other all day. There is a sense of father-and-son intimacy after their separate wandering. Eventually, Leopold is reunited with Molly after Stephen refuses his invitation to stay.

Ulysses uses parody, pastiche, literary allusions, punning and ventriloquism to create a very deep portrait of human experience over a single day. It is also loosely structured to correspond to the main episodes and characters of Homer's *The Odyssey*. The ironic parallel could not be more stark between the heroic adventures of Ulysses around the Aegean for twenty years and the average meanderings of Leopold and Steven around Dublin for a single day. *Ulysses* also includes an encyclopedic view of Dublin and its people, native Irish mythology and history.

The novel starts with Stephen's day in a mainly comprehensible way. This does not last long. The central technique Joyce uses for conveying the characters' internal experience moment by moment throughout the day is called 'stream of consciousness'. This involves writing down exactly what is going through the character's head, moment by moment. Every spontaneous image, emotion and memory all land on the page in the same logical–illogical way that they go through the brain. The last eight paragraphs, documenting Molly Bloom's thoughts as she lies in bed, last for almost eighty pages and have no punctuation marks whatsoever. This was a whole new and innovative way of writing reality—to abandon syntax, and focus instead on the strange inconsequential associations and unusual rhythms of internal life, which (mostly) produce their own cohesion.

The reaction to *Ulysses* has been hugely varied. Those readers who persevere to the book's end can emerge feeling amazed or dazed or infuriated or exhilarated. It is fairly safe to say that few books in English literature have been so frequently thrown across rooms, treasured, stamped on, and lovingly read aloud.

Activities

1 During your next shower, listen to all your thoughts as you have them.

a How are they structured?

b How logical, coherent or structured are they?

Immediately after your shower try to write down all the thoughts that you had. Write in a realistic fashion; for instance, with no tidying, neatening and structuring. Pretend a microphone was recording what you thought.

c What difficulties did you have in writing them down?

d How different is this writing from the writing that you generally read in novels? Which one better describes 'reality'?

2 Write the stream of consciousness of one of the following situations:

a walking into your English class

b robbing a bank

c your first kiss

d being in a car accident

e leaving home.

What difficulties did you have in representing these thoughts in writing?

ULYSSES: EXTRACT I

Stately, plump Buck Mulligan came from the stairhead, bearing a bowl of lather on which a mirror and a razor lay crossed. A yellow dressing-gown, ungirdled, was sustained gently behind him by the mild morning air. He held the bowl aloft and intoned:

—*Introibo ad altare Dei.* [I will go into the alter of God.]

Halted, he peered down the dark winding stairs and called out coarsely:

—Come up, Kinch! Come up, you fearful jesuit.

Solemnly he came forward and mounted the round gunrest. He faced about and blessed gravely thrice the tower, the surrounding country and the awaking mountains. Then, catching sight of Stephen Dedalus, he bent towards him and made rapid crosses in the air, gurgling in his throat and shaking his head. Stephen Dedalus, displeased and sleepy, leaned his arms on the top of the staircase and looked coldly at the shaking gurgling face that blessed him, equine in its length, and at the light untonsured hair, grained and hued like pale oak.

1 What is difficult about this passage? What is comprehensible about it?

2 Does knowing that Joyce had a background in theology (religion) influence your reading of this scene? If so, how?

3 Are there any images or descriptions in this passage that you find striking? Explain your answer.

The extract below refers to Sirens, who were enchanting and deadly sea-maidens that sang to seamen so beautifully that they would jump overboard trying to reach them, and drown. Homer's Odysseus (Ulysses) has his crew tie him to the mast rather than stop his ears to the sound of the Sirens' call. The focus in this section is on sound. This is appropriate as is it set in a concert room.

ULYSSES: EXTRACT 2

Bronze by gold heard the hoofirons, steelyringing.
Imperthnthn thnthnthn.
Chips, picking chips off rocky thumbnail, chips.
Horrid! And gold flushed more.
A husky fifenote blew.
Blew. Blue bloom is on the.
Goldpinnacled hair.
A jumping rose on satiny breasts of satin, rose of Castille.
Trilling, trilling: Idolores.
Peep! Who's in the ... peepofgold?
Tink cried to bronze in pity.
And a call, pure, long and throbbing. Longindying call.
Decoy. Soft word. But look: The bright stars fade. Notes chirruping
answer. O rose! Castile. The morn is breaking.
Jingle jingle jaunted jingling.
Coin rang. Clock clacked.
Avowal. *Sonnez.* I could. Rebound of garter. Not leave thee. Smack.
La cloche! Thigh smack. Avowal. Warm. Sweetheart, goodbye!
Jingle. Bloo.
Boomed crashing chords. When love absorbs. War! War!
The tympanum.

Questions

1 In groups, try to make sense of the passage. Focus on what is happening, what is being felt and what information is being conveyed. Compare your answers. If you can, come to some sort of consensus in the class.

2 How is sound conveyed in this extract? What language techniques are being used?

3 What is your overall opinion about this extract?

ULYSSES: EXTRACT 3
This extract is a record of the stream of consciousness of the character Molly while lying in bed.

… O that awful deepdown torrent O and the sea the sea crimson sometimes like fire and the glorious sunsets and the figtrees in the Alameda gardens yes and all the queer little streets and the pink and blue and yellow houses and the rosegardens and the jessamine and geraniums and cactuses and Gibraltar as a girl where I was a Flower of the mountain yes when I put the rose in my hair like the Andalusian girls used or shall I wear a red yes and how he kissed me under the Moorish wall and I thought well as well him as another and then I asked him with my eyes to ask again yes and then he asked me would I yes to say yes my mountain flower and first I put my arms around him yes and drew him down to me so he could feel my breasts all perfume yes and his heart was going like mad and yes I said yes I will Yes.

Questions

1 What is your first impression of this piece of writing?

2 What is Molly thinking about? How are her memories conveyed? What dominates her memory?

3 In your view, does Joyce find a language that is suitable for Molly's expressions of her sexual experience? If so, in what way? You may want to think about the rhythm of sentences, the lack of punctuation and the specific images used.

4 How effectively do you think this passage captures the stream of consciousness of someone lying in her bed?

5 How does this passage compare to the stream of consciousness piece you wrote earlier?

6 What language features provide structure in this extract?

7 What do you think about the repetition of the word 'yes'?

Overall questions

1 On the basis of these extracts, what is your personal response to Joyce's writing? Do you suspect that this writing is fraudulent nonsense, a hugely significant advance in the way writing represents experience, or something in between? Should we canonise Joyce, dismiss him or do something in between? How is your own response shaped by everything you have read up until now, and your own expectations when reading?

2 Do you think language is capable of conveying reality and experience in the way that Joyce and other modern writers are attempting or are we coming to the limits of what language can do?

Activities

1 Rewrite either extract 2 or extract 3 as a more 'traditional' text. What is gained and what is lost?

2 Use a search engine, such as Google (images. google.com) to locate copyright-free images that convey what Joyce was attempting in extracts 2 or 3. Create a collage of these images. What is gained and what is lost from this alternative representation of the characters' experiences? Could you represent the experience using sounds instead? If so, how?

Woolf and *To the Lighthouse*

Virginia Woolf (1882–1941)

Adeline Virginia Stephen was born in 1882 into a large, talented and difficult family. She had a productive, richly creative and sometimes tragic life, struggling with a difficult childhood, a number of significant personal losses and mental illness. Unlike the solitary expatriate Joyce, Woolf was part of a vibrant modernist network—the Bloomsbury Group—a set of intellectual and artistic friends who met at the house she shared with her sister in Bloomsbury, London. The group opposed Victorian puritanism and embraced the modernist fashion for experimentation in literature and art. The set included EM Forster and her husband-to-be, Leonard Woolf, whom she married in 1912. The Woolfs set up the Hogarth Press, which published TS Eliot and later Sigmund Freud.

Virginia Woolf.

In an essay called 'Modern Fiction', Woolf wrote that each day 'the 'mind receives a myriad of impressions—trivial, fantastic, evanescent or engraved with the sharpness of steel'. The novelist, attempting to work with this 'incessant shower of innumerable atoms', is forced to recognise that a new style is required. Woolf was interested in conveying something of the 'luminous halo' of life, which she saw as different from the aims of previous fiction, such as Victorian realism. As a result, she moved away from materialistic accounts of the external world and towards a kind of intensely poetic, lyrical impressionism.

In 1925, she represented the consciousness of one woman in one day in *Mrs Dalloway*. In 1927, *To the Lighthouse* confirmed and refined her modernist style, which was then extended to *The Waves* (1931). One of her main aims was to reduce the external elements of her novels as far as possible and increase the internal elements. Like Joyce, Woolf pioneered new techniques to capture the characters' typical internal experience—in her case, a use of extreme free indirect speech in order to capture the inner life of her characters. Large caves of memory and reflection open out from the characters' present moment when some small events might be happening in the outside world, such as watching cricket, or knitting. Woolf used this technique to deal with issues such as the importance of art, desire and revelation in everyday life.

Woolf is often seen as more accessible than Joyce, although equally important. She believed that art should communicate. Woolf also believed that there was a specific kind of experience that was feminine. She saw that women's experience had not historically been represented because it was different from male experience and required a different style. Mrs Dalloway's experience in *Mrs Dalloway* introduced into fiction the idea that female experience was specific and valuable. Female experience was also a topic Woolf wrote and spoke about very powerfully, most notably her published lectures to Cambridge women students, *A Room of One's Own* (1929).

Throughout her life, Woolf was known as a lively wit. However, her recurrent mental illness always lay beneath. In 1941, she was terrified about World War II and feared losing her mind permanently. Apparently, rather than be a burden to her husband, she chose to drown herself in the river Ouse.

Activity

Watch the film *The Hours*. (You may prefer to concentrate only on the sections of the film that feature Virginia Woolf.)

a How does it represent Virginia Woolf?

b Are there aspects of her from the biography above that the film downplays?

c What does the film suggest about the experience of being female in the twentieth century?

d Read extracts from Woolf's *Mrs Dalloway* to familiarise yourself with that novel. What are the ways in which the film interacts with (that is, relates to) *Mrs Dalloway* and how effectively do you think these interactions are achieved?

e What issues are there in using the textual form of a popular Hollywood film as a way of gaining an impression of an important modern writer?

To the Lighthouse

In *To the Lighthouse*, the setting is the house used for holidays by Mr and Mrs Ramsay. The novel dispenses with plot and is organised in three parts dominated by two symbols. The first is the lighthouse out at sea. The second is the painter Lily Briscoe's painting of the house, with Mrs Ramsay sitting in the window with her son James. What would normally be seen as major events, such as deaths of family members, are secondary to symbols. Thus, these incidents only appear in square brackets in the narrative; for example, '[A shell exploded. Twenty or thirty young men were blown up in France, among them Andrew Ramsay, whose death, mercifully, was instantaneous.]'.

The first part of the novel is dominated by the intuitive, imaginative and reassuring Mrs Ramsay. The mysterious lighthouse flashing through the darkness is associated with her. The second part of the novel corresponds to the war years 1914–18. In it Mrs Ramsay dies, and the pages concern the empty house, which is subject to the flux of time. In part three, Lily Briscoe seeks to use art to anchor the constantly changing relationships of people and objects in a single painting.

TO THE LIGHTHOUSE: EXTRACT I

This is from the first part of the novel called 'The Window'. In it Mrs Ramsay reflects on a dinner party she has just hosted for her family and guests.

It was windy, so that the leaves now and then brushed open a star, and the stars themselves seemed to be shaking and darting light and trying to flash out between the edges of the leaves. Yes, that was done then, accomplished; and as with all things done, became solemn. Now one thought of it, cleared of chatter and emotion, it seemed always to have been, only was shown now and so being shown, struck everything into stability. They would, she thought, going on again, however long they lived, come back to this night; this moon; this wind; this house: and to her too. It flattered her, where she was most susceptible of flattery, to think how, wound about in their hearts, however long they lived she would be woven; and this, and this, and this, she thought, going upstairs, laughing, but affectionately, at the sofa on the landing (her mother's); at the rocking-chair (her father's); at the map of the Hebrides. All that would be revived again in the lives of Paul and Minta; 'the Rayleys'—she tried the new name over; and she felt, with her hand on the nursery door, that community of feeling with other people which emotion gives as if the walls of partition had become so thin that practically (the feeling was one of relief and happiness) it was all one stream, and chairs, tables, maps, were hers, were theirs, it did not matter whose, and Paul and Minta would carry it on when she was dead.

Questions

1 What is your overall impression of the writing?

2 What is happening in this extract?

3 Explore how this passage reflects the modernist concerns of Woolf that are explained in the introduction.

Activities

1 Break into groups. Each group should spend some time commenting on one of the following points:

a the descriptive quality of the passage

b the 'snapshot' of what is in Mrs Ramsay's mind

c the importance of stability

d the importance of relations with others

e the kinds of details described in the house

f the quality of Woolf's sentences.

Then come back together into one class and report your findings.

2 Alternative readings:

a How would you describe Mrs Ramsay?

b Experiment with re-reading and rewriting this passage but with the main character as a man: *Mr* Ramsay.

c How would you describe the Mr Ramsay you have just written? Is the impression any different from that of Mrs Ramsay? If your impression of Mr Ramsay is at all different, what does this tell you about your reading of gender?

TO THE LIGHTHOUSE: EXTRACT 2

This sequence comes from part three of To the Lighthouse, *and is narrated from the point of view of Lily Briscoe. Lily, a painter, is trying to finish, from memory, a portrait of Mrs Ramsay with her young son James. She is recalling days before the war and Mrs Ramsay's death. At the same time, James (now older) and Mr Ramsay are finally rowing to the lighthouse.*

'Like a work of art,' she repeated, looking from her canvas to the drawing-room steps and back again. She must rest for a moment. And, resting, looking from one to the other vaguely, the old question which traversed the sky of the soul perpetually, the vast, the general question which was apt to particularise itself at such moments as these, when she released faculties that had been on the strain, stood over her, paused over her, darkened over her. What is the meaning of life? That was all—a simple question; one that tended to close in on one with years. The great revelation had never come. The great revelation perhaps never did come. Instead there were little daily miracles, illuminations, matches struck unexpectedly in the dark; here was one. This, that, and the other; herself and Charles Tansley and the breaking wave; Mrs Ramsay bringing them together; Mrs Ramsay saying, 'Life stand still here'; Mrs Ramsay making of the moment something permanent (as in another sphere Lily herself tried to make of the moment something permanent)—this was of the nature of a revelation. In the midst of chaos there was shape; this eternal passing and flowing (she looked at the clouds going and the leaves shaking) was struck into stability. Life stand still here, Mrs Ramsay said. 'Mrs Ramsay! Mrs Ramsay!' she repeated. She owed this revelation to her.

All was silence …

1 What kinds of ideas seem to occur to Lily Briscoe in this passage?

2 What turns out to be the answer to the meaning of life?

3 How does this passage employ modernist techniques?

4 How is the quality of Lily's thinking different from Mrs Ramsay's (from extract 1)?

5 Re-read the section on feminist criticism in Unit 1 (pages 15–16).
   a What concepts do you think help you understand both extracts?
   b Do you think that Woolf creates a specific language to represent female experience?
   c What seems to be the important aspects of life for these female characters? How does this relate to the figure of the female artist in Woolf's text?

Eliot and 'The Love Song of J Alfred Prufrock'

TS Eliot (1888–1965)

Thomas Stearns Eliot was born far from the cultural centres of modernism, in St Louis, Missouri. After being educated in Boston, notably Harvard University, he studied philosophy in Marburg, Paris and Oxford. He married an English woman in June 1915 and settled in England, where his first volume of poetry, *Prufrock and other Observations*, appeared in 1917.

Commentators such as Ezra Pound thought that this volume, particularly the title poem, established modern poetry in English. Ezra Pound and Eliot went on to have an important and fruitful relationship, especially in terms of Eliot's famous long modernist poem, *The Waste Land*. Eliot is famous for his coining of the term 'objective correlative'. This term describes a certain kind of symbol—a concrete or specific situation, location or thing that evokes a particular emotion in the reader (as opposed to attempting to describe the emotion itself). This technique was part of Eliot's mission to make great poetry 'impersonal'.

Apart from his contribution to modernist poetry, he also had an important role as editor, critic and literary scholar. He almost single-handedly revived the reputation of the metaphysical poet John Donne. As a director of the publishing house Faber and Faber he built up a very influential list of modern poets. His reputation and power made him something of a 'Godfather' of modern poetry.

In the early 1930s he turned to drama, with plays such as *Murder in the Cathedral*. He won the Nobel Prize for Literature in 1948 and married in 1957, at the sprightly age of sixty-nine. He died in 1965. If he had lived another decade or two he would have seen his classic book of children's verse *Old Possum's Book of Practical Cats* (1939) turned into the upbeat and stupendously successful Andrew Lloyd Weber musical *Cats*. This adaptation may or may not have pleased the twentieth century's foremost chronicler of modernist angst.

'The Love Song of J Alfred Prufrock'

His early poetry, including 'The Love Song of J Alfred Prufrock' ('Prufrock'), deals with spiritually exhausted people who exist in an impersonal modern city. 'Prufrock' was written in 1911. It is famous for a range of reasons: for the intensity and complexity of feeling that is conveyed, its command of the rhythms of colloquial speech, and also for the way in which it seemed to capture the alienated, sensitive and paralysed male speaker in a bewildering modern world. It is also famous for what became Eliot's trademark modernist interest in fragmentation and juxtaposition.

'Prufrock' is a dramatic monologue in which there is a single poetic speaker saying something to a silent, assumed audience. Prufrock is an elusive and complex character dramatised through a kaleidoscope of scenes and manners of speech. In it, Prufrock is speaking to himself in silent isolation, rather than directing his thoughts to any other person. He is engaged in anxious self-scrutiny. This is poetry that is a long way in form and theme from rapt Romantic poets in awe of sublime landscapes.

A brief reading of 'Prufrock'

At the beginning of this 'love song', Prufrock delivers an invitation that is ambiguous and rather unattractive, evoking an atmosphere of isolation and discomfort, tedium and even suffering. The tone of the speaker is also strange, both badgering and halting, in a rather anti-Romantic and despairing mode. The poem progresses both downward and inward, until we arrive at a series of water images that are confusing and about which Prufrock is eventually inarticulate and pessimistic. The poem is full of unnerving images of enervation and paralysis, such as the evening described as 'etherised', immobile. One part of Prufrock would like to be startled out of his meaningless life, but to accomplish this he would have to risk disturbing his 'universe'—indeed, leaving his room. The latter part of the poem captures his sense of defeat for failing to act courageously. Hamlet, the great procrastinator of western literature, serves as a parallel, but Prufrock decides that he is not even that decisive, he is like Hamlet's foolish adviser Polonius, or an even lesser character, such as 'an attendant lord'.

THE LOVE SONG OF J ALFRED PRUFROCK

Let us go then, you and I,
When the evening is spread out against the sky
Like a patient etherised upon a table;
Let us go, through certain half-deserted streets,
The muttering retreats   5
Of restless nights in one-night cheap hotels
And sawdust restaurants with oyster shells:
Streets that follow like a tedious argument
Of insidious intent

》

To lead you to an overwhelming question ...   10
Oh, do not ask, 'What is it?'
Let us go and make our visit.

In the room the women come and go
Talking of Michelangelo.

The yellow fog that rubs its back upon the window panes,   15
The yellow smoke that rubs its muzzle on the windowpanes
Licked its tongue into the corners of the evening,
Lingered upon the pools that stand in drains,
Let fall upon its back the soot that falls from chimneys,
Slipped by the terrace, made a sudden leap,   20
And seeing that it was a soft October night,
Curled once about the house, and fell asleep.

And indeed there will be time
For the yellow smoke that slides along the street,
Rubbing its back upon the window panes;   25
There will be time, there will be time
To prepare a face to meet the faces that you meet;
There will be time to murder and create,
And time for all the works and days of hands
That lift and drop a question on your plate;   30
Time for you and time for me,
And time yet for a hundred indecisions,
And for a hundred visions and revisions,
Before the taking of a toast and tea.

In the room the women come and go   35
Talking of Michelangelo.

And indeed there will be time
To wonder, 'Do I dare?' and, 'Do I dare?'
Time to turn back and descend the stair,
With a bald spot in the middle of my hair—   40
(They will say: 'How his hair is growing thin!')
My morning coat, my collar mounting firmly to the chin,
My necktie rich and modest, but asserted by a simple pin—
(They will say: 'But how his arms and legs are thin!')
Do I dare   45
Disturb the universe?
In a minute there is time

                                                                                »

For decisions and revisions which a minute will reverse.
For I have known them all already, known them all:—
Have known the evenings, mornings, afternoons,   50
I have measured out my life with coffee spoons;
I know the voices dying with a dying fall
Beneath the music from a farther room.
So how should I presume?

And I have known the eyes already, known them all—   55
The eyes that fix you in a formulated phrase,
And when I am formulated, sprawling on a pin,
When I am pinned and wriggling on the wall,
Then how should I begin
To spit out all the butt-ends of my days and ways?   60
And how should I presume?

And I have known the arms already, known them all—
Arms that are braceleted and white and bare
(But in the lamplight, downed with light brown hair!)
Is it perfume from a dress   65
That makes me so digress?
Arms that lie along a table, or wrap about a shawl.
And should I then presume?
And how should I begin?

Shall I say, I have gone at dusk through narrow streets   70
And watched the smoke that rises from the pipes
Of lonely men in shirt-sleeves, leaning out of windows? ...

I should have been a pair of ragged claws
Scuttling across the floors of silent seas.

And the afternoon, the evening, sleeps so peacefully!   75
Smoothed by long fingers,
Asleep ... tired ... or it malingers,
Stretched on the floor, here beside you and me.
Should I, after tea and cakes and ices,
Have the strength to force the moment to its crisis?   80
But though I have wept and fasted, wept and prayed,
Though I have seen my head (grown slightly bald) brought in upon a
platter,

»

I am no prophet—and here's no great matter;
I have seen the moment of my greatness flicker,
And I have seen the eternal Footman hold my coat, and snicker,   85
And in short, I was afraid.

And would it have been worth it, after all,
After the cups, the marmalade, the tea,
Among the porcelain, among some talk of you and me,
Would it have been worth while,   90
To have bitten off the matter with a smile,
To have squeezed the universe into a ball
To roll it toward some overwhelming question,
To say: 'I am Lazarus, come from the dead,
Come back to tell you all, I shall tell you all'—   95
If one, settling a pillow by her head,
Should say: 'That is not what I meant at all.
That is not it, at all.'

And would it have been worth it, after all,
Would it have been worth while,   100
After the sunsets and the dooryards and the sprinkled streets,
After the novels, after the teacups, after the skirts that trail along
    the floor—
And this, and so much more?—
It is impossible to say just what I mean!
But as if a magic lantern threw the nerves in patterns on a screen: 105
Would it have been worth while
If one, settling a pillow or throwing off a shawl,
And turning toward the window, should say:
'That is not it at all,
That is not what I meant, at all.'   110

No! I am not Prince Hamlet, nor was meant to be;
Am an attendant lord, one that will do
To swell a progress, start a scene or two,
Advise the prince; no doubt, an easy tool,
Deferential, glad to be of use,   115
Politic, cautious, and meticulous;
Full of high sentence, but a bit obtuse;
At times, indeed, almost ridiculous—
Almost, at times, the Fool.

»

I grow old ... I grow old ...   120
I shall wear the bottoms of my trousers rolled.

Shall I part my hair behind? Do I dare to eat a peach?
I shall wear white flannel trousers, and walk upon the beach.
I have heard the mermaids singing, each to each.

I do not think that they will sing to me.   125

I have seen them riding seaward on the waves
Combing the white hair of the waves blown back
When the wind blows the water white and black.

We have lingered in the chambers of the sea
By sea-girls wreathed with seaweed red and brown   130
Till human voices wake us, and we drown.

Questions

1 What is your overall impression of this poem?
   What mood does it create for you?

2 What impression do we gain of the city in lines
   1–10? How is this impression created?

3 In what ways is the fog personified in lines
   15–25? What animal does it evoke to you? Why?

4 Re-read the introductory notes about 'objective
   correlative' (page 187). Find an example of it
   in the poem and explain why you think it is an
   objective correlative.

5 How is a sense of uncertainly built up in lines
   28–34?

6 What sort of impression does Prufrock give of
   himself in lines 37–44?

7 'Do I dare disturb the universe' (lines 45–6) is
   one of the more famous lines of the twentieth

century. Why do you think this is so? In what
ways does it encapsulate (sum up) the modern
outlook?

8 How does Prufrock characterise his relationship
   with other people in lines 49–69? What aspects
   of modernism does this relate to?

9 Why do you think that Prufrock feels he should
   be 'a pair of ragged claws' in line 73?

10 In your own words, explain what Prufrock's
   doubts are about in lines 87–98.

11 Pick a line from among lines 99–110 that you
   think best encapsulates the modern condition.
   Justify your choice of that line. You may prefer to
   pick two consecutive lines.

12 What is the effect of the last line? How
   effectively does it round off the poem?

   »

13 Why do you think Prufrock sees himself as a marginal attendant rather than as a central Hamlet? What characteristics do you think he wants to display and how does this add to our understanding of Prufrock?

14 How does Eliot use the language of poetry to convey a sense of urban alienation throughout this poem? In what ways does it reflect or challenge the spirit of the early twentieth century (see the 'Context of the period' section at the start of this unit)?

15 Identify sections that you think convey a sense of sexual anxiety or physical uncomfortableness. What are their effect on the overall poem?

16 Compare this poem with William Wordsworth's 'Tintern Abbey' (pages 96–100). Which one do you prefer and why? How is your preference affected by your general attitude, likes and dislikes? If you could put one of these two poems in a space shuttle to send to a distant species as a representative of earth's poetry which one would you choose and why?

Activities

1 Choose a section of the poem and get different members of the class to read it in different tones of voice, such as strong, weak, afraid and angry. Which one do you find most effective? Why?

2 The desires about which Prufrock explicitly speaks are social and intellectual ones. In what ways are other kinds of desires (such as sexual) expressed in the poem; for example, by the use of symbol or metaphor? How does this focus upon his unconscious desires affect your overall interpretation of the poem? Before answering this, re-read the section about psychoanalytic criticism in Unit 1 (pages 16–17).

3 Imagine that you are able to make a one-minute animation of 'The Love Song of J Alfred Prufrock'. You are not committed to the animation being chronologically the same as the poem. What images will you use from the poem and how will you represent them? Storyboard the animation.

4 Make a tableau or a silent dramatisation of four sections of the poem. Present them to the rest of the class one after the other without revealing which sections you are dramatising. See how many of them can be identified by the other members of the class.

1 Imagine that you just finished the modernism unit in this book when suddenly you are unexpectedly transported back in time. You find yourself in Thomas Malory's prison cell, just as he is finishing writing the *Morte D'Arthur* (extracted on pages 47–8). He asks you your opinion of his work. You tell him that his work is okay, but not a patch on some of the more modern texts you have read. Naturally jealous, he asks you for advice on how to turn the *Morte D'Arthur* into something more modern; something that Virginia Woolf or TS Eliot would be proud of. Advise him, and experiment with rewriting some of his piece so that it is more 'modern'. In your answer reflect on how the changed time period would lead to changed values being reflected in the text.

2 'Modern texts are fascinating because they are about the mapping of an unstable and frightening new world.' Do you agree? Where, for you, does the interest in modern texts lie?

3 Only one of the major modernists we have looked at originally came from England (although they all wrote their major works in England). Conrad was Polish, Yeats and Joyce were Irish and Eliot was American. In addition, Woolf, the only English person, was a woman. What does this lead you to speculate about attempting to write literature that is a break from the cultural norm? (Consider also Renaissance and Romantic literature if you can.)

4 Imagine you are a high-energy motivational speaker and life coach who is convinced that a healthy diet and lots of exercise are the answers to all personal problems. You really have no time for endless introspection and think that this just weighs people down in the busy, bustling twenty-first century. TS Eliot and one other author send you samples of their work and then they come to you for some life coaching.

Script the meeting that takes place when they enter your 'high-motivation studio'. The script should include:
- an alternative reading of their texts from your point of view, showing where you disapprove of their modern assumptions
- a chance for them to respond.

5 Explain how philosophical, cultural and literary values have shaped the modern texts that you have studied.

Bushmen, Stars & the Big Smoke

AUSTRALIAN LITERATURE

Highlights

¶ *Wild brumbies escape*

¶ *Poisonous snake menaces woman*

¶ *Woman watches lovers at Watsons Bay*

¶ *Men catch stars from row boat*

¶ *Fraud poet exposed*

Note: Australian History is compulsory in schools in each state. This unit draws upon some of the students' background knowledge of the historical context of Australian literature.

Outcomes

By the end of this unit you should have:

¤ developed an understanding of the relationship between the texts and their Australian context (including the literary, cultural and historical contexts)

¤ gained an appreciation of the way in which the texts can be seen as cultural products of both their authors and their society

¤ engaged in detailed textual interpretation of a number of Australian pieces and developed an understanding of how language forms and/or techniques shape the meaning of these pieces

¤ challenged and evaluated some of the cultural assumptions that exist in Australian texts and considered 'alternative' readings of some texts come to a personal view about valuing the texts and Australian literature based on your own context and preferences

¤ engaged with the texts in a number of ways, including writing essays and poems, participating in group activities and using visual representation

¤ gained enjoyment through exposure to the texts and their ideas and contexts.

Harpur and 'A Midsummer Noon in the Australian Forest'

Paterson and 'The Man from Snowy River'

Lawson and 'The Drover's Wife'

Mackellar and 'My Country'

Richardson and *The Fortunes of Richard Mahoney*

Visions of the outback

AUSTRALIAN LITERATURE

The big smoke: modernism and urban Australian

Newer voices in poetry

Contemporary novels

Slessor and *Five Bells*

Stead and *For Love Alone*

The Ern Malley affair

Wright and 'At Cooloolah'

Harwood and 'Estuary'

Winton and *Cloudstreet*

National canons

In the English-speaking world, when we think of lists of 'great works', we often tend to think about works produced by English authors or set in England. In fact, a great number of people (particularly older people) who can read English and are interested in the classics of English literature have spent their youth and adult lives reading about hedgerows, badgers, home counties and London's fog even though they grew up in Mumbai or Wagga Wagga or on the Kenyan plains. This experience is an interesting feature of postcolonial life.

Sometimes, via mechanisms such as the Nobel Prize for Literature, non-English people are able to participate in the 'Anglo' canon. In the twentieth century many international figures have been introduced into the canon of works of English literature in this way. An Australian example is Patrick White, who may be little read generally but is much regarded by critics.

It is worth remembering that each major western nation-state in the nineteenth and twentieth centuries has produced its own internal list of great works as part of nationalist projects. (Examples are WB Yeats in Ireland and Mark Twain in the USA.) This is particularly true for ex-colonies of Britain (such as Canada and India) that use literature to assert their own identity independent from Britain. It is also useful to remember that in the Middle Ages, Britain itself was producing vernacular works as part of a nationalistic programme to show independence from its French colonisers.

In Australia, recognition of the importance of having a list of great works that helps us to define and understand Australian place and identity began as early as Federation in 1901, gained momentum in the 1920s and 1930s, and continues today. Since 1901 there has been a general anxiety about having a list of great works and specific anxieties about what should be included on that list. This concern is part of being a settler colony that was so strongly affiliated with 'home' (England) from 1788 to 1901. From 1901, Australians began to find more local affiliations with landscape, idiom and some aspects of Indigenous culture. Australians also found fundamental stories (such as pioneer life, Ned Kelly and the ANZACs) that marked, and even created, a difference between themselves and the 'mother country'.

The construction of an Australian literary canon has excluded oral literatures, such as those of Indigenous peoples. This echoes the construction of the Australian nation-state on the notion of terra nullius (empty land), which was eventually overturned by the Mabo case. The proper, respectful inclusion of the artistic work of Australia's Indigenous peoples is a continuing issue for teachers and students. Dynamic and difficult questions about the study of Indigenous texts include those concerning authorship, ownership and copyright of stories, as well as genre and critical recognition. The related questions about who speaks for or about Indigenous experience also continue to challenge Indigenous and non-indigenous readers.

Questions

1 RECAP: Explain, in your own words, the relationship between:

a the literature of England and Australian people

b literature and nationalism.   »

Visions of the outback

For colonial Australians, representing the Australian bush was a much harder task than it sounds. People in Australia with an aesthetic sensibility had usually been schooled in English poetry: the landscapes and images of Wordsworth and Keats (see pages 87–117), for example. European Australian artists and writers were confronted by the wild, untamed, ancient force that is the Australian bush and outback. New language and new ways of seeing were needed in order to represent this landscape. In the mid-nineteenth century, there was an early group of poets that we now know as the colonial poets.

These poets included Charles Harpur (see page 198). They used the prevailing European and English norms of poetry of their time to try to evoke their experience of Australia.

Ideas about what Australian literature ought to be were implemented and stage-managed by AG Stephens, an early editor of the Sydney *Bulletin*, a popular periodical established in 1880. His idea about Australian identity and writing was based on strong, conservative stereotypes about men and women and the city and the bush. As the end of the nineteenth century approached, two writers emerged in Australia who began to further define this sense of 'Australianness' in writing. They were Banjo Paterson and Henry Lawson. Not only were these writers incredibly popular in their own time, they have become 'Australian classics' of

Colonial Australians found it difficult to represent the wild, untamed, ancient force that is the Australian bush and outback.

the type you buy in bound editions for your grandfather for Christmas. Their work with ballad and short story forms has influenced all kinds of stories and images produced by Australians since the roaring nineties (the 1890s).

Charles Harpur (1813–1868)

Harpur is now regarded as an important Australian nineteenth-century poet. Born in Australia as the son of Irish convicts, he was one of the first writers to use Australian subject matter in the elevated form of poetry. Here is part of one famous example of his work.

A MIDSUMMER NOON IN THE AUSTRALIAN FOREST
Extracted

Not a sound disturbs the air,
There is quiet everywhere;
Over plains and over woods
What a mighty stillness broods!

All the birds and insects keep   5
Where the coolest shadows sleep;
Even the busy ants are found
Resting in their pebbled mound;
Even the locust clingeth now
Silent to the barky bough: 10
Over hills and over plains
Quiet, vast and slumbrous, reigns …

ooooo

Of a vermeil-crusted seal
Dusted o'er with golden meal.
Only there's a droning where
Yon bright beetle shines in air,
Tracks it in its gleaming flight   25
With a slanting beam of light,
Rising in the sunshine higher,
Till its shards flame out like fire …

Questions

1 What is your first impression of this poem? What elements of the Australian outback is it concentrating on?

2 Speculate on what could be important about the poem's main themes (landscape and death) for

»

a nineteenth-century outback Australian reader and writer.

3 How vividly does it evoke Australia to you? Read the poem again and imagine that it is describing a field in England. What, if anything, from the poem disrupts this reading? What conclusions can you draw from this?

4 Read what the postcolonial section in Unit 1 (pages 14–15) has to say about 'hybridity'. Comment on hybridity in this poem.

Andrew Barton (Banjo) Paterson (1864–1941)

Paterson grew up near Orange and Yass and knew many bush characters: drovers, bush-rangers and squatters. He was admitted to practice as a solicitor, but after his literary fame really took off in 1895, he led a life travelling and working as a journalist. He had the kind of luck and good health that eluded his contemporary, Henry Lawson. Paterson's *The Man from Snowy River and Other Verses* (1895) was the first Australian bestseller, selling 10 000 copies in its first year of publication. This was an amazing amount; poetry never makes the bestseller lists anymore. Paterson's popularity rested, to a certain extent, on his vision of the bush as a place of freedom and adventure.

Banjo Paterson.

THE MAN FROM SNOWY RIVER
Extracted

There was movement at the station, for the word had passed around
That the colt from old Regret had got away,
And had joined the wild bush horses—he was worth a thousand pound,
So all the cracks had gathered to the fray.
All the tried and noted riders from the stations near and far   5
Had mustered at the homestead overnight,
For the bushmen love hard riding where the wild bush horses are,
And the stock-horse snuffs the battle with delight.

ooooo

[The man from Snowy River and the other horsemen chase the horses and arrive at the top of a mountain.]

When they reached the mountain's summit, even Clancy took a pull— 65
It well might make the boldest hold their breath;
The wild hop scrub grew thickly, and the hidden ground was full
Of wombat holes, and any slip was death.

»

But the man from Snowy River let the pony have his head,
And he swung his stockwhip round and gave a cheer,   70
And he raced him down the mountain like a torrent down its bed,
While the others stood and watched in very fear.
He sent the flint-stones flying, but the pony kept his feet,
He cleared the fallen timber in his stride,
And the man from Snowy River never shifted in his seat—   75
It was grand to see that mountain horseman ride.
Through the stringy barks and saplings, on the rough and
    broken ground,
Down the hillside at a racing pace he went;
And he never drew the bridle till he landed safe and sound
At the bottom of that terrible descent.   80

He was right among the horses as they climbed the farther hill,
And the watchers on the mountain, standing mute,
Saw him ply the stockwhip fiercely; he was right among them still,
As he raced across the clearing in pursuit.
Then they lost him for a moment, where two mountain
    gullies met   85
In the ranges—but a final glimpse reveals
On a dim and distant hillside the wild horses racing yet,
With the man from Snowy River at their heels.

And he ran them single-handed till their sides were white
    with foam;
He followed like a bloodhound on their track,   90
Till they halted, cowed and beaten; then he turned their heads
    for home,
And alone and unassisted brought them back.
But his hardy mountain pony he could scarcely raise a trot,
He was blood from hip to shoulder from the spur;
But his pluck was still undaunted, and his courage fiery hot,   95
For never yet was mountain horse a cur.

And down by Kosciusko, where the pine-clad ridges raise
Their torn and rugged battlements on high,
Where the air is clear as crystal, and the white stars fairly blaze
At midnight in the cold and frosty sky,   100
And where around the Overflow the reed-beds sweep and sway
To the breezes, and the rolling plains are wide,
The man from Snowy River is a household word today,
And the stockmen tell the story of his ride.

1 Explore the rhyme and the rhythm of this poem. How do you think these help in a poem about mustering horses?

2 What impression does the extract give of the Australian outback?

3 In what ways would it be a significant poem for readers in Australia in the years leading up to Federation in 1901?

4 Pick two of the poem's striking images and explain why they are powerful.

5 This poem has more iconic status in Australia than any other. It is certainly well loved by many today. What features in it do you find that could evoke this response? Do you think it is 'good poetry'?

6 Material such as this helped define and shape Australian masculinity.

a What assumptions does the poem make about masculinity and how men act? What aspects of it would we agree with in the twenty-first century?

b Where are the women in this poem? Does this mean they are marginalised?

c Rewrite the poem (changing as little as possible) so that it is a group of women going out to look for the horse. What effect, if any, does this have on your reading of the poem?

7 A deconstructive reading of 'The Man From Snowy River' would be interested in the way in which Banjo Paterson values what he writes about. Fill in the other half of the binaries below.

a independence   _____
b bush life   _____
c masculine self-reliance _____
d hardship   _____
e wildness   _____

Is Paterson's dominant ideology still prevalent in Australian culture today? What values are being marginalised? Re-read the section on deconstructive criticism in Unit 1 (page 18) before you answer this question.

Henry Lawson (1867–1922)

Lawson was born near Grenfell and grew up near Mudgee, New South Wales. His parents separated in 1883. His mother, Louisa, moved to Sydney, where she became active in publishing and the women's movement. Lawson's childhood was full of the trials of poverty. He wrote verse until 1890, but then he turned his attention to the short story form. The collection of short stories generally regarded as his best, *While the Billy Boils*, was published in 1896. Unfortunately, from about this time, his life was increasingly dogged by his battle with alcohol, which eventually ruined his marriage, his health, his work and his writing.

Henry Lawson.

Lawson's short stories grew from his journalistic interest in 'sketches from life', which used vivid detail, a straightforward tone and distinct character portraits of well-known bush stereotypes, rather than a strong sense of plot. He was interested in a 'natural' effect in his stories, including a natural and colloquial narrative voice and sympathy for his characters. The 'natural' took quite a lot of construction. In general, Lawson was less convinced than Paterson about the romantic freedom of the bush, preferring a more pessimistic view.

One of his most famous stories, 'The Drover's Wife', is about a woman whose husband has gone away to look for work, leaving her alone to raise the children in their outback house. In the extract below, a snake has entered the house and so the mother and the dog are keeping watch while the children sleep.

THE DROVER'S WIFE

Near midnight. The children are all asleep and she sits there still, sewing and reading by turns. From time to time she glances round the floor and wall-plate, and whenever she hears a noise she reaches for the stick. The thunderstorm comes on, and the wind, rushing through the cracks in the slab wall, threatens to blow out her candle. She places it on a sheltered part of the dresser and fixes up a newspaper to protect it. At every flash of lightning, the cracks between the slabs gleam like polished silver. The thunder rolls, and the rain comes down in torrents.

Alligator lies at full length on the floor, with his eyes turned towards the partition. She knows by this that the snake is there. There are large cracks in that wall opening under the floor of the dwelling-house.

She is not a coward, but recent events have shaken her nerves. A little son of her brother-in-law was lately bitten by a snake, and died. Besides, she has not heard from her husband for six months, and is anxious about him.

Questions

1 What impression does the extract give of the Australian outback?

2 Find and explore evidence of the 'naturalistic' style that Lawson uses.

3 How does this piece's tone and attitude contrast with those of the previous two extracts?

4 How would these texts have linked in with the historical push towards Federation in the late nineteenth century?

Dorothea Mackellar (1885–1968)

If there is a poem that rivals 'The Man From Snowy River' as Australia's sentimental favourite, it is probably Dorothea Mackellar's 'My Country', published in 1908. Mackellar's literary influence does not extend beyond this piece, although she wrote several other volumes of poetry before abandoning writing in the mid-1920s due to ill health. 'My Country' was written when she was nineteen. The poem is significant for the way in which Mackellar contrasts the Australian environment (stanzas 2, 3 and 4) with the traditional English landscape (stanza 1). This is an important step in embracing the Australianness of the landscape in a nationalistic sense.

MY COUNTRY
Extracted

The love of field and coppice,
Of green and shaded lanes,
Of ordered woods and gardens
Is running in your veins;
Strong love of grey-blue distance,   5
Brown streams and soft, dim skies—
I know but cannot share it,
My love is otherwise.

I love a sunburnt country,
A land of sweeping plains,   10
Of ragged mountain ranges,
Of droughts and flooding rains,
I love her far horizons,
I love her jewel sea,
Her beauty and her terror—   15
The wide brown land for me ...

ooooo

Core of my heart, my country!   25
Her pitiless blue sky,
When sick at heart around us
We see the cattle die—
But when the grey clouds gather
And we can bless again   30
The drumming of an army,
The steady, soaking rain ...

ooooo

An opal-hearted country,
A wilful, lavish land—
All you who have not loved her,
You will not understand—
Though Earth holds many splendours,   45
Wherever I may die,
I know to what brown country
My homing thoughts will fly.

Questions

1 What is your overall impression of this poem?

2 Draw up a piece of paper with the phrase 'gentle images' on the left-hand side and 'hard images' on the right-hand side. Write eight key lines across the page from most to least gentle. What impression is Mackellar giving about the Australian environment?

3 What is Mackellar's attitude to the English environment? How does she contrast the English and the Australian landscapes?

4 What is the difference between stressing the word 'love' and the word 'sunburnt' when reading out line 9?

5 Describe, in your own words, the role this poem could play in an emerging sense of Australian identity. Re-read the section on postcolonial criticism in Unit 1 (pages 14–15) before completing this task.

6 Explore a reading of this poem that an Indigenous Australian may have made in 1908.

7 Does this poem arouse any feelings about Australia for you? Why or why not? Do you think this is a good poem to study in the twenty-first century?

Henry Handel Richardson (1870–1946)

About twenty years after 'My Country', and from a different angle, Henry Handel Richardson (the pen-name of Ethel Florence Lindesey Robertson, nee Richardson) produced a trilogy about pioneer Australian life and landscape called *The Fortunes of Richard Mahony* (1917–29). It was predominantly realist in mode. Her general sense of pessimism and tragedy links her to Lawson. However, Richardson's themes are often broader; she writes about the nature of migrant experience, the importance of the idea of home amidst feelings of dislocation, and the idea of nationality. Her account of the life of Richard Mahony commences in the nation-making milieu of the Australian goldfields.

THE FORTUNES OF RICHARD MAHONY

Under a sky so pure and luminous that it seemed like a thinly drawn veil of blueness, which ought to have been transparent, stretched what, from a short way off, resembled a desert of pale clay. No patch of green offered rest to the eye; not a tree, hardly a stunted bush had been left standing, either on the bottom of the vast shallow basin itself, or on the several hillocks that dotted it and formed its sides. Even the most prominent of these, the Black Hill, which jutted out on the Flat like a gigantic tumulus, had been stripped of its dense timber, feverishly disembowelled, and was now

»

become a bald protuberance strewn with gravel and clay. The whole scene had that strange, repellent ugliness that goes with breaking up and throwing into disorder what has been sanctified as final, and belongs, in particular, to the wanton disturbing of earth's gracious, green-spread crust. In the pre-golden era this wide valley, lying open to sun and wind, had been a lovely grassland, ringed by a circlet of wooded hills; beyond these, by a belt of virgin forest. A limpid river and more than one creek had meandered across its face; water was to be found there even in the driest summer. She-oaks and peppermints had given shade to the flocks of the early settlers; wattles had bloomed their brief delirious yellow passion against the grey-green foliage of the gums. Now, all that was left of the original 'pleasant resting-place' and its pristine beauty were the ancient volcanic cones of Warrenheip and Buninyong. These, too far off to supply wood for firing or slabbing, still stood green and timbered, and looked down upon the havoc that had been made of the fair, pastoral lands.

Seen nearer at hand, the dun-coloured desert resolved itself into uncountable pimpling clay and mud-heaps, of divers shade and varying sizes: some consisted of but a few bucketfuls of mullock, others were taller than the tallest man. There were also hundreds of rain-soaked, mud-bespattered tents, sheds and awnings; wind-sails, which fell, funnel-like, from a kind of gallows into the shafts they ventilated; flags fluttering on high posts in front of stores. The many human figures that went to and fro were hardly to be distinguished from the ground they trod. They were coated with earth, clay-clad in ochre and gamboge. Their faces were daubed with clauber; it matted great beards, and entangled the coarse hairs on chests and brawny arms. Where, here and there, a blue jumper had kept a tinge of blueness, it was so besmeared with yellow that it might have been expected to turn green. The gauze neck-veils that hung from the brims of wide-awakes or cabbage-trees were become stiff little lattices of caked clay.

Questions

1 How does this extract compare with the extract from 'The Drover's Wife'?

2 What sort of life and atmosphere do you think it evokes of the goldfields? How are language structures and features employed to create this effect?

3 What is the cumulative effect of the punctuation extending the sentences in the first section of paragraph two?

4 Explore how pieces such as this have disrupted the idealistic image of the landscape and of 'bronzed Aussie' men?

Questions

Overall questions

1 What struggles did Australians have representing their landscape in the nineteenth and early twentieth centuries? How did they attempt to resolve these struggles?

2 Which of the preceding extracts most closely evokes a sense of Australia with which you are familiar? Why?

3 In your view, how important is literature in contributing to a sense of 'national identity' and why?

4 Re-read the section about postcolonialism in Unit 1 (pages 14–15). What key concepts from this introduction do you find useful when thinking about colonial Australian writing?

Activities

1 Write a piece of prose or poetry in which you evoke a sense of the outback. If possible, focus on a landscape with which you are familiar.

2 Using multimedia presentation software (such as PowerPoint) and copyright-free images located using a search engine (such as Google), create a slide show that displays the tension between the English and Australian landscapes. Be as creative as you can when representing these landscapes; your pictures don't have to be limited to those of actual landscapes.

The big smoke: modernism and urban Australia

As modernism emerged and took hold in England and the USA during the early twentieth century, Australians stuck relatively firmly to the importance of landscape and the pioneer days in literature. In fact, it was not until the 1950s that Patrick White introduced major experimental writing into Australian literature. However, modernism in poetry did sneak in through the work of Kenneth Slessor. Until this time, Norman Lindsay and other influential literary figures had criticised modernism and attempted to keep it out of Australian poetry.

Question

Read the section on modernism in Unit 5 (pages 162–4) and make notes on its distinguishing features.

Kenneth Slessor (1901–1971)

Kenneth Slessor was born in Orange, New South Wales. As an adult he lived in the eastern suburbs of Sydney and a number of his poems evoke this area. He was a journalist for most of his life. During World War II he worked as the official war correspondent with the Australian Army, but he resigned in 1944 after disagreements with army officials. At about this time he stopped writing poetry, describing himself as 'an extinct volcano'. His journalistic career, however, continued and flourished. Over the years he was leader writer and literary editor of the *Sun*, the *Telegraph* and the *Sunday Telegraph* and also was the president of the Sydney Journalists' Club from 1956 to 1965.

Slessor was affected by the modernism of poems such as TS Eliot's *The Waste Land*. In his poem 'Stars', Slessor describes the stars not as romantic or beautiful lights, but as 'bottomless, black cups of space', 'tunnels of nothingness' and 'infinity's trap-door, eternal and merciless'. He also embraced the grinding modern harshness of urban life in his poem 'William Street'. The sense of meaninglessness and alienation in much of modern poetry can also be found in some of Slessor's work.

Slessor's most widely acknowledged work is *Five Bells*, an elegy for his friend Joe Lynch who drowned when he fell off a ferry between Circular Quay and the north side of the Harbour. This poem reflects on meaning and existence. It refers to existence as a blunt, meaningless force that annihilates. Yet at the same time it holds out memories, images and even poetry itself as possible, fragile defences to this force.

North Sydney wharf, which lies opposite Circular Quay. Slessor's friend Joe Lynch drowned when he fell off a ferry between Circular Quay and the north side of Sydney Harbour.

FIVE BELLS

Note: The five bells are being rung by a ship on the harbour to indicate that it is half past ten

... Deep and dissolving verticals of light
Ferry the falls of moonshine down. Five bells
Coldly rung out in a machine's voice. Night and water   10
Pour to one rip of darkness, the Harbour floats
In the air, the Cross hangs upside-down in water.

Why do I think of you, dead man, why thieve
These profitless lodgings from the flukes of thought
Anchored in Time? You have gone from earth,   15
Gone even from the meaning of a name;
Yet something's there, yet something forms its lips
And hits and cries against the ports of space,
Beating their sides to make its fury heard.   »

Are you shouting at me, dead man, squeezing your face   20
In agonies of speech on speechless panes?
Cry louder, beat the windows, bawl your name!

But I hear nothing, nothing ... only bells; ...

∞∞∞∞∞

The night you died, I felt your eardrums crack,
And the short agony, the longer dream,
The Nothing that was neither long nor short;
But I was bound, and could not go that way,
But I was blind, and could not feel your hand.   115
If I could find an answer, could only find
Your meaning, or could say why you were here
Who now are gone, what purpose gave you breath
Or seized it back, might I not hear your voice?

I looked out of my window in the dark   120
At waves with diamond quills and combs of light
That arched their mackerel-backs and smacked the sand
In the moon's drench, that straight enormous glaze,
And ships far off asleep, and Harbour-buoys
Tossing their fireballs wearily each to each,   125
And tried to hear your voice, but all I heard
Was a boat's whistle, and the scraping squeal
Of seabirds' voices far away, and bells,
Five bells. Five bells coldly ringing out.
Five bells.   130

Questions

1 The poem begins by evoking Sydney Harbour. How does it do this? Are they attractive images?

2 What does Slessor wonder about Joe Lynch in this poem?

3 What creates the chilling tone in the line 'But I hear nothing, nothing ... only bells' (line 23)?

4 What is Slessor suggesting about the meaning and purpose of life in the second extracted section of the poem? Look at the line 'The Nothing that was neither long nor short ...' (line 113).

5 How is water used in the poem?

6 How has Slessor used language features to evoke a sense of nihilism and blackness in this poem?

7 What is of most significance to you in this poem: a sense of emotional meaningless, a touching sense of Slessor's grief for the loss of a friend, or something else? Explain your answer.

Christina Stead (1902–1983)

Another Australian was writing a certain kind of modernism from overseas: the expatriate Australian Christina Stead. She spent most of her life overseas, but much of her early writing was devoted to evoking scenes from her Australian upbringing. These were often about life in the modern city, but Stead also had quite an eye for the lyrical aspects of Sydney landscapes. Her work is an interesting combination of the surreal and the lyrical.

Stead has only reluctantly been claimed as an important Australian writer because she spent most of her eighty-one years outside Australia (which she left in 1928, aged twenty-six, for Europe) and because some of her work has international aspects. This attitude towards Stead's identity and stature as a writer is typical of a kind of conservatism obvious in Australia in the 1950s and even later, which held fast to the idea that to be an Australian writer you had to be *in* Australia and write *only* about Australia.

Critics now argue that Stead's work has the same standing as Patrick White's. The fact that Stead was a woman who went away from Australia and mainly stayed away, as well as the challenges of her major works, is responsible for the delayed recognition.

Stead's novel *For Love Alone* (extracted below) is a semi-autobiographical novel about a young woman who leaves parochial Sydney for London in search of love and fulfilment.

FOR LOVE ALONE

It was high tide at nine-thirty that night in February and even after ten o'clock the black tide was glassy, too full for lapping in the gullies. Up on the cliffs, Teresa could see the ocean flooding the reefs outside, choking the headland and swimming to the landing platforms of jetties in the bays. It was long after ten when Teresa got to the highest point of the seaward cliffs and turning there, dropped down to the pine-grown bay by narrow paths and tree-grown boulders, trailing her long skirt, holding her hat by a ribbon. From every moon-red shadow came the voices of men and women; and in every bush and in the clumps of pine, upon unseen wooden seats and behind rocks, in the grass and even on the open ledges, men and women groaned and gave shuddering cries as if they were being beaten. She passed slowly, timidly, but fascinated by the strange battlefield, the bodies stretched out, contorted, with sounds of the dying under the fierce high moon…

Some fishermen came slowly up through the rocks to the edge of the curved lipped platform over which they began casually to drop down by the iron footholds to the lowest ledges, wet by the unusual tides, and from these they waded out smoothly to their fishing posts on the side of the square-cleaving shale. The bay, the ocean, were full of moonstruck fish, restless, swarming, so thick in places that the water looked oily; their presence, the men thought, with other signs, meant storms at hand.

Questions

1 How does this excerpt compare with the excerpt from Henry Handel Richardson's *The Fortunes of Richard Mahony*? Which do you think is more experimental with language? Why do you have this view?

2 How are language features used to convey the quality of the water?

3 How is human sexuality conveyed in this extract? Is it positive or negative? How does Teresa react to 'the strange battlefield'?

4 What elements in the extract would allow a local to recognise the setting as Sydney Harbour, specifically Watsons Bay? Is this a typical description of Sydney Harbour?

5 Stead's book suggests that female sexuality is an important creative force. Does this idea participate in patriarchal ideology or resist it? Re-read the section on feminist criticism in Unit 1 (pages 15–16) before you answer this question.

Patrick White (1912–1990)

Patrick White, winner of the Nobel Prize for Literature, wrote about Australia, its social history and its people's sense of isolation. However, he sought to evoke a spiritual dimension in this secular and pragmatic (practical) culture by making his style dense with symbols and myths. He complained of the 'dreary dun-coloured offspring of journalistic realism' and his work broke the hold of the ghost of Henry Lawson as the writer whose language most suited the evocation of Australia.

Activity

Take two of White's books, read the blurbs on their back covers, and then read their first two pages. What strikes you as significant about the pages you have read? Do you find the features explained above in your selection? Explain your response. Examples of White's novels are:

- *The Tree of Man* (1955)
- *Voss* (1957)
- *Riders in the Chariot* (1961)
- *The Solid Mandala* (1966)
- *The Twyborn Affair* (1979).

Fraud of the century: the Ern Malley affair

The relatively small world of Australian poetry broke up into three warring camps in the middle of last century. There was agreement that Australians had to get away from the British model and find their own voice. The disagreement was where to find it.

The first group, the Jindyworobaks, which included Rex Ingamells, thought that we should look to Aboriginal vernacular, which led to Ingamells writing poetry that sounded like a sunburnt *Jabberwocky* without any of the humour. For example, his poem 'Moorwathimerring' begins as shown on the following page.

> Into Moorwathimerring
> where atinga dare not tread
> leaving wurly for a wilban
> tallabilla, you have fled

A second group, based in Melbourne, was called the Angry Penguins. They embraced modernism and surrealism. Led by Max Harris, they confronted local puritans with their avant-garde writings about sexual throbbings and so on.

The third group, Hermes, was based in Sydney. They thought that the Angry Penguins wrote pretentious rubbish, and said of Max Harris: '[He is] morally sick and discusses his symptoms with the gusto of an old woman showing the vicar her ulcerated leg'.

This rivalry between the groups erupted in the Ern Malley affair. Two members of the Hermes group—James McAuley and Harold Stewart—got together one afternoon and threw together what they thought was a fairly random collection of pretentious jottings and 'free association' poetry. Then they sent it off to Max Harris for publication in his journal. However, they didn't send it as themselves. Instead, they sent it with a covering letter from a fictional woman called 'Mrs Ethel Malley'. The hoax letter said that Ethel had a brother, Ern, a motor mechanic who had recently been tragically killed. 'Mrs Malley' went on to say that she had found the poems under Ern's bed when she was clearing up his things. She said she was sending them to Harris to see what he thought of them.

Harris thought he had unearthed a tragically dead genius. He rhapsodised about how wonderful the poetry was. He devoted a whole issue of his *Angry Penguins* journal to Malley in 1944. Ern Malley, the motor mechanic, was the shining light of Australian modernism.

And then McAuley and Stewart sprang their trap. In a full double-page feature in the *Sun* newspaper they exposed the fraud of Malley and admitted that they had written the poems, badly, in a single afternoon. Harris was 'exposed' as someone who couldn't tell real poetry from a pile of drunken ramblings. He tried to claim that the poems really were good and that McAuley and Stewart had written better poems than they even knew. But few people listened to him. His influence was over. But was his judgment impaired? You can judge for yourself in the following activity.

Activities

1 Three of the poetic extracts on page 212 are taken from Malley's (fraud) collection of poems called *The Darkening Ecliptic*. The other three are from TS Eliot's towering triumph of modernism, *The Waste Land*. Which are which? (The answer is given on page 223.)

2 Read Peter Carey's *My Life as a Fake*, which is about this incident. (In Carey's novel, the Ern Malley character rises to life, Frankenstein style, to haunt the McAuley character.) Where do your sympathies lie in this reading? How has Carey adapted the Malley story?

»

a

'My nerves are bad to-night. Yes, bad. Stay with
    me.
'Speak to me. Why do you never speak? Speak.
'What are you thinking of? What thinking? What?
'I never know what you are thinking. Think.'

I think we are in rats' alley
Where the dead men lost their bones.

'What is that noise?'
The wind under the door.
'What is that noise now? What is the wind doing?'
Nothing again nothing.
'Do
'You know nothing? Do you see nothing?
    Do you remember
'Nothing?'

I remember
Those are pearls that were his eyes.
'Are you alive, or not? Is there nothing in your
    head?'

b

There are ribald interventions
Like spurious seals upon
A Chinese landscape-roll
Or tangents to the rainbow.
We have known these declensions,
Have winked when Hyperion
Was transmuted to a troll.
We dubbed it a sideshow.

c

After the torchlight red on sweaty faces
After the frosty silence in the gardens
After the agony in stony places
The shouting and the crying
Prison and place and reverberation
Of thunder of spring over distant mountains
He who was living is now dead
We who were living are now dying
With a little patience

d

April is the cruellest month, breeding
Lilacs out of the dead land, mixing
Memory and desire, stirring
Dull roots with spring rain.
Winter kept us warm, covering
Earth in forgetful snow, feeding
A little life with dried tubers.
Summer surprised us, coming over the
    Starnbergersee
With a shower of rain; we stopped in the
    colonnade,
And went on in sunlight, into the Hofgarten,
And drank coffee, and talked for an hour.

e

I had often, cowled in the slumberous heavy air,
Closed my inanimate lids to find it real,
As I knew it would be, the colourful spires
And painted roofs, the high snows glimpsed at
    the back,
All reversed in the quiet reflecting waters —
Not knowing then that Dürer perceived it too.
Now I find that once more I have shrunk
To an interloper, robber of dead men's dream,
I had read in books that art is not easy
But no one warned that the mind repeats
In its ignorance the vision of others. I am still
the black swan of trespass on alien waters.

f

I have avoided your wide English eyes:
But now I am whirled in their vortex.
My blood becomes a Damaged Man
Most like your Albion;
And I must go with stone feet
Down the staircase of flesh
To where in a shuddering embrace
My toppling opposites commit
The obscene, the unforgivable rape.

1 If you confused the writings of the twentieth century's greatest poet with the random, fraudulent jottings made by two men on a drunken afternoon what does this indicate to you: the nature of poetry, your own understanding of poetry, or something else?

2 Max Harris suggested that Ern Malley's poems were better than the fakers knew themselves. Would you agree with him?

3 Link the story of this fraud with the context of Australian society at the time. Do you think the same thing could have happened in England at that time? Why or why not? (Answering this question may require further research into the social context of both Australia and England at the time of the fraud.)

4 Re-read the section about new historicism in Unit 1 (pages 17–18). How is cultural history important in understanding the meanings of the Ern Malley affair? What kinds of social and cultural power are at stake in the production and reception of the Ern Malley poems; for example, who has the power to say what is 'good' and 'real' poetry?

Newer voices in poetry

Judith Wright (1915–2000)

Wright was born in the New England tablelands to a wealthy pastoralist family who had originally settled in the Hunter Valley in the 1820s. In some respects, Wright's early work seemed to be a continuation of the expression of the importance of rural traditions: bush settlers and bush epiphanies; that is, strong, almost spiritual realisations about something of importance. Yet her diction was modern, and her interests more spiritual than material. She wrote prolifically about the environment and Indigenous affairs in her poetry and prose. Her work is considered to be both lyrical and emotionally forthright.

European Australians found Australian landscapes beautiful and powerful, but also a source of unease about ownership and possession.

AT COOLOOLAH

The blue crane fishing in Cooloolah's twilight
has fished there longer than our centuries.
He is the certain heir of lake and evening,
and he will wear their colour till he dies;

»

But I'm a stranger, come of a conquering people.   5
I cannot share his calm, who watch his lake,
being unloved by all my eyes delight in
and made uneasy, for an old murder's sake.

Those dark-skinned people who once named Cooloolah
knew that no land is lost or won by wars,   10
for earth is spirit; the invader's feet will tangle
in nets there and his blood be thinned by fears.

Riding at noon and ninety years ago,
my grandfather was beckoned by a ghost—
a black accoutred warrior armed for fighting,   15
who sank into bare plain, as now into time past.

White shores of sand, plumed reed and paperbark,
clear heavenly levels frequented by crane and swan—
I know that we are justified only by love,
but oppressed by arrogant guilt, have room for none.   20

And walking on clean sand among the prints
of bird and animal, I am challenged by a driftwood spear
thrust from the water; and, like my grandfather,
must quiet a heart accused by its own fear.

Questions

1 How is the blue crane made to feel like part of the environment in stanza 1?

2 How are the insights and attitudes of the original people who lived around Cooloolah contrasted with that of Wright and other more recent arrivals?

3 How is Wright's relationship with the land in this poem made to seem unstable and problematic?

4 Explain the meaning of the final two stanzas of the poem. How do they summarise the poem's concerns?

5 Contrast this poem with one of the nineteenth-century poems you have studied in this unit. What does this tell you about the changing values of society?

Gwen Harwood (1920–1995)

Harwood was born in Brisbane. From a musical family, she became a music teacher in Brisbane. She learned German and read widely in German poetry and philosophy. She married

William Harwood in 1945 and moved to Tasmania, where she raised four children. She used the pseudonyms Walter Lehmann and Miriam Stone when she first began to publish poetry. Her first book of verse was *Poems* (1963), and she published six more collections of her poetry. She was awarded the Robert Frost award (1977) and the Patrick White award (1978). Her fourth book, *Bone Scan* (1989), won the Victorian Premier's Literary Prize for poetry. She identified her themes as love, art, friendship and memory, and she had an obvious and wonderful gift for the natural landscape as well as the landscapes of childhood memory.

ESTUARY
To Rex Hobcroft

Wind crosshatches shallow water.
Paddocks rest in the sea's arm.
Swamphens race through spiky grass.
A wire fence leans, a crazy stave
with sticks for barlines, wind for song.   5
Over us, interweaving light
with air and substance, ride the gulls.

Words in our undemanding speech
hover and blend with things observed.
Syllables flow in the tide's pulse.   10
My earliest memory turns in air:
Eclipse. Cocks crow, as if at sunset;
Grandmother, holding a smoked glass,
says to me, '*Look. Remember this.*'

Over the goldbrown sand my children   15
run in the wind. The sky's immense
with spring's new radiance. Far from here,
lying close to the final darkness,
a great-grandmother lives and suffers,
still praising life: another morning   20
on earth, cockcrow and changing light.

Over the skeleton of thought
mind builds a skin of human texture.
The eye's part of another eye
that guides it through the maze of light.   25
A line becomes a firm horizon.
All's as it was in the beginning.
Obscuring symbols melt away.

》

'*Remember this.*' I will remember
this quiet in which the questioning mind   30
allows reality to enter
its gateway as a friend, unchallenged,
to rest as a friend may, without speaking;
light falling like a benediction
on moments that renew the world.   35

Questions

1 Rex Hobcroft was a pianist. What is significant about the dedication of the poem to him?

2 How are language, music and memories being threaded into the environment in stanzas 1 and 2? What effect does this have on the evocation of the environment?

3 How are the forces of life and death evoked and contrasted in stanza 3?

4 Harwood writes of 'another eye' in stanza 4 (line 24). What do you think this other eye is? How does this help you make sense of all of stanza 4?

5 What is meant by 'moments that renew the world' (line 35)? How does ending the poem on the notes of freshness and renewal affect your understanding of the whole poem?

6 What do you think is the overall tone of this poem? What is Harwood attempting to communicate? How are language forms and features used to do this?

Les Murray (1938–)

Murray was born in 1938 into a farming community near Bunyah, north of the Myall Lakes, close to Taree. His family was poor, but prided itself on its connection to the first Scottish pioneers who opened up the district in the nineteenth century. Scottish Presbyterianism and Celtic culture and language have survived as elements in Murray's writing. They gave him a sense of independence and an understanding of minority cultures.

Activity

Locate Murray's 'The Broad Bean Sermon'. It can be found at the Lyrikline website (www.lyrikline.org/en/homepage.aspx). What do you think Murray's main concerns are in this poem? How would you contrast it with Wright's?

Contemporary novels: where are we now?

The 1970s, particularly after the election of Gough Whitlam as Labor prime minister in 1972, heralded a fresh and exciting era in Australian publishing. A new level of confidence and interest in Australian authors started to be expressed by publishers and reviewers. Women's writing, especially short stories, began to be published and migrant writing started to find an audience. Helen Garner's 1977 novel, *Monkey Grip*, about urban relationships developing in the shadow of drug addictions, was a significant indicator of the new styles and themes in Australian writing.

The publication of Indigenous writers was comparatively slow by comparison with migrant and women's writing. There were several breakthrough publications in the 1980s, culminating in Sally Morgan's memoir, *My Place*, in 1988. This has been followed by increasingly ambitious and striking writing from Indigenous writers. The most recent publications by novelist Kim Scott (who won the Miles Franklin Literary Award with *Benang* in 1999) indicate the power and dexterity of contemporary Indigenous fiction. Indigenous poetry is also an exciting area, with voices such as Lisa Bellear and Lionel Fogarty representing the dynamics of politics, land, gender and culture in their work. Contemporary Indigenous poetry is partnered by the strength and popularity of Indigenous song lyrics.

The 1970s laid the foundation for a continuing interest in Australian writing in the 1980s, which was supported by an increasing number of local writers winning prizes and receiving positive reviews overseas. The 1980s was the decade in which the careers of the most significant contemporary writers began to prosper. They include Peter Carey, David Malouf, Tim Winton and Kate Grenville. Their work demonstrated a new focus on history, national identity, experimental styles and international influences.

For example, Winton and Malouf are interested in writing about the spiritual relationship that people can have with the Australian landscape—just as Patrick White was. In other words, they are interested in the concept of 'transcendence' in this landscape. Writing about transcendence while trying to use a realistic style would be extremely difficult. Thus, Winton and Malouf modify their writing styles to try to generate this spiritual sense. An example of this is provided in the following extract from Winton's *Cloudstreet*.

Question

The authors of this textbook have great regard for Kim Scott's Miles Franklin Literary Award-winning novel *Benang* (1999). We believe it stands up to any literary analysis or criticism. Nonetheless, it is not as well known as the other novels in the preceding discussion.

a Should we include *Benang* on our list of possible 'great Australian novels' (see page 220)?

b Are we unfairly (or fairly) shaping the canon by including it?

c Should we only pick the best-known novels?

d What other criteria should we use?

Tim Winton (1960–)

Tim Winton was born in 1960 in Western Australia, where he still lives. He attended a Creative Writing Course at Curtin University in Perth, and it was while there that he began his first novel, *An Open Swimmer*. This was entered for *The Australian*/Vogel Literary Award in 1981. It won the award and Winton has never looked back. His more recent novels include *The Riders* and *Dirt Music*. Tim Winton has also written the *Lockie Leonard* series for younger readers. An extract from Winton's 1991 novel *Cloudstreet* appears below. This novel is about two families living together in a large, rambling house during the 1940s.

CLOUDSTREET

Out past Claremont, out past somewhere—Quick doesn't know anymore—he just stops. He sits back and ships the oars and gives it away. Fish is curled at his feet, sleepy.

Well, Quick says. He sits a few moments. In the starlight he can make out Fish's features. He has his eyes open. What are you thinkin?

I can hear the water

We're on the river, you dill.

I can hear it.

Yeah. Quick twists about in his seat. Up on the hills there's houselights and even the dimmed lamps of cars. You cold?

No.

I'm knackered.

You wanna sing, Quick? Let's sing.

It's quiet for a few moments and then they begin to sing, and once they start it's hard to give it up, so they set up a great train of songs from school and church and wireless, on and on in the dark until they're making them up and starting all over again to change the words and the speed. Quick isn't afraid and he knows Fish is alright. He lies back with his eyes closed. The whole boat is full of their songs—they shout them up at the sky until Fish begins to laugh. Quick stops singing. It's dead quiet and Fish is laughing like he's just found a mullet in his shorts. It's a crazy sound, a mad sound, and Quick opens his eyes to see Fish standing up in the middle of the boat with his arms out like he's gliding, like he's a bird sitting in an updraught. The sky, packed with stars, rests just above his head, and when Quick looks over the side he sees the river is full of sky as well. There's stars and swirl and space down there and it's not water anymore—it doesn't even feel wet. Quick stabs his fingers in. There's nothing there. There's no lights ashore now. No, there's no shore at all, not that he can see. There's only sky out there, above and below, everywhere to be seen. Except for Fish's giggling, there's no sound at all. Quick

»

knows he is dreaming. This is a dream. He feels a turn shunting against his sphincter. He's awake, alright. But it's a dream—it has to be.

Are we in the sky, Fish?

Yes. It's the water.

What dyou mean?

The water. The water. I fly.

Questions

1 What is noticeable to you about the relationship between the characters and the narrative description of the stars?

2 How does the narrative move from the literal to the figurative?

3 How are the sky and the water fused in this extract?

4 How effectively do you think that Winton has used language features to write 'transcendently'? Explain your answer.

5 Re-read the section on psychoanalytic criticism in Unit 1 (pages 16–17). What do you think Fish's desire for the water could be? What do his cries of ecstasy about the water mean?

Activity

Write your own creative piece in which a simple cultural activity that is important to you is made to seem magical and 'transcendent'.

1 Explore the ways in which literature has reflected and shaped a sense of Australia and an Australian national identity.

2 For decades Australian academics, readers and writers have searched for 'the great Australian novel': the one novel we would save if every library in the world was burning down and we could only pluck one Australian book from the burning shelves; the one book that says most about who and what 'we' are. Now you, as a class, will get to decide (tentatively) which novel this would be.

You will decide by using the tried and true method of 'literary survivor'. You will vote books *off* the list two at a time until there is only one book left: the great Australian novel.

The list to choose from is as follows:
* Patrick White's *The Tree of Man*
* Peter Carey's *True History of the Kelly Gang* or *Oscar and Lucinda*
* David Malouf's *An Imaginary Life* or *The Great World*
* Tim Winton's *Cloudstreet* or *Dirt Music*
* Christina Stead's *For Love Alone* or *The Man Who Loved Children*
* Frank Moorhouse's *Dark Palace*
* Thomas Keneally's *Schindler's Ark* or *The Chant of Jimmie Blacksmith*
* Janette Turner Hospital's *The Last Magician*
* Helen Garner's *Monkey Grip*
* Kate Grenville's *The Secret River*
* Kim Scott's *Benang*.

The class should break into eleven groups. Each group will be allocated one of the books listed above. Each group is to make a presentation to the class about how important and wonderful their chosen book is. The presentation should include a brief biography of the author and a summary of the book. Then each group should read out a passage that best represents how wonderful their novel is. The passage should be half a page to a page in length.

During the presentation all other members of the class should take some notes so that they remember each text when it comes time to vote.

Then let the voting begin. Each person is voting for which two novels should be *excluded* from the list. In the first round the list should go from eleven to nine, and then from nine to seven, and so on. Finally the list will be reduced from three to one.

At the end of this activity you will have your class's 'great Australian novel'.

Note: Perhaps this process is not quite as valid as a recommendation made by someone who has actually *read* all eleven books, but it's a start. Furthermore, it provides you with an idea of some Australian novels to read over the next few years.

a How appropriate is it for you (and your class) to 'decide' for yourself which is the great Australian novel on the basis of this process? Explain your response.

b Why do you think the activity was set?

3 How can three Australian texts that you have studied be seen as products of the time in which they were produced? In your answer explore the linguistic and structural features of your texts.

4 Judith Wright and Gwen Harwood rise from the beyond in order to come to your classroom to write for you the 'quintessential Australian landscape poem'. However, they want you to tell them what to write about. They will arrive in twenty minutes. You need to be ready to give them the 'specifications' for their poem.

a In groups, pool your memories of different Australian landscapes. For each landscape (such as beach and bush) make up mind maps that include memories of:

- what you did there and who you did them with
- how the landscapes feel when you are there with other people
- how the landscapes feel when you are there on your own.

Which of these memories should be included in the 'quintessential Australian landscape poem'?

b What issues about the Australian landscape do you think could be covered in this poem? (Examples of issues are Indigenous relationships and the environment.)

c Combine your group's responses to tasks (a) and (b) above in order to create your 'specifications' for Harwood and Wright.

d Imagine that Harwood and Wright mysteriously do not appear at your lesson. You decide to have a go at writing this poem yourself. Use all the language techniques at your disposal to evoke (not just list or describe) a sense of the landscape as well as you can.

5 What has this unit and the texts it contains made you think about Australia and being Australian? In what ways do you value these texts? How is your response shaped by your own context, such as your family, culture and school?

Glossary

Note: This is a list of many of the literary terms used in this book. It is not intended to be an exhaustive list of literary terms.

allegory a narrative in which the characters, plot and so on symbolise, or act as an extended metaphor for, another idea or story

alliteration the repetition of a consonant at the beginning of a series of words

alliterative verse verse in which alliteration is the primary way in which each line is organised

allusion a reference (implied or explicit) in a text to another well-known text or to famous people or events, for example

apostrophe a metaphor in which an inanimate object or concept is directly addressed by a speaker; an address to an absent person

binary opposition the fundamental contrasts (such as good/bad) used in linguistic analysis, criticism, anthropology and feminism

bon mot a witty phrase or saying

bourgeois in Marxist theory, a member of the property-owning class; a capitalist

canon in literary studies, a collection of great works by classic authors that represents the tradition of a national literature

capitalist a supporter of capitalism; an investor of capital in business

conceit a type of metaphor in which apparently very unlike things are compared, often in witty and clever ways

connotation the wider associations of a given word

construction the way a text has been assembled and the values embedded in it. This includes factors the author could not control, such as his or her ideology and culture

cumulation the built-up effect of a series of words, phrases or ideas

diction words; in particular, the way in which something is expressed in words

discontinuity the state of a text that contains interruptions, breaks or fragmentation

discourse a system of ideas or knowledge inscribed in a specific vocabulary, such as psychoanalysis, anthropology or literary studies

dominant reading an interpretation that accepts or favours dominant values and beliefs

dramatic monologue a poem that is the monologue of a single character. In the course of the poem, often the character will unintentionally reveal something significant about him or herself

elegiac a plaintive, melancholic or wistful mood

epic a long, narrative poem that has a serious subject and is told in a formal (elevated) manner. It often contains a grand hero whose actions determine the fate of many others

epigram a short, polished poem, often with a surprising or satirical end

eponymous a character after which a book, film or other work is named

ethnicity a composite of the shared values, beliefs, norms, tastes, experiences, memories and loyalties of an ethnic group; a term used to account for human variation based on culture, tradition, language, social patterns and ancestry rather than on fixed, genetically determined biological types

fragmentation separation into pieces; the presentation of only a part of the whole

free verse verse that lacks the rhythm and rhyme of more traditional poetry, while usually still maintaining a more controlled sense of rhythm than ordinary prose

hegemony domination by consent; the power of the ruling class to convince other classes that the ruling class's interests are the interests of all

heroic couplets pairs of rhyming iambic pentameter lines

homoerotic concerning, or tending to arouse, homo-sexual desire

hybridity the creation of a new form from previously distinct elements; mixed, eclectic or mongrel; the disintegration of pure or fixed forms of culture

iambic pentameter verse of ten-syllable lines in which the stresses lie on the second, fourth, sixth, eighth and tenth syllables

ideology the collection of ideas, opinions, values, beliefs and preconceptions that contribute to the mind-set of a group of people; the intellectual framework through which the group views everything, and which colours all their attitudes and feelings, including assumptions about power and authority

idiom a type of speech that is particular to a national or regional group

imagism the use of exact images in order to create clarity of expression

imperialistic containing the values of an empire

impressionism writing that attempts to convey the general idea and feeling of a scene, place or character without including specific details

irony occurs when the *apparently* stated meaning is different from (often opposite to) the *actual* meaning of the author. The purpose of an ironic piece is often to ridicule the position it is apparently supporting

juxtaposition the placing of two contrasting ideas or words close to each other, often to highlight their differences

liberal a political philosophy with an emphasis on individual freedoms and social justice

lyric poetry poetry that expresses a speaker's (usually the poet's) feelings and state of mind

marginality existence at the periphery; exclusion from the centre

meditation sustained, often gentle, mental contemplation about a topic

metonymy replacing the name of something with the name of something closely associated with it

metre the regular rhythm of a line; usually made up of a regular pattern of stressed and unstressed syllables

nihilism a philosophy that considers that no system of politics or philosophy has any true meaning; often equated with meaninglessness

nouveau riche 'new rich'; one who has become recently rich, as opposed to one whose family has been wealthy for generations; sometimes associated with spending patterns and taste that are considered by the 'old rich' to be excessive

Oedipus complex in psychoanalysis, a subconscious sexual desire in a child, especially a male child, for the parent of the opposite sex, usually accompanied by hostility to the parent of the same sex

paradox an apparent contradiction which, on closer examination, may be seen to contain some truth

pastiche the fusing together of different texts, styles or genres in a single work

pastoral a type of poem that nostalgically idealises a 'natural', simple, rural style of life

patriarchal dominated by values considered to be masculine

patriarchy an androcentric (man-centred) social and political system organised so as to give power and prestige to men, and regarded by many men as the natural order of things

performativity the idea that gender is a daily, habitual, learned act based on cultural norms of femininity and masculinity

postmodernism in terms of literature, of or relating to works that react against earlier modernist principles; for example, by resisting modernism's seriousness with playfulness, or by carrying modernist styles or practices to extremes

post-structuralism any of various theories or methods of analysis (including deconstruction and some psychoanalytic theories) that deny the validity of structuralism's method of binary opposition and maintain that meanings and intellectual categories are shifting and unstable

projection attribution of one's own faults to another

realism most frequently thought of as concerned with exploring the humdrum, dreary and often disappointing side of day-to-day existence (as opposed to Romantic or escapist fiction); applies to writers who show explicit concern to convey an authentic impression of actuality, either by their narrative style or by their serious approach to their subject matter

repartee witty speech and replies

repression desires, mainly sexual, that are in conflict with social norms and are censored and pushed into the subconscious

resistant reading a reading of a piece that is different (such as ideologically different) from the mainstream reading

rhetoric eloquent use of language, often in an attempt to persuade

romance a story, usually in verse, that idealises the life of a chivalric figure, such as a knight

satire the use of witty scorn and amused contempt to denigrate a subject and make it look ridiculous

sublimation the directing of unconscious drives and fixations towards non-sexual goals

subvert to undermine a piece, often by highlighting the ideological assumptions it has made

surrealism a form of literature that attempts to represent dreamlike experiences or visions

symbolism the representation of things not through a literal description but through the use of other things (symbols) that can be associated with it in some way

transference emotional reactions that are stimulated by one individual being expressed towards another

utopian ideal, but often impractical, solutions to social and political issues, often aimed at creating a 'perfect' society

vernacular the particular language used by a local (often indigenous) group

Note: In activity 1 on pages 211 and 212, poems B, E and F are Malley's, and A, C and D are from The Waste Land.

Selected bibliography

Alexander, M, *A History of English Literature*, Palgrave, Hampshire, 2000.

Allen, Y, *The Age of Chaucer*, Cambridge University Press, Cambridge, 2004.

Appignanesi, R, *Introducing Marx*, Icon Books, Cambridge, 1999.

Appignanesi R and O Zarate, *Freud for Beginners*, Icon Books, Cambridge, 1992.

Ashcroft, B, H Tiffin and G Griffith, *Key Concepts in Post-colonial Studies*, Routledge, London and New York, 1989.

Barnet, S and WE Cain, *A Short Guide to Writing about Literature*, 9th edn, Longman, New York, 2003.

Bennett, A and N Royle, *Introduction to Literature, Criticism and Theory*, Prentice Hall, New York, 1999.

Bennett, B and J Strauss (eds), *The Oxford Literary History of Australia*, Oxford University Press, Melbourne, 1998.

Bertens, H, *Literary Theory: The Basics*, Routledge, London and New York, 2001.

Bloom, H, *The Western Canon: The Books and School of the Ages*, Berkley Publishing Group, New York, 1994.

Bradford, R (ed.), *Introducing Literary Studies*, Prentice Hall, Hemel Hempstead, 1996.

Brannigan, J, *New Historicism and Cultural Materialism*, St Martin's Press, New York, 1998.

Butler, M, *Romantics, Rebels and Reactionaries: English Literature and its Background 1760–1830*, Oxford University Press, Oxford, 1981.

Carter, R and J McRae, *The Routledge History of Literature in English (Britain and Ireland)*, Routledge, London, 1997.

Childs, P, *The Twentieth Century in Poetry: A Critical Survey*, Routledge, London and New York, 1999.

Coote, S, *The Penguin Short History of English Literature*, Penguin, London, 1993.

Culler, J, *Literary Theory: A Very Short Introduction*, Oxford University Press, Oxford, 1997.

Curran, S (ed.), *The Cambridge Companion to British Romanticism*, Cambridge University Press, Cambridge, 1993.

Davidson, CN, *Revolution and the Word: The Rise of the Novel in America*, Oxford University Press, New York, 1986

Drabble, M and J Stringer, *Oxford Concise Companion to English Literature*, Oxford University Press, Oxford, 2003.

Eagleton, T, *Literary Theory: An Introduction*, Blackwell, Oxford, 2003.

Everest, K, *English Romantic Poetry*, Open University Press, Buckingham, 1990.

Fuery, P and N Mansfield, *Cultural Studies and the New Humanities: Concepts and Controversies*, Oxford University Press, Melbourne, 1997.

Gallagher, C and S Greenblatt, *Practicing New Historicism*, The University of Chicago Press, Chicago, 1997.

Gibson, R, *Shakespearean and Jacobean Tragedy*, Cambridge University Press, Cambridge, 2000.

Gilbert, S and S Gubar, *The Madwoman in the Attic: The Woman Writer and the Nineteenth Century Literary Imagination*, Yale University Press, Yale, 1979.

Gray, M, *A Dictionary of Literary Terms*, Longman, London, 1992.

Guillory, J, *Cultural Capital: The Problem of Literary Canon Formation*, The University of Chicago Press, Chicago, 1993.

Lee-Browne, P, *The Modernist Period: 1900–1945*, Evans Brothers, London, 2003.

Lee-Browne, P, *The Renaissance*, Evans Brothers, London, 2003.

Levenson, M (ed.), *The Cambridge Companion to Modernism*, Cambridge University Press, Cambridge, 1999.

Macey, D, *The Penguin Dictionary of Critical Theory*, Penguin, London, 2000.

Peck, J and M Coyle, *A Brief History of English Literature*, Palgrave, Hampshire, 2002.

Rogers, P (ed.), *The Oxford Illustrated History of English Literature*, Oxford University Press, Oxford, 1987.

Sage, L, *The Cambridge Guide to Women's Writing in English*, Cambridge University Press, Cambridge, 1989.

Said, EW, *Culture and Imperialism*, Random House (Vintage), New York, 1994.

Said, EW, *Orientalism: Western Conceptions of the Orient*, Routledge and Kegan Paul, New York, 1978.

Sanders, A, *The Short Oxford History of English Literature*, (revised edn), Clarendon Press, London, 1996.

Selden, R, P Widdowson and P Brooker, *A Reader's Guide to Contemporary Literary Theory*, Prentice Hall, New York, 1997.

Stevens, D, *Romanticism*, Cambridge University Press, Cambridge, 2004.

Swisher, C (ed.), *Victorian Literature*, Greenhaven Press, California, 2000.

Veeser, HA (ed.), *The New Historicism*, Routledge, London, 1989.

Webby, E (ed.), *The Cambridge Companion to Australian Literature*, Cambridge University Press, Cambridge, 2000.

Wilmott, R, *Metaphysical Poetry*, Cambridge University Press, Cambridge, 2002.

Wynne-Davies, M, *The Bloomsbury Guide to English Literature*, Bloomsbury, London, 1989.

Index